AUTO-BIOGRAPHY

G000272628

This page enables you to compile a list of useful data on your car, so that whether you're ordering spares or just checking the tyre pressures, all the key information - the information that is 'personal' to your car - is easily within reach.

Registration number: ....

Model: ....

Body colour: ....

Paint code number: ....

Date of first registration: ....

Date of manufacture (if different): ....

VIN (or 'chassis') number: ....

Engine number: ....

Ignition key number: ....

Door lock key/s number/s: ....

Fuel locking cap key number (if fitted): ....

Alarm remote code (if fitted): ....

Alarm remote battery type: ....

Radio/cassette security code (if fitted): ....

Tyre size

Front: ....Rear: ....

Tyre pressure (normally laden)

Front: ....Rear: ....

Tyre pressure (fully laden)

Front: ....Rear: ....

Insurance

    Name and address of insurer:..

    ....

    Policy number:..

Modifications

    Information that might be useful when you need to purchase parts:.......................................

    ....

    ....

Suppliers

    Address and telephone number of your garage and parts suppliers:.......................................

    ....

    ....

First published in 1995 by Porter Publishing Ltd.

Porter Publishing Ltd.
The Storehouse
Little Hereford Street
Bromyard
Hereford HR7 4DE
England

British Library Cataloguing in Publication Data.

A catalogue record for this book is available from the British Library.

ISBN 1-899238-15-8

Series Editor: Lindsay Porter
Design: Martin Driscoll, Lindsay Porter and Lyndsay Berryman
Layout and Typesetting: Pineapple Publishing, Worcester
Cover photography: Jeremy Gale
Printed in England by The Trinity Press, Worcester.

Titles in this Series:

Absolute Beginners' Service Guide
Caravan Owner's Manual & Service Guide
Classic 'Bike Service Guide
Diesel Car Engines Service Guide
Ford Escort (Front Wheel Drive) & Orion Service Guide
Ford Fiesta (All models to 1995) Service Guide
Land Rover Series I, II, IIA & III Service Guide
Land Rover Defender, 90 & 110 Service Guide

Metro (1980-1990) Service Guide
Mini (all models 1959-1994) Service Guide
MGB (including MGC, MGB GT V8 and MG RV8) Service Guide
Vauxhall Astra & Belmont (All models-1995) Service Guide
Vauxhall Cavalier Service Guide
VW Beetle Service Guide

- With more titles in production -

Ford Sierra & Sapphire

Service Guide & Owner's Manual

by

Andy MacQuillan & Lindsay Porter

OIL AND WATER DON'T MIX

It is important to remember that even a small quantity of oil is harmful to water and wildlife. And tipping oil down the drain is as good as tipping it into a river. Many drains are connected directly to a river or stream and pollution will occur.

Each year the National Rivers Authority deals with over 6,000 oil related water pollution incidents. Many of these are caused by the careless disposal of used oil.

The used oil from the sump of just one car can cover an area of water the size of two football pitches, cutting off the oxygen supply and harming swans, ducks, fish and other river life.

OIL POLLUTES WATER
USE YOUR BRAIN-
NOT THE DRAIN!

Follow the Oil Care Code

◆ *When you drain your engine oil - don't oil the drain!* Pouring oil down the drain will cause pollution. It is also an offence.

◆ Don't mix used oil with other materials, such as paint or solvents, because this makes recycling very difficult.

◆ Take used oil to an oil recycling bank. Telephone FREE on 0800 663366 to find the location of your nearest oil bank, or contact your local authority recycling officer.

OIL CARE
FOLLOW THE CODE

This book is produced in association with Castrol (U.K.) Ltd.

"Cars have become more and more sophistated. But changing the oil and brake fluid, and similar jobs are as simple as they ever were. Castrol are pleased to be associated with this book because it gives us the opportunity to make life simpler for those who wish to service their own cars. Castrol have succeeded in making oil friendlier and kinder to the environment by removing harmful chlorine from our range of engine lubricants which in turn prolong the life of the catalytic convertor (when fitted), by noticeably maintaining the engine at peak efficiency. In return, we ask you to be kinder to the environment too... by taking your used oil to your Local Authority Amenity Oil Bank. It can then be used as a heating fuel. Please do not poison it with thinners, paint, creosote or brake fluid because these render it useless and costly to dispose of."

Castrol (U.K.) Ltd

CONTENTS

Introduction

Over the years, I have run any number of cars, from superb classic cars and modern cars, to those with one foot in the breakers yard. And I know only too well that any car is only enjoyable to own if it's safe, reliable and basically sound - and the only way of ensuring that it stays that way is to service it regularly. That's why we have set about creating this book, which aims to show the owner interested in DIY car servicing that there's nothing to fear; you really can do it yourself!

Making It Easy! Porter Publishing Service Guides are the first books to give you all the service information you might need, with step-by-step instructions, along with a complete Service History section for you to complete and fill in as you carry out regular maintenance on your car over the months ahead. Using the information contained in this book, you will be able to:

◆ see for yourself how to carry out every Service Job, from weekly and monthly checks, right up to longer-term maintenance items.
◆ carry out regular body maintenance and rustproofing, saving a fortune in body repairs over the years to come.
◆ enhance the value of your car by completing a full Service History of every maintenance job you carry out on your car.

I hope you enjoy keeping your car in trim while saving lots of money by servicing your car yourself, with the help of this book. Happy motoring!

Lindsay Porter
Porter Publishing Ltd

Lindsay Porter

Andrew MacQuillan

Acknowledgements

Writing this guide has been both a pleasure and an eye-opener: a pleasure because I'm a Sierra 'fan' and have been for some years, and an eye-opener because I've found out so much more about them in the course of studying all the background literature Ford have kindly made available to us. The Sierra has been an unqualified success for Ford, despite some initial concern over the 'jelly-mould' styling when first introduced in 1982, but the simple sturdy construction coupled with a range of well-proven engines soon overcame any reservations and the styling quickly became accepted for what it was - stylish, practical and the shape of things to come.

My preparation for this guide would have been incomplete without the help of Central Motors (Leicester) whose Service Manager Ray Russell was helpful to a point way beyond mere 'duty' - he's an enthusiast too! - and in terms of the facilities made available for much of the photography. Thanks are also due to Adie Hodgekinson's Mum, whose car was used for many of the pictures.

Thanks must go also to the staff at Porter Publishing, for their help and guidance in the early days of preparation, and all the hard work of making sense of my manuscript and 'knocking' it into shape afterwards; perhaps my contribution is the easy part!

Of course, no acknowledgements would be complete without mention of my wife, whose support and forbearance made this book possible, and my daughters Megan and Lizzie, who make it all worthwhile.

Andy MacQuillan

SPECIAL THANKS

The Publisher would like to thank: Ford Motor Company for their advice and use of illustrative material - Robert Iles who contributed to chapters other than Chapter 3, including taking the photographs for Chapter 8 - Douglas Seaton Ltd of Yeovil for their assistance with Chapter 8 - Dave Smith and John Taylor from the A44 Garage, Worcester for their assistance with the photography for the front cover - Gunsons for equipment, line drawings and advice - Dinitrol for their kind assistance with Chapter 5 - and our good friends at Castrol for their continuing support, assistance and advice.

CHAPTER 1 - SAFETY FIRST!

You must always ensure that safety is the first consideration in any job you carry out. A slight lack of concentration, or a rush to finish the job quickly can easily result in an accident, as can failure to follow the precautions outlined in this Chapter. Whereas skilled motor mechanics are trained in safe working practices you, the home mechanic, must find them out for yourself and act upon them.

Remember, accidents don't just happen, they are caused, and some of those causes are contained in the following list. Above all, ensure that whenever you work on your car you adopt a safety-minded approach at all times, and remain aware of the dangers that might be encountered.

Be sure to consult the suppliers of any materials and equipment you may use, and to obtain and read carefully any operating and health and safety instructions that may be available on packaging or from manufacturers and suppliers.

PART I: IMPORTANT POINTS

Vehicle Off Ground

ALWAYS ensure that the vehicle is properly supported when raised off the ground. Don't work on, around, or underneath a raised vehicle unless axle stands are positioned under secure, load bearing underbody areas, or the vehicle is driven onto ramps, with the wheels remaining on the ground securely chocked to prevent movement.

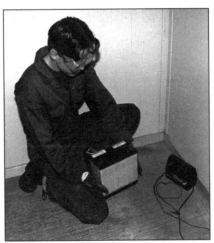

ALWAYS ensure that the safe working load rating of any jacks, hoists or lifting gear used is sufficient for the job, and that lifting gear is used only as recommended by the manufacturer.

NEVER attempt to loosen or tighten nuts that require a lot of force to turn (e.g. a tight oil drain plug) with the vehicle raised, unless it is safely supported. Take care not to pull the vehicle off its supports when applying force to a spanner. Wherever possible, initially slacken tight fastenings before raising the car off the ground.

ALWAYS wear eye protection when working under the vehicle and when using power tools.

Working On The Vehicle

ALWAYS seek specialist advice unless you are justifiably confident about carrying out each job. The safety of your vehicle affects you, your passengers and other road users.

DON'T lean over, or work on, a running engine unless it is strictly necessary, and keep long hair and loose clothing well out of the way of moving mechanical parts. Note that it is theoretically possible for fluorescent striplighting to make an engine fan appear to be stationary - double check whether it is spinning or not! This is the sort of error that happens when you're really tired and not thinking straight. So...

...DON'T work on your car when you're over tired.

ALWAYS work in a well ventilated area and don't inhale dust - it may contain asbestos or other harmful substances.

REMOVE your wrist watch, rings and all other jewellery before doing any work on the vehicle - and especially when working on the electrical system.

DON'T remove the radiator or expansion tank filler cap when the cooling system is hot, or you may get scalded by escaping coolant or steam. Let the system cool down first and even then, if the engine is not completely cold, cover the cap with a cloth and gradually release the pressure.

NEVER drain oil, coolant or automatic transmission fluid when the engine is hot. Allow time for it to cool sufficiently to avoid scalding you.

ALWAYS keep antifreeze, brake and clutch fluid away from vehicle paintwork. Wash off any spills immediately.

TAKE CARE to avoid touching any engine or exhaust system component unless it is cool enough not to burn you.

Running The Vehicle

NEVER start the engine unless the gearbox is in neutral (or 'Park' in the case of automatic transmission) and the hand brake is fully applied.

NEVER run catalytic converter equipped vehicles without the exhaust system heat shields in place.

TAKE CARE when parking vehicles fitted with catalytic

SAFETY FIRST!

converters. The 'cat' reaches extremely high temperatures and any combustible materials under the car, such as long dry grass, could be ignited.

Personal Safety

NEVER siphon fuel, antifreeze, brake fluid or other such toxic liquids by mouth, or allow contact with your skin. There is an increasing awareness that they can damage your health. Best of all, use a suitable hand pump and wear gloves.

BEFORE undertaking dirty jobs, use a barrier cream on your hands as a protection against infection. Preferably, wear thin gloves, available from DIY outlets.

WEAR GLOVES for sure when there is a risk of used engine oil coming into contact with your skin. It can cause cancer.

WIPE UP any spilt oil, grease or water off the floor immediately, before there is an accident.

MAKE SURE that spanners and all other tools are the right size for the job and are not likely to slip. Never try to 'double-up' spanners to gain more leverage.

SEEK HELP if you need to lift something heavy which may be beyond your capability. Don't forget that when lifting a heavy weight, you should keep your back straight and bend your knees to avoid injuring your back.

NEVER take risky short-cuts or rush to finish a job. Plan ahead and allow plenty of time.

BE METICULOUS and keep the work area tidy - you'll avoid frustration, work better and lose less.

KEEP children and animals right-away from the work area and from unattended vehicles.

ALWAYS tell someone what you're doing and have them regularly check that all is well, especially when working alone on, or under, the vehicle.

PART II: HAZARDS

Fire!

Petrol (gasoline) is a dangerous and highly flammable liquid requiring special precautions. When working on the fuel system, disconnect the vehicle battery earth (ground) terminal whenever possible and always work outside, or in a very well ventilated area. Any form of spark, such as that caused by an electrical fault, by two metal surfaces striking against each other, by a central heating boiler in the garage 'firing up', or even by static electricity built up in your clothing can, in a confined space, ignite petrol vapour causing an explosion. Take great care not to spill petrol on to the engine or exhaust system, never allow any naked flame anywhere near the work area and, above all, don't smoke.

Invest in a workshop-sized fire extinguisher. Choose the carbon dioxide type or preferably, dry powder but never a water type extinguisher for workshop use. Water conducts electricity and can make worse an oil or petrol-based fire, in certain circumstances.

DON'T disconnect any fuel pipes on a fuel injected engine while the ignition is switched on. The fuel in the line is under very high pressure - sufficient to cause serious injury. Remember that many injection systems have residual pressure in the pipes for days after switching off. Consult the workshop manual or seek specialist advice before carrying out any work.

Fumes

In addition to the fire dangers described previously, petrol (gasoline) vapour and the types of vapour given off by many solvents, thinners, and adhesives are highly toxic and under certain conditions can lead to unconsciousness or even death, if inhaled. The

risks are increased if such fluids are used in a confined space so always ensure adequate ventilation when handling materials of this nature. Treat all such substances with care, always read the instructions and follow them with care.

Always ensure that the car is out of doors and not in an enclosed space when the engine is running. Exhaust fumes contain poisonous carbon monoxide, even when the car is fitted with a catalytic converter, since 'cats' sometimes fail and don't function when the engine is cold.

Never drain petrol (gasoline) or use solvents, thinners adhesives or other toxic substances in an inspection pit as the extremely confined space allows the highly toxic fumes to concentrate. Running the engine with the vehicle over the pit can have the same results. It is also dangerous to park a vehicle for any length of time over an inspection pit. The fumes from even a slight fuel leak can cause an explosion when the engine is started. Petrol fumes are heavier than air and will accumulate in the pit.

Mains Electricity

Best of all, avoid the use of mains electricity when working on the vehicle, whenever possible. For instance, you could use rechargeable

tools and a DC inspection lamp, powered from a remote 12V battery - both are much safer. However, if you do use mains-powered equipment, ensure that the appliance is wired correctly to its plug, that where necessary it is properly earthed (grounded), and that the fuse is of the correct rating for the appliance is fitted. For instance, a 13 amp fuse in lead lamp's plug will not provide adequate protection. Do not use any mains powered equipment in damp conditions or in the vicinity of fuel, fuel vapour or the vehicle battery.

Also, before using any mains powered electrical equipment, take one more simple precaution - use an RCD (Residual Current Device) circuit breaker. Then, if there is a short, the RCD circuit breaker minimises the risk of electrocution by instantly cutting the power supply. Buy one from any electrical store or DIY centre. RCDs fit simply into your electrical socket before plugging in your electrical equipment.

The Ignition System
You should never work on the ignition system with the ignition switched on, or with the engine being turned over on the starter, or running.

Touching certain parts of the ignition system, such as the HT leads, distributor cap, ignition coil etc, can result in a severe electric shock. This is especially likely where the insulation on any of these components is weak, or if the components are dirty or damp. Note also that voltages produced by electronic ignition systems are much higher than those produced by conventional systems and could prove fatal, particularly to people with cardiac pacemaker implants. Consult your handbook or main dealer if in any doubt.

An additional risk of injury can arise while working on running engines, if the operator touches a high voltage lead and pulls his or her hand away on to a sharp, conductive or revolving part.

The Battery
Never cause a spark, smoke, or allow a naked light near the vehicle's battery, even in a well ventilated area. Highly explosive hydrogen gas will be given off as part of the charging process.

Battery terminals on the car should be shielded, since a battery contains energy and a spark can be caused by any metal object which touches the battery's terminals or connecting straps.

Before working on the fuel or electrical systems, always disconnect the battery earth (ground) terminal. (But before doing so, read the relevant FACT FILE in *Chapter 3* regarding saving computer and radio settings.)

When using a battery charger, care should be taken to avoid causing a spark by switching off the power supply before the battery charger leads are connected or disconnected. Before charging the battery from an external source, disconnect both battery leads before connecting the charger. If the battery is not of the 'sealed-for-life' type, loosen the filler plugs or remove the cover before charging. For best results the battery should be given a low rate trickle charge overnight. Do not charge at an excessive rate or the battery may burst.

Always wear gloves and goggles when carrying or when topping up the battery. Even in diluted form (as it is in the battery) the acid electrolyte is extremely corrosive and must not be allowed to contact the eyes, skin or clothes.

Brakes and Asbestos
Obviously, a car's brakes are among its most important safety related items. ONLY work on your vehicle's braking system if you are trained and competent to do so. If you have not been trained in this work, but wish to carry out the jobs described in this book, we strongly recommend that you have a garage or qualified mechanic check your work before using the car.

Whenever you work on the braking system's mechanical components, or remove front or rear brake pads or shoes: i) wear an efficient particle mask; ii) wipe off all brake dust from the brakes after spraying on a proprietary brand of brake cleaner (never blow dust off with compressed air); iii) dispose of brake dust and discarded shoes or pads in a sealed plastic bag; iv) wash your hands thoroughly after you have finished working on the brakes and certainly before you eat or smoke; v) replace shoes and pads only with asbestos-free shoes or pads. Note that asbestos brake dust can cause cancer if inhaled.

Brake Fluid
Brake fluid absorbs moisture rapidly from the air and can become dangerous resulting in brake failure. Castrol (U.K.) Ltd. recommend that you should have your brake fluid tested at least once a year by a properly equipped garage with test equipment and you should change the fluid in accordance with your vehicle manufacturer's recommendations or as advised in this book if we recommend a shorter interval than the manufacturer. You should buy no more brake fluid than you need, in smaller rather than larger containers. Never store an opened container of brake fluid. Dispose of the remainder at your Local Authority Waste Disposal Site, in the designated disposal unit, not with general waste or with waste oil.

Engine Oils
Take care to observe the following precautions when working with used engine oil. Apart from the obvious risk of scalding when draining the oil from a hot engine, there is the danger from contamination contained in all used oil.

Always wear disposable plastic or rubber gloves when draining the oil from your engine. i) Note that the drain plug and the oil are often hotter than you expect. Wear gloves if the plug is too hot to touch and keep your hand to one side so that you are not scalded by the spurt of oil as the plug comes away; ii) There are very real health hazards associated with used engine oil. In the words of one manufacturer's handbook "Prolonged and repeated contact may cause serious skin disorders, including dermatitis and cancer." Use a barrier cream on your hands and try not to get oil on them. Always wear gloves and wash your hands with hand cleaner soon after carrying out the work. Keep oil out of the reach of children; iii) NEVER, EVER dispose of old engine oil into the ground or down a drain. In the UK, and in most EC countries, every local authority must provide a safe means of oil disposal. In the UK, try your local Environmental Health Department for advice on waste disposal facilities.

Plastic Materials
Work with plastic materials brings additional hazards into workshops. Many of the materials used (polymers, resins, adhesives and materials acting as catalysts and accelerators) contain dangers in the form of poisonous fumes, skin irritants, and the risk of fire and explosions. Do not allow resin or 2-pack adhesive hardener, or that supplied with filler or 2-pack stopper, to come into contact with skin or eyes. Read carefully the safety notes supplied on the can, tube or packaging and always wear impervious gloves and goggles when working with them.

Jacks and Axle Stands
Throughout this book you will see many references to the correct use of jacks, axle stands and similar equipment - and we make

SAFETY FIRST!

no apologies for being repetitive. This is one area where safety cannot be overstressed - your life could be at stake!

Special care must be taken when any type of lifting equipment is used. Jacks are made for lifting the vehicle only, not for supporting it while it is being worked on. Never work under the car using only a jack to support the weight. Jacks must be supplemented by adequate additional means of support, positioned under secure load-bearing parts of the frame or underbody. Axle stands are available from most auto. parts stores. Drive-on ramps are limiting because of their design and size but they are simple to use, reliable and offer the most stable type of support. We strongly recommend their use.

Full details on jacking and supporting the vehicle will be found near the beginning of *Chapter 3.*

Fluoroelastomers

MOST IMPORTANT! PLEASE READ THIS SECTION!

If you service your car in the normal way, none of the following may be relevant to you. Unless, for example, you encounter a car which has been on fire (even in a localised area), subject to heat in, say, a crash-damage repairer's workshop or a vehicle breaker's yard, or if any second-hand parts have been heated in any way.

Many synthetic, rubber-like materials used in motor cars contain a substance called fluorine. These materials are known as fluoroelastomers and are commonly used for oil seals, wiring and cabling, bearing surfaces, gaskets, diaphragms, hoses and 'O' rings. If they are subjected to temperatures greater than 315 degrees C, they will decompose and can be potentially hazardous. Fluoroelastomer materials will show physical signs of decomposition under such conditions in the form of charring of black sticky masses. Some decomposition may occur at temperatures above 200 degrees C, and it is obvious that when a car has been in a fire or has been dismantled with the assistance of a cutting torch or blow torch, the fluoroelastomers can decompose in the manner indicated above.

In the presence of any water or humidity, including atmospheric moisture, the by-products caused by the fluoroelastomers being heated can be extremely dangerous. According to the Health and Safety Executive, "Skin contact with this liquid or decomposition residues can cause painful and penetrating burns. Permanent irreversible skin and tissue damage can occur". Damage can also be caused to eyes or by the inhalation of fumes created as fluoroelastomers are burned or heated.

After a vehicle has been exposed to fire or high temperatures:

1. Do not touch blackened or charred seals or equipment.

2. Allow all burnt or decomposed fluoroelastomer materials to cool before inspection, investigations, tear-down or removal.

3. Preferably, don't handle parts containing decomposed fluoroelastomers, but if you must, wear goggles and PVC (polyvinyl chloride) or neoprene protective gloves whilst doing so. Never handle such parts unless they are completely cool.

4. Contaminated parts, residues, materials and clothing, including protective clothing and gloves, should be disposed of by an approved contractor to landfill or by incineration according to national or local regulations. Oil seals, gaskets and 'O' rings, along with contaminated material, must not be burned.

PART III: GENERAL WORKSHOP SAFETY

1. Always have a fire extinguisher of the correct type at arm's length when working on the fuel system.

If you do have a fire, DON'T PANIC. Use the extinguisher effectively by directing it at the base of the fire.

2. NEVER use a naked flame anywhere in the workplace.

3. KEEP your inspection lamp well away from any source of petrol (gasoline) such as when disconnecting a carburettor float bowl or fuel line.

4. NEVER use petrol (gasoline) to clean parts. Use paraffin (kerosene), white spirits, or a proprietary degreaser.

5. NO SMOKING. There's a risk of fire or of transferring dangerous substances to your mouth and, in any case, ash falling into mechanical components is to be avoided.

6. BE METHODICAL in everything you do, use common sense, and think of safety at all times.

FACT FILE: FOUR WHEEL DRIVE CARS WITH PERMANENT 4WD

Whenever you have to raise a wheel off the ground and turn it by hand, always ensure that the opposite-side's wheel to the one being lifted is also off the ground and free to turn and that both wheels remaining on the ground are held by the parking brake (if possible) and securely chocked in both directions. ALWAYS have the gearbox in neutral.

CHAPTER 2 - BUYING GUIDE

In this Chapter, we show you how to go about buying a second hand car. We also look at which parts wear out, and we explain when they are likely to need replacement, so that whether you are giving your own car the once-over, or you're looking at a prospective purchase, you'll know what to expect; and we examine the best ways of buying parts for your pride and joy.

PART I: BUYING A SECOND-HAND CAR

In general, the safest - but also the most expensive - way of buying second hand is through a main dealer: NOT the same as a general second-hand dealer, whose standards are almost certain to be lower! We *strongly* recommend the use of HPI Autodata checks mentioned on page 110, because even main dealers can make 'mistakes', but once you've done that, and selected the main-dealer car you want, it's better to have an AA or RAC inspection carried out rather than carry out your own checks. But for many people, it's a question of saving money and buying privately, and that's what this Chapter is mainly about. But don't find yourself with the *worst* of both worlds...

Spot The Rogue Trader

One of the biggest dangers with buying privately is that you might encounter a real cheat: a trader masquerading as a private seller. Cars offered by such people are likely to be among the worst on offer, they may have had their mileometers tampered with and deep seated faults may have been cleverly concealed. Here's how to spot them:

• take note of the way traders often word their advertisements. Key phrases include: "a very clean car", "very straight", "a beautiful motorcar" and other glib phrases.

• when you telephone in response to an ad., *always* say, "I'm calling about the car..." If the person on the other end asks, "Which car?", put the 'phone down before the spiel starts.

• if you get past the telephone stage, take careful note of the attitude of the seller. Part-time, 'black economy' dealers often seem blase, even bored by the whole thing, and slicker than most private sellers.

• insist on looking at the Registration Document. If the seller isn't the registered keeper, why not?

How To Inspect A Used Vehicle

STAGE ONE: Even if you know very little about cars, you can root out the obvious no-hopers before arranging for a local main agent, AA or RAC inspection. The text in italics explains the problems.

• catch the light along all sides of the car. Can you see any ripples? Check for overspray inside wheel arches, inside engine bay and on tyres and trim. Does all the paint match? *All indicate poorly carried out crash repairs.*

• Look at the gaps between panels. Also, look very carefully inside the engine bay and inside the boot for evidence of rippling in the metal. Look low down, mainly in the vicinity of structural members. *Tell-tale signs of crash damage.*

STAGE TWO: If your car passes Stage One, look more closely at the bodywork - the most expensive part to repair.

• check the sills by lifting the carpets just inside the doors and also check the footwells, especially around the edges. *Rust!*

• look inside the engine bay especially at the tops of struts. *Check for corrosion.*

• check the bottoms of wings, the 'skirts' beneath front and rear bumpers and the tops of wing panels for corrosion. *Rust covered with filler will quickly burst through again.*

SPECIALIST SERVICE: It's hardly worth trying to check beneath a car without the use of a hoist. Leave it to the pro. inspection mentioned earlier, or see if you can persuade a local garage to lend or hire their hoist:

• check around spring mountings, the joints between floors and sills, all box-section 'chassis' members and anywhere that suspension components are fixed to the car's body structure.

• check all brake pipes and hoses. *Look for rubbing or corrosion.*

• look at the shock absorbers. *Fluid leakage means failure.*

• check the exhaust. *Look for rust, holes or patches.*

• examine each tyre carefully for bulges or splits. *Tyres worn more on one side than the other might mean that the car's tracking needs checking - easily adjustable - or it might indicate suspension damage, maybe from an accident.*

---

making it easy! If you are buying an older car which needs work doing to it, try making the owner an offer 'subject to MoT test'. Then, you can have the car tested as an inexpensive (though not necessarily complete) condition check.

Mechanical Components

• before starting up, remove the oil filler cap. *Grey sludge around the cap is a certain indicator that the engine is on its last legs.*

• pull out the dipstick. Is the oil level very low? Is the oil a dirty black and does it feel gritty between finger and thumb? *Not a well maintained car!* Does it have droplets of water on it? *Big problems! Probably a blown head gasket.*

• check inside the radiator cap (ONLY if the engine is cold!). Do you see anti-freeze colour? *Good!* Do you see rust? *Bad!* Do you see droplets of oil? *Disastrous! See previous paragraph.*

• start the car and note whether the starter motor sounds lively or whether it is struggling to keep up. *Could be duff battery; or tired starter motor.*

• undo and remove the oil filler cap again. (N.B. Most engines spray oil around in *copious* quantities. Ensure that you don't get covered!) *If oil mist chugs out, the engine bores are badly worn. Also...*

• ...look at the exhaust. Steam (especially in colder weather) and even water dripping out is no problem, although it should go away after the car has been driven. 'Rev' the engine, hard and several times. *If you see puffs or even clouds of black smoke (not grey steam), the engine is probably on the slippery slope.*

• does the oil pressure warning light flicker with engine cold? *Low oil pressure equals an engine rebuild?*

• bonnet open. Does the 'top' of the engine rattle on start up? *Mechanical tappets: adjustment needed.* If the rattle continues after 30 seconds, *the engine may need an expensive replacement camshaft.* Hydraulic tappets: *noise is always expensive!*

• rev the engine. Does it rattle in a deep, growly way, low down in the engine? *The big end and/or main bearings are gone - replacement engine time!*

Static Checks

• are the carpets wet? *water is leaking in. Windscreen seal leaks can often be cured easily. But if the car is old the screen surround may have corroded, requiring expensive welding. Alternatively, water coming in from beneath suggests that the car's lower structure has as much future as an old car park ticket. If water is leaking from the heater, remember that it can be expensive and tricky to replace.*

• seat rips can be a pain and devalue the car. *It can be difficult to find the right colour match on second hand seats.* Do your knees come up as your backside goes down. *The seat springing has gone.*

• can you live with headlining rips or severe discolouration? *It's difficult to clean easily and replacement is usually expensive.*

• take a *close* look at seat belts and mountings. *Life saver - and quite expensive to replace.*

• check that the heater works properly. *Or you'll end up hating the car!*

• take time to check every switch, accessory and electrical fitting on the car. *Replacements can be expensive.* Check that the stereo works - and check that it's included with the car!

• don't accept lame excuses when things don't work! *If things are so easy to fix, why haven't they been done already?*

• check the spare wheel and the condition (existence?) of the jack and toolkit. *More expense!*

• open and close windows and sunroof. *(Also look for stains around sunroof aperture - they can leak!)*

Finally, but perhaps most important of all, make sure that the person who is selling the car actually owns it!

• ask to see the Registration Document. *If it's not available it could be: the 'owner' has a) lost it; b) has it but it doesn't show the 'owner's' name because he is a trader; c) the car doesn't belong to the seller. If you can't see the Registration Document, walk away!*

• ask to see the owner's original purchase receipt and check that the car is owned by the 'owner' and is not subject to a finance agreement. See below. *IMPORTANT NOTE: You may be amazed to learn that, if you pay for a car that is subsequently found to belong to someone else, you will lose the car and the money!*

• check that the VIN (Vehicle Identification Number) shown on the Registration document is the same as those on the VIN plate riveted to the car. See "Fact File" later in this chapter for the precise location of these numbers. *If any of the numbers in these three locations are different, missing, or have obviously been tampered with, then under no circumstances consider buying the car unless the seller can provide an explanation, in writing, satisfactory to a third party, such as an AA or RAC inspector, or the Police!*

Spot The Rogue Car

Before buying *any* used car, check it out with HPI Autodata. (See Page 110.) A postal or telephone enquiry (cheques or credit card payments accepted) will (i) confirm that the vehicle details shown (make, model, colour, engine size, fuel type) are all correct, (ii) tell you if the vehicle is reported as stolen, or subject to an outstanding finance agreement, (iii) tell you if the vehicle has been logged as having a major insurance claim (not foolproof; many don't show up), (iv) identify vehicles which have had a registration plate change.

PART II: WHAT WEARS, AND WHEN

The following list provides a great way of checking what is *likely* to be worn on your Ford Sierra, and at what stage it is likely to need replacement - useful when checking your own car, or when buying another. Please bear in mind that the mileages shown are only intended as an approximation of the lifespan of each component. In real life, some will wear out faster and some slower of course, but the chart below provides a useful rough guide.

> **SAFETY FIRST!**
> **Read and take note of Chapter1, Safety First! and the Safety information in Chapter 3 before carrying out any of these checks.**

COMPONENT:	COULD NEED REPLACEMENT AT:	CHECKS OR SYMPTOMS:
Alternator	80,000 - 100,000 miles	Fails without warning or the ignition warning light could glow dimly for a few miles.
Battery	4 to 7 years (original); 1 to 5 (non-original)	Goes flat, even though disconnected.
Brake Pads - Front	15 - 20,000 miles	See Job 67.
Brake Pads/Shoes - Rear	Check linings at 12 - 24,000 miles	See Job 68.
Cambelt	36,000 miles - if fitted, depending on model	Should be renewed - check service history.
Clutch	Up to 75,000 normally	Check for slipping when pulling away, hill climbing.
Diesel Glowplugs	60,000 miles	Engine reluctant to start from cold and smokes (even though battery in good condition).
Diesel Injectors	75,000 miles	Excessive smoke; engine misfires.
Exhaust mountings	Rears go every year or two	Examine visually, twist manually.
Exhaust pipe (Ford parts) (non-original parts)	Up to 4 years 1 to 3 years	Examine visually, listen for blowing.
Shock absorbers (front) Shock absorbers (rear)	40,000 miles 50,000 miles	Clean off and look for oil leaks. Grasp and twist, looking for wear in bushes top and bottom.
Starter motor	150,000 miles	Turns engine slowly *when battery and connections in good condition.*
Tyres (most models)	15 - 20,000 miles	
Tyres - High performance models	7 - 10,000 miles	Check visually, especially inside tyre walls, and also spare.

PART III - BUYING SPARES

One of the great advantages of DIY servicing is that you can choose which parts you buy, where you buy your parts, and how much you pay for them, whereas if the dealer services your car you buy their parts at their prices!

Of course, you must take care not to buy poor quality parts, but it's worth bearing in mind that many of the car makers' parts are the same as those available from 'independents'.

Buying The Right Parts

All manufacturers change the parts they use on the production line, often with startling frequency. The only way of ensuring that the parts you buy are the right ones for your car is to take your car's Vehicle Identification Number (VIN) and engine number with you when buying spares.

Main Dealers

Main dealers more than anyone else should be able to match your car's VIN number to the precise part you need, so have it to hand. This can also be the key to a more helpful approach by some Parts Department staff! Also, try to avoid calling on the parts department in the early mornings and other busy periods, and you may find that staff have more time to help you. Consumable items are almost certain to be too expensive from your main dealer. Try high street auto accessory stores or out-of-town Superstores for best prices.

Auto Accessory Stores

Local parts factors and big-name motor accessory shops can be extremely useful for obtaining servicing parts at short notice - many 'accessory' outlets open late in the evening, and on both days at weekends. You'll find that the high-street shops and Superstores will usually be open when you need them, their prices are usually the keenest of all, because they can buy-in in great quantities, and the quality of the parts is excellent from the best-known shops, since they use the same big-name manufacturers as many of the original car makers.

Buying Second-Hand

Purchasing any safety-related items second-hand - braking, steering or suspension parts - is something to avoid. That's not to decry buying second-hand altogether. Replacing a worn out distributor or carburettor, for instance, with a second-hand component that you know to be 'low mileage' can make a lot of sense. Equally, non-performance related items, such as wheel trims, interior trim and other interior parts can often be obtained at a fraction of the 'new' cost.

Reconditioned Parts

These are best obtained from reputable retail suppliers. When buying, always enquire about the terms of the guarantee. Don't buy if there isn't a good one! 'Exchange' alternators and starter motors are good value - but only buy from a reputable source.

Steering racks are invariably available as exchange items. Ensure that you rotate the operating shaft fully from lock to lock, feeling for any undue free play, roughness, stiffness, or 'notchiness' as you do so. Reject any units showing signs of any of these problems.

Tyres

We recommend buying only good quality radial ply tyres. Cheaper tyres rarely perform as well as top brands, even when they are the cheaper brand of a top manufacturer. Your car may steer more erratically, have less grip on cornering and braking and be noisier than if you pay the small extra amount required for top brand tyres - and they usually last longer, too. Remould tyres are available at lower initial cost, but life expectancy is not as long as with new tyres and we don't recommend them.

Shopping Around

If you want to buy good quality parts *and* save money, you must be prepared to shop around. Ring each of your chosen suppliers with a shopping list to hand, and your car's personal data, from the Auto-Biography at the front of this book, in front of you. Keep a written note of prices - including VAT, delivery etc - whether the parts are proper 'brand name' parts or not and - most importantly! - whether or not the parts you want are in stock. Parts expected 'soon' have been known never to materialise. A swivel pin in the hand is worth two in the bush. (Bad pun!)

FACT FILE: IDENTIFICATION NUMBERS

All manufacturers change the parts they use on the production line, often with startling frequency. The only way of ensuring that the parts you buy are the right ones for your car is to take your car's Vehicle Identification Number (VIN) and engine number with you when buying spares.

There are three main numbers you will need to know in order to buy parts and touch-up paint for your car. The VIN is your car's internationally unique number and tells your parts supplier *exactly* which model and year the car is. Quote the VIN whenever you buy spares for your car.

1. The Sierra's VIN plate (A) is positioned on the front or 'slam' panel of the engine bay and the number should be the same as that shown on your vehicle documents.

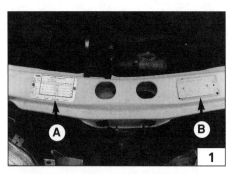

INSIDE INFORMATION: If you need an exact paint colour match, you'll need the car's paint code number. The paint code plate (B) is also situated on the front 'slam' panel, to the right of the VIN plate and is usually painted in the body colour. Most aerosol paints won't relate to this number, although at least one brand claims to be able to produce cans matched to your car's code colour, to special order.

Alternatively, have your local paint factor mix a small quantity of matching paint for you. He will also be able to tell whether your paint

is cellulose or synthetic-based - an important point in avoiding the potential disaster of applying cellulose paint over synthetic!

2. The VIN number is also stamped onto the floor-pan at manufacture and is found beneath a small flap in the carpet between the drivers' seat and the door sill. Make sure it is the same as that shown on the VIN plate!

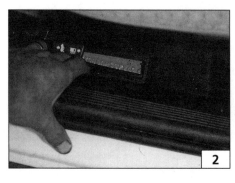

3. The engine number will usually be found stamped on the engine block, on a small flat area on the lefthand-side of the engine as you look to the rear of the car, near the No. 1 cylinder position.

V6 ENGINES

The V6 engine number is stamped into a 'flat' on the engine block, towards the front and on the right-hand side as you look to the rear of the car. However, due to the design of the engine it is awkward to see and requires the use of a small mirror and torch to locate and read it.

DIESEL ENGINES

The diesel engine number is found on the right-hand side of the engine, near the top of the block, and between the fuel pump and the oil filter.

Please read the whole of the Introduction to this Chapter before carrying out any work on your car.

SERVICING YOUR CAR

CHAPTER 3 - SERVICING YOUR CAR

Everyone wants to own a car that starts first time, runs reliably and lasts longer than the average. And there's no magic about how to put your car into that category, it's all a question of thorough maintenance! If you follow the Service Jobs listed here or even if you have a garage or mechanic do it for you - you can almost *guarantee* that your car will still be going strong when others have fallen by the wayside... or the hard shoulder.

If you want your car to be as well looked after as possible, you'll follow the Jobs shown here, but if you don't want to go all the way, you can pick and choose from the most essential items in the list. But do bear in mind that the Jobs we recommend are there for some very good reasons:

♦ **body maintenance** is rarely included in most service schedules. We believe it to be essential.

♦ **preventative maintenance** figures very high on our list of priorities. And that's why so many of our service jobs have the word "Check..." near the start!

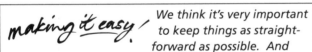 *We think it's very important to keep things as straight-forward as possible. And where you see this heading, you'll know there's an extra tip to help 'make it easy' for you!*

The 'Catch-up' Service

When you first buy a used car, you never know for sure just how well it's been looked after. Even one with a full service history is unlikely to have been serviced as thoroughly as one with a Porter Manual Service History! So, if you want to catch-up on all the servicing that may have been neglected on your car, just work through the entire list of Service Jobs listed for the longest term servicing jobs listed in this Manual, and your car will be bang up to date and serviced as well as you could hope for. Do allow several days for all of this work, not least because it will almost certainly throw up a number of extra jobs - potential faults that have been lurking beneath the surface - all of which will need putting right before you can 'sign off' your car as being in tip-top condition.

The Service History

Those people fortunate enough to own a new car, or one that has been well maintained from new will have the opportunity to keep a 'Service History' of their car, usually filled in by a main dealer. Now you can keep your own complete record, using the tick list in the Appendix at the back of this book.

Your car's Service History will then be more complete and detailed than any manufacturer's service record, with the extra bonus that there is space for you to keep a record of all those extras: New tyres; replacement exhaust; extra accessories, so if your battery goes down only 11 months after buying it, you'll be able to look up where and when you bought it.

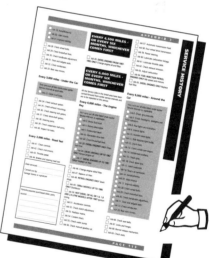

SAFETY FIRST!
SAFETY FIRST! information must always be read with care and always taken seriously. In addition, please read the whole of Chapter 1, Safety First! before carrying out any work on your car. There are many hazards associated with working on a car but all of them can be avoided by adhering strictly to the safety rules. Don't skimp on safety!

RAISING THE CAR

RAISING THE CAR

Raising The Car Before Working On It

Raising a Car - Safely!
You will often need to raise your car off the ground in order to carry out the Service Jobs shown here. To start off with, here's what you must never do - never work beneath a car held on a jack, not even a trolley jack. Quite a number of deaths have been caused by a car slipping off a jack while someone has been working beneath. On the other hand, the safest way is by raising a car on a proprietary brand of ramps. Sometimes, there is no alternative but to use axle stands. Please read all of the following information and act upon it!

When using car ramps:

(I) Make absolutely certain that the ramps are parallel to the wheels of the car and that the wheels are exactly central on each ramp.

Always have an assistant watch both sides of the car as you drive up. Drive up to the end 'stops' on the ramps but never over them!

Apply the hand brake firmly, put the car in first or reverse gear, or 'Park', in the case of an automatic.

(II) Chock both wheels remaining on the ground, both in front and behind so that the car can't move in either direction.

INSIDE INFORMATION: Wrap a strip of carpet into a loop around the first 'rung' of the ramps and drive over the doubled-up piece of carpet on the approach to the ramps. This prevents the ramps from skidding away, as they are inclined to do, as the car is driven on to them.

On other occasions, you might need to work on the car while it is supported on an axle stand or a pair of axle stands. These are inherently less stable than ramps and so you must take much greater care when working beneath them. In particular:

• ensure that the axle stand is on flat, stable ground, never on a surface where one side can sink in to the ground.

• ensure that the car is on level ground and that the hand brake is off and the transmission in neutral.

• raise the car with a trolley jack - invest in one if you don't already own one; the car's wheel changing jack is often too unstable. Place a piece of cloth over the head of the jack if your car is nicely finished on the underside. Ensure that the floor is sufficiently clear and smooth for the trolley jack wheels to roll as the car is raised and lowered, otherwise it could slip off the jack.

(IIIa) **SIERRA AND SAPPHIRE:** These are Ford's recommended jacking points (A) and areas where you place additional supports or a trolley jack (B).

(IIIb) **P100 PICK-UP:** These are the P100 jacking points (A) and areas where you place additional supports or a trolley jack (B).

I

II

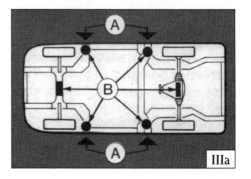

IIIa

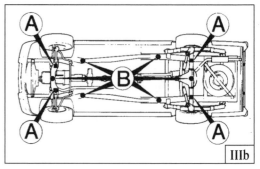

IIIb

IIIc

IV

(IIIc) Place the jack beneath the front sub-frame or another load-bearing area, such as immediately behind the wheel-change jacking point, with a block of wood to spread the load when raising the front of the car...

(IV) ...and place the axle stands beneath body-mounts or suspension mounts, but NEVER under the engine or gearbox.

(V) At the rear of the car, place the jack head, beneath the rear body jacking points or rear suspension mounting points, or beneath the rear 'axle'/torsion beam.

(VI) Take care to locate the top of the axle stands on a strong, level, stable part of the car's underside: you should never use a movable suspension part (because the part can move and allow the axle stand to slip) or the floor of the car (which is just too weak).

V

Just as when using ramps - only even more importantly! - apply the hand brake firmly, put the car in first or reverse gear (or 'Park', in the case of an automatic) and chock both wheels remaining on the ground, both in front and behind.

Be especially careful when applying force to a spanner or when pulling hard on anything, when the car is supported off the ground. It is all too easy to move the car so far that it topples off the axle stands. And remember that if a car falls on you, **YOU COULD BE KILLED!**

Whenever working beneath a car, have someone primed to keep an eye on you! If someone pops out to see how you are getting on every quarter of an hour or so, it could be enough to save your life!

Do remember that, in general, a car will be more stable when only one wheel is removed and one axle stand used than if two wheels are removed in conjunction with two axle stands. You are strongly advised never to work on the car with all four wheels off the ground, on four axle stands. The car would then be very unstable and dangerous to work beneath.

VI

Before lowering the car to the ground, remember to remove the chocks, release the hand brake and place the transmission in neutral.

Raising The Car In An Emergency

It happens too often - a roadside puncture, probably in the dark, probably in the rain, the spare is flat, you don't know where the car jack is, or the wheelbrace, and even if you did you don't know where the jack should go, and the wheel nuts are far too tight to be shifted by that bit of bent rod they call a wheelbrace! If you've never done it before, changing a wheel is a daunting prospect, so practise the wheel-change routine at home, before the worst happens to you.

SAFETY FIRST!
Wheel changing jacks are dreadfully unstable! Take great care not to get any part of your body under the car when supported by one of these jacks.

RAISING THE CAR

(VIIa) START by finding where the jack and the wheelbrace are normally stowed - below the boot carpet on all Sierra cars. (See XII below for P100.) CHECK that the spare hasn't gone flat: you should check it every week, along with the other wheels/tyres! PREPARE by ensuring that in the boot and/or glovebox you have an old waterproof, something to kneel on, rag to clean your hands if necessary, but also protective gloves, and a torch. The spare is here, in the boot, in Sierra and Sapphire cars.

VIIa

(VIIb) It's under the rear of the P100. Use the wheelbrace to slacken the bolt and lift/unhook the spare wheel carrier.

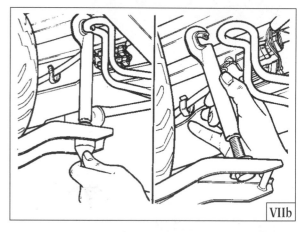

VIIb

(VIII) Wheel nuts should be done up to a specified degree of tightness, but all too often they're done up by a chap behaving like a gorilla with a toothache! Give yourself a better chance by buying one of these extendible wrenches, complete with the right-sized socket to fit your wheel nuts. Its superior strength and leverage will shift wheel nuts that the car-kit brace wouldn't even look at - it's an absolute 'must', not just for those who haven't got the strength of a raging gorilla but to replace that feeble wheel brace in the boot, for everyone!

VIII

(IX) In many instances, you will first have to lever off a wheeltrim. The car-kit wheelbrace might have a flattened end made for the job, otherwise find yourself perhaps a suitable screwdriver (keep it in the car) and lever carefully around the circumference of the trim: note where the tyre valve protrudes through, making a pencil mark if necessary. Once the wheeltrim is partly unclipped - it often needs vigorous levering, so watch that bodywork! - you may be better off donning your gloves and pulling.

IX

(X) With the wheel still on the ground, loosen the wheel nuts. For your physical wellbeing you should always bear down on the wheelbrace, rather than pull it upwards - if you're stuck with that bent-rod car-kit brace, you'll probably need a length of pipe to slip over it to extend its leverage but it will probably be a struggle to keep it on the bolt... If you try slackening the wheel nuts *after* you've raised the wheel, all you'll do is rotate the wheel, not the bolt!

(XI) Make sure now that you know exactly where and how the car jack locates, and how it is operated. If you are unsure, check your handbook or seek the advice of your car dealer. Do it NOW, so that you'll know when you need it! On all Sierras, the wheel-changing jack locates at one of these positions (identical on both sides of the car).

(XII) On the P100, place the scissors jack (found in the cab, behind the passenger seat) beneath the front suspension crossmember...

(XIII) ...or an outer end of the rear axle.

Remember to carry a piece of timber in the boot that can be placed beneath the jack to spread the load and prevent it from sinking into soft ground. Have the handbrake on, and there are purpose-made chocks you can buy that you can wedge each side of the wheel opposite to the one you are changing, to guard against the car rolling. In an emergency, use an old piece of wood or brick that you can find. Wind the jack handle until the wheel is clear of the ground, remembering if it's flat that you need enough clearance for a wheel with a fully pumped up tyre. Do not put any part of your body beneath a car which is supported only on a jack.

Once the required wheel is clear of the ground, fully undo the nuts, leaving the one 'at the top' until last so you can get your balance and a secure grip before lifting away the wheel. Nip the nuts up finger-tight, then lower the wheel to the ground for final tightening, working diagonally, a little at a time, on each nut: do them up as tight as you can, using all your strength if you're using the car-kit wheelbrace, slightly less than full strength if it's the extended wrench.

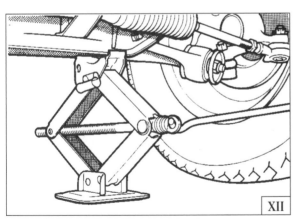

(XIV) SAFETY FIRST! and INSIDE INFORMATION
Always place the spare wheel, or the wheel you've just removed, under the car: partly for safety to help guard against being crushed; partly so that if the car topples off the wheel-change jack (and they DO, especially on soft ground) you'll be able to reposition the jack and start again.

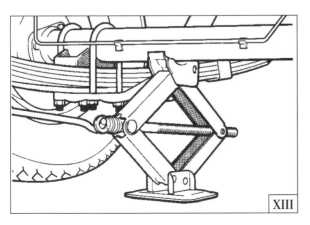

FACT FILE: ENGINE BAY LAYOUTS

These are typical Sierra engine bay Service-item layouts. Please note that some minor variations may occur, depending on the model, its age, and the number of options fitted.

1.3, 1.6 & 2.0 litre OHC Engines

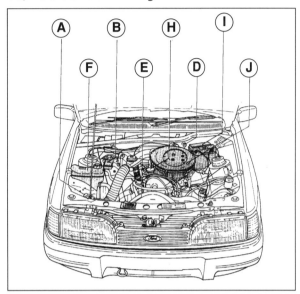

A. Windscreen washer fluid reservoir
B. Brake fluid reservoir
C. Power steering fluid reservoir
D. Engine oil dipstick
E. Vehicle identification plate

2.0 litre DOHC (injection) from 1989

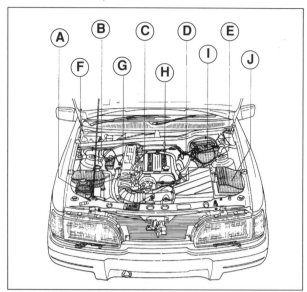

F. Engine coolant reservoir
G. Automatic transmission fluid dipstick
H. Engine oil filler cap
I. Battery
J. Air cleaner

2.3, 2.8 & 2.9 litre V6 Engines

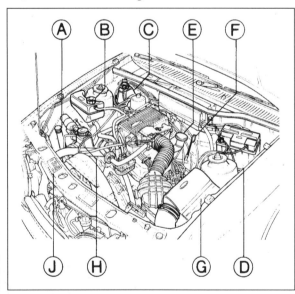

A. Windscreen/tailgate/headlamp washer
B. Engine coolant reservoir
C. Brake fluid reservoir
D. Battery
E. Engine oil filler cap

Non-Turbo Diesel Engines

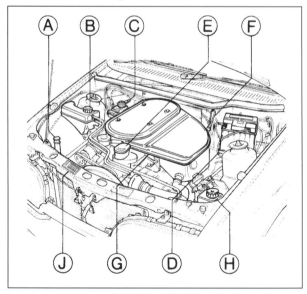

F. Engine oil dipstick
G. Air cleaner
H. Power steering fluid reservoir
J. Vehicle identification plate

Every 500 Miles, Weekly, or Before a Long Journey

These are the regular checks that you need to carry out to help keep your car safe and reliable. They don't include the major Service jobs but they should be carried out as an integral part of every 'proper' service.

Every 500 Miles - The Engine Bay

☐ **Job 1. Engine oil level.**

Although some engines barely need their sump oil topping-up between major services, even healthy ones sometimes have an unusual appetite for it while worn ones will certainly burn it. Even the best maintained engine can develop an oil leak and an engine low on oil runs the risk of internal damage, overheating and possible seizure - all of them ruining the engine.

Before you check the oil level, the engine should be switched off and left standing for a while to ensure that all oil has returned to the sump - probably the best time to do this is first thing in the morning after the car has been standing overnight.

INSIDE INFORMATION : Never overfill the engine with oil as any excess could find its way past an overloaded oil seal, or lead to over-heating and other problems.

If you're not sure where the dipstick on your engine is located, refer to FACT FILE: ENGINE BAY LAYOUTS on page 20.

1A. Make sure the car is on level ground when you check the dipstick, which on nearly all Sierras is coloured yellow. Carefully lift the dipstick out.

1B. Wipe the measuring end clean with a piece of cloth or tissue, put it back in and lift out again. The oil level should be clearly visible on the lower part of the 'stick' but if not, wipe clean and try again, turning the stick so that it goes into the tube at a different angle.

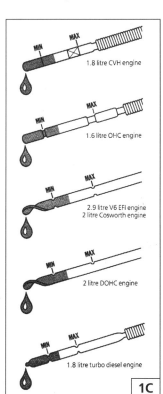

1C. Dipstick design varies according to model, but will be similar to one of those shown here. The oil 'film' adhering to the dipstick indicates the level of oil in the sump, and should be between the marks, as indicated. NOTE: Approximately one litre of oil will raise the level from the MIN to the MAX markings, so making it easy to gauge how much is needed for intermediate readings. (Illustration, courtesy Ford Motor Co.)

1D. If you need to top-up or add oil, first remove the oil filler cap, again referring to the Engine Layouts on page 20 for the location of the filler on your car. All engines except the CVH, DOHC and diesel have a push-fit filler cap that is simply pulled upwards and off; the exceptions mentioned use a cap that has to be unscrewed anti-clockwise, like that shown.

1E. Add the oil a little at a time and allow a minute or so for the fresh oil to drain down into the sump before you check the level, not forgetting to start with a clean dipstick again.

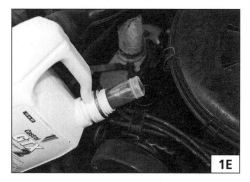

1F. For topping-up when only small quantities of oil are required, a small measuring jug, plastic bottle or funnel-measure like that shown here, is useful to pour the oil in; spills are less likely and you can also keep a check on oil consumption between service intervals.

☐ Job 2. Check coolant level.

> **SAFETY FIRST!**
> **i) The coolant level should only ever be checked WHEN THE SYSTEM IS COLD. If you remove the pressure cap when the engine is hot, the release of pressure can cause the liquid in the system to quickly boil and spurt several feet into the air, with the risk of severe scalding. ii) Take precautions to prevent antifreeze coming into contact with the skin or eyes. If this should happen rinse immediately with plenty of clean water.**

Again, this is a check that should be made first thing in the morning, before the engine has been run. There are two reasons for this: (i) Hot coolant expands, so you'll only get true level reading when it's cold; (ii) Hot coolant (like a boiling kettle) can be extremely dangerous, and removal of the filler cap can release a scalding blast of steam and liquid. See *Safety First!* above.

It is important that all engines have the correct proportion of antifreeze in the coolant. This not only helps prevent freezing in the winter, but also overheating in summer temperatures. In addition, it also helps to prevent internal engine corrosion.

If coolant is required in an emergency, use distilled water or, in extreme circumstances, rain water. NEVER use salt water or water which may have a salt content, regardless of the presence of an antifreeze content. Doing so will certainly result in engine corrosion.

DIESEL ENGINES ONLY

INSIDE INFORMATION: Because of the high rate of heat transfer around the injector nozzles, diesel engines should NEVER be run without coolant, even for short periods of time. Serious injector damage could result.

2A. Having located the position of the coolant header tank for your model from the Engine Layout section on page 20, check the coolant level against the mark on the outside of the tank (all Sierras use a translucent tank similar to that shown).

2B. If topping-up is required, turn the cap a quarter-turn anticlockwise to release any slight pressure in the system, then turn fully and remove. NEVER ATTEMPT TO REMOVE THE FILLER CAP WHEN THE ENGINE IS HOT. If, in an emergency, the cap needs to be removed before the engine has completely cooled, wrap rag around both the cap and your hands and open the cap in two stages, the first quarter turn to release any remaining internal pressure.

2C. With the cap removed, add coolant from a measuring jug or bottle. If only a small quantity is required it is quite permissible to use neat antifreeze straight from the bottle as here, which saves the trouble of mixing it with water. There is no danger of increasing the concentration of antifreeze - water is added merely for reasons of economy, provided that you don't go over about 60% antifreeze to water.

When the level is correct, replace the cap, making sure it is not cross-threaded and that it is fully tightened down, otherwise coolant leakage could lead to overheating and serious engine damage.

> *making it easy!* The coolant header tank on all models is made from semi-transparent material in order for the coolant level to be readily seen without needing to remove the cap. However, the inner surface of the tank often becomes discoloured making this impossible, but it is easily cured by cleaning the inner surface with a long-handled brush, such as those used in the kitchen for washing dishes.

INSIDE INFORMATION: Although the word ' Antifreeze' is used throughout this book as a generic term, it is more strictly correct to refer to it as 'Antifreeze/Summer Coolant' due to the corrosion-inhibiting qualities of most good-quality modern products. Modern engines need inhibitors on an all-year-round basis, even in temperate countries where frost isn't present. Ford recommend a mixture of 50/50 ratio which is easy to remember and mix!

SAFETY FIRST!
i) If brake fluid should come into contact with the skin or eyes, rinse immediately with plenty of water. ii) It is acceptable for the brake fluid level to fall slightly during normal use, but if it falls significantly below the bottom of the filler cap neck, it indicates a leak or an internal seal failure. Stop using the car and seek specialist advice immediately. iii) If you get dirt into the hydraulic system it can cause brake failure. Wipe the filler cap clean before removing. iv) You should only ever use only new brake fluid from an airtight container. Old fluid absorbs moisture and this could cause the brakes to fail when carrying out an emergency stop or other heavy use of the brakes - just when you need them most and are least able to do anything about it, in fact!

☐ Job 3. Check brake fluid level.

Check/top-up brake fluid level as required.

3A. Even though all models are fitted with a device to monitor the brake fluid level in the reservoir and operate a warning lamp on the instrument panel when the level drops below the MIN mark, it is wise to check the level physically while carrying out these other checks, as failure of the warning-light system (i.e. the bulb!) could go unnoticed. There's no need to remove the cap on the reservoir which is translucent, making the fluid level easily seen.

If you are unsure of the brake fluid reservoir location, see the Engine Layouts section on page 20 for details of your car.

3B. If the cap is to be removed (after cleaning!), hold the centre section of the cap and the sensor wires steady while the outer part is unscrewed anticlockwise.

3C. Before lifting the cap clear of the reservoir, allow the fluid contained in the sensor 'tube' on the underside of the cap to drain away - remember, brake fluid is damaging to paintwork, even that in the engine bay! When drained, place the cap on a piece of rag or tissue to catch any remaining drips.

3D. Before adding fresh fluid position a piece of rag around the filler neck to catch any spillages. Don't overfill the reservoir, and remember to leave some space to allow for the displacement of fluid by the sensor tube when the cap is replaced afterwards.

INSIDE INFORMATION: i) Check the ground on which the car has been parked, especially beneath the engine bay and inside each road wheel, for evidence of oil, or brake fluid leaks. If any are found, investigate further before driving the car.

3A

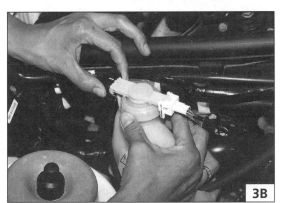
3B

SAFETY FIRST!
If the brake fluid level in the reservoir drops quite markedly over a short period, the cause must be investigated immediately - it could be dangerous to drive the car until the fault is found and rectified. Modern dual-circuit hydraulic brake systems should always give some braking ability provided any leakage is confined to just one of the circuits.

Note that on all disc-braked cars a gradual drop in the fluid level over a lengthy period is normal. This is because, as the disc pads' friction material wears, the pad backing plates move nearer to the disc, the brake caliper pistons (in contact with the backing plates) move further out of their bores, the fluid follows the pistons, and more fluid from the reservoir flows into the system to fill the extra space thus created.

3C

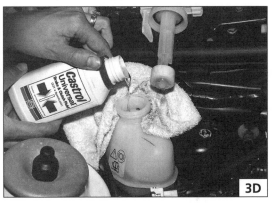
3D

☐ Job 4. Check battery electrolyte.

SAFETY FIRST!
i) The gas given off by a battery is highly explosive. Never smoke, use a naked flame or allow a spark to occur in the battery compartment. Never disconnect the battery (it can cause sparking) with the battery caps removed. ii) Batteries contain sulphuric acid. If the acid comes into contact with the skin or eyes, wash immediately with copious amounts of cold water and seek medical advice. iii) Do not check the battery levels within half an hour of the battery being charged with a separate battery charger because the addition of fresh water could then cause the highly acid and corrosive electrolyte to flood out of the battery. Many vehicles were fitted by the manufacturer with a 'sealed for life' or low-maintenance type of battery, but it is possible that yours may have a 'normal' item, fitted by a subsequent owner. If yours is the former type, then no maintenance is required. This section relates to the common type of replacement battery.

FACT FILE: DISCONNECTING THE BATTERY

Many vehicles depend on a constant power supply from the battery and you can find yourself in all sorts of trouble if you simply disconnect the battery on those vehicles. You might find that the car alarm will go off, you could find that the engine management forgets all it has ever "learned" and the car will feel very strange to drive until it has re-programmed itself, and you could find that your radio refuses to operate again unless you key in the correct code. And if you've bought the car second-hand and don't know the code, you would have to send the set back to the manufacturer for re-programming. So, you must ensure that the vehicle has a constant power supply even though the battery is removed. To do so, you will need a separate 12 volt battery supply. You *could* put a self tapping screw into the positive lead near the battery terminal before disconnecting it, and put a positive connection to your other battery via this screw. But you would have to be EXTREMELY CAREFUL to wrap insulation tape around the connection so that no short is caused. The negative terminal on the other battery would also have to be connected to the car's bodywork.

A better way is to use something like the

Sykes-Pickavant Computer Saver shown here. Clip the cables to your spare battery and plug it into your cigarette lighter. (You may have to turn the ignition switch to the "Auxiliary" setting to allow the cigarette lighter to function.)

You have to hold in the red button on the Computer Saver while inserting it into the cigarette lighter, and if two green lights still show after the button is released, you have a good connection and your battery can now be disconnected and removed.

Be sure not to turn on any of the car's equipment while the auxiliary battery is connected.

Where the battery has screw caps to the individual cells, or a removable strip which plugs into or over a number of cells at a time, it is obviously intended that its electrolyte content should be topped up as and when required. Note that some so-called 'maintenance-free' batteries may have flush-fitting strips over its cells which can be prised up for the addition of electrolyte, perhaps prolonging its life beyond general expectation!

Most Sierras were fitted with a 'maintenance-free' battery when new, but that doesn't mean they are sealed-for-life like some other makes; although evaporation of the electrolyte is much reduced, over a period of time there are occasions when the addition of distilled water is required. The provision of cell caps at least means it is possible to test the electrolyte with a hydrometer - see Job 4D.

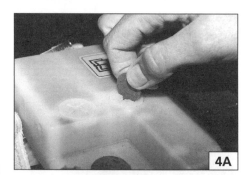

4A

making it easy! 4A. Use a coin to undo cell caps, rather than a screwdriver. The slots are very wide made of very soft plastic and just chew up if you try to use an ordinary screwdriver.

4B. 'Ordinary' batteries: If the battery case is translucent, look for a level mark scribed or moulded on the side, otherwise a general recommendation is that the electrolyte level should be just above the tops of the plates which you can see with the cell caps or strips removed.

4B

INSIDE INFORMATION: Note that here is an instance where it is preferable that the battery should be warm, such as after a run, before checking the level, since the electrolyte expands with heat. If it were topped up while cold there is a danger that later the fluid would overflow, leading to corrosion of the terminals and accumulated dirt.

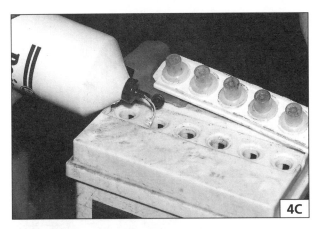

4C

4C. Top up only with distilled (de-ionised) water, never ordinary tap water, which may contain impurities which would damage the plates and shorten the battery's life. Mop up any accidental spillage immediately, and make sure the entire battery exterior is clean and dry. You can buy de-ionised water from the auto accessory shop, either in handy top-up bottles or in bulk containers - note that it is highly recommended, for steam irons!

4D. Here's how to check the 'specific gravity' of the battery electrolyte, which in turn indicates the degree of 'charge' in the battery by reference to a scale printed on the hydrometer. Draw a small amount of electrolyte into the transparent tube and observe the number of beads that 'float' in the liquid. Check each cell in turn and if one or more of the cells gives a reading significantly lower than the others, the battery is probably defective and likely to become unusable at any time - have the battery checked out by a specialist, or you could find yourself with a car that refuses to start one morning!.

4D

Check the tightness of the battery clamp. A loose, rattling battery will have a shorter life than one that is held down securely.

If checking now reveals corroded terminals (typically, a white powdery growth) refer to *Job 80, Battery terminals*.

☐ Job 5. Check screenwash level.

Check screenwash fluid level reservoir and top-up if necessary.

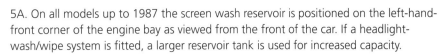

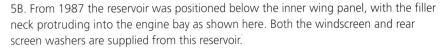

It can be positively dangerous to run out of screenwash fluid in mid-journey, so check the washer bottle level regularly!

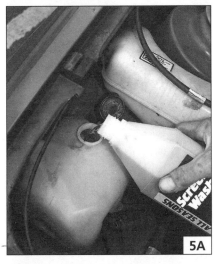

5A

5A. On all models up to 1987 the screen wash reservoir is positioned on the left-hand-front corner of the engine bay as viewed from the front of the car. If a headlight-wash/wipe system is fitted, a larger reservoir tank is used for increased capacity.

5B. From 1987 the reservoir was positioned below the inner wing panel, with the filler neck protruding into the engine bay as shown here. Both the windscreen and rear screen washers are supplied from this reservoir.

5C. On early saloon and estate models, the rear screen washer reservoir is situated alongside the tailgate opening on the nearside.

Make sure the reservoir is kept fully topped up, using a good brand of screenwash additive that promises not to freeze up in winter and helps clean the screen in summer. Stick to the recommended concentration and never add cooling system antifreeze, since, like brake fluid, this is also an effective paint stripper!

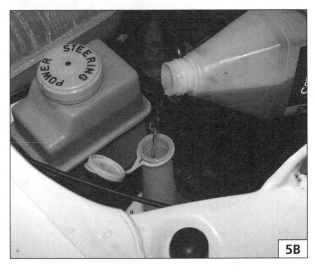

5B

5C

Every 500 Miles - Around the Car

☐ **Job 6. Check tyre pressures.**

6A

This is another job that is best done 'cold', for certainly after any appreciable run the tyres will have warmed up and the air inside will have expanded, giving you a higher pressure reading.

Correct tyre pressures will not only prolong tyre life, they will also make for safer driving. The tyre pressures for the various tyre sizes are shown in *Chapter 8, Facts and Figures*.

6A. Garage airline readings can be unreliable, so use a good quality gauge of your own to check that the tyre pressures accord with your handbook recommendations. Provided the garage is little more than 'just down the road', you can drive there to use the airline, checking afterwards with your own gauge that you have got the pressures right. Of course, having your own foot pump, of a good make, is also a good idea! Observe the utmost cleanliness, and don't forget to replace the valve caps afterwards.

6B. Don't forget to check the spare wheel in the boot, otherwise it may not be usable when you need it! The 'pencil' type gauge shown here is available quite cheaply from most accessory shops and is sufficiently accurate if not mistreated.

P100 MODELS ONLY

6C. The spare wheel is a little more difficult to get at on this model, being situated beneath the cargo area floor - but that doesn't make it any less vital to check!

6B

☐ **Job 7. Check headlights, sidelights and front indicators.**

SPECIALIST SERVICE: It is not possible to set headlight alignment accurately at home. They will need to be checked by a garage with proper headlight beam setting equipment.

> *SAFETY FIRST!*
> *i) It is important, for reasons both of safety and legality, that your car's lights work correctly and that the reflectors and lenses are in good condition. Replace faulty bulbs as soon as possible and get any damaged lens renewed. ii) If removing a headlight bulb, be aware that these items get extremely hot in use and are capable of burning fingers for some minutes after switching off; allow at least five minutes for the bulbs, and their holders, to cool before attempting to remove them. NEVER hold a headlight bulb while it is switched on - it will burn you before you can let it go!*

6C

Check that ALL lights operate correctly and with equal brightness on each side of the car; in other words, that both left and right-hand sidelights for instance, are equally bright.

making it easy! When checking the rear lights it helps to have an assistant stand at the rear of the car to confirm each light is working, but the job can be done alone if the car is reversed close to a garage door or wall so that the reflections of the lights can be seen from the driver's seat. Also, test the stop-lights with the sidelights already switched on, then the indicators with the stoplights held on; this test causes maximum current to flow through the earth circuit of the rear-light clusters, which occasionally suffer from poor earth connections.

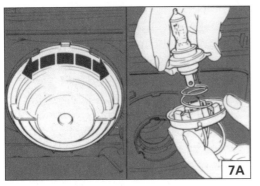

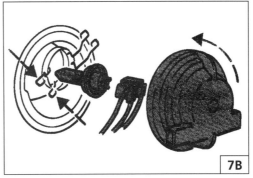

HEADLIGHT BULB REPLACEMENT

MODELS UP TO 1987

7A. The headlight and sidelight bulbs are replaced from within the engine bay after first removing the dust cover from the rear of the headlight unit by turning it anticlockwise. Carefully pull off the wiring plug, then turn the spring-loaded bulb retainer anticlockwise and remove it from the unit. The headlight bulb can now be removed. When re-fitting the bulb, make sure the locating lugs on the bulb flange are engaged with the recesses in the holder before re-fitting the bulb retainer clip and dust cover. (Illustration, courtesy Ford Motor Co.)

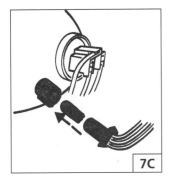

MODELS FROM 1987

7B. From inside the engine bay, turn and lift-away the plastic cover and disconnect the wiring plug from the rear of the bulb; squeeze the ends of the wire retainer spring together and swing it out of the way, then lift out the bulb. When you fit a replacement bulb, ensure the locating lugs on the bulb 'skirt' engage the recesses in the light unit before refitting the spring clip. (Illustration, courtesy Ford Motor Co.)

INSIDE INFORMATION: i) On some V6 engine models you will need to remove part of the air cleaner assembly to get at the rear of the nearside headlight - this is described in Job 78. ii) NEVER touch the glass envelope of a headlight bulb, as this can cause the bulb to 'blow' when switched on; always handle such bulbs by the metal base-cap. New bulbs are usually supplied with a paper or card tube protecting the glass envelope - don't remove it until you are about to fit the bulb to the light unit. iii) If you DO accidentally touch the glass envelope, clean it with methylated spirit before fitting.

FRONT SIDELIGHT BULBS

7C. These are contained within the headlight reflector; to renew the bulb, first remove the moulded dust cover from the rear of the light unit by twisting anticlockwise. (Illustration, courtesy Ford Motor Co.)

7D. The sidelight bulbholder is a push-fit in the reflector, as is the bulb in the holder itself.

FRONT DIRECTION INDICATOR LIGHT BULBS

UP TO 1987 ONLY

7E. Remove the direction indicator light assembly from the front bumper by pressing the outside edge of the unit inwards until the plastic retaining clip (A) can be heard to lock in the depressed position, when the unit can be removed. On Ghia models, press the release lever (B) upwards as shown to release the light unit. (Illustration, courtesy Ford Motor Co.)

Turn the bulb holder anticlockwise to release it; the bulb is extracted by pushing slightly into the holder then turning to the left and lifting out. To refit the assembly, push the light into its opening until the locking tab can be heard to engage.

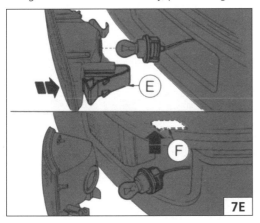

LATER MODELS 1987 ON

7F. From inside the engine bay, release the retaining spring and pull the unit forwards from outside the car. Turn the bulbholder anticlockwise to release it

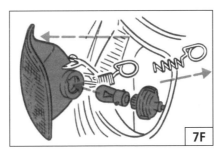

and remove the bulb by pushing slightly into the holder and turning to the left. Check that the bulb holder is clean and dry then fit the bulb and re-assemble the light unit. (Illustration, courtesy Ford Motor Co.)

AUXILIARY DRIVING LIGHTS (IF FITTED)

7G. Swing the wire clip forwards and remove the protective cap. Compress the retaining spring securing the bulb and swing it aside. Pull out the bulb and disconnect the wire terminal. If renewing the bulb, be careful not to touch the glass envelope - see *INSIDE INFORMATION* above. (Illustration, courtesy Ford Motor Co.)

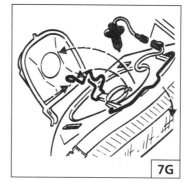

7G

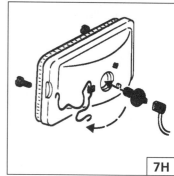

7H

7H. Front fog lights are those fitted beneath the bumper: The light unit is secured by two crosshead screws - removing these allows the unit to be pulled forward. The bulb is retained by a wire spring which is moved sideways and up, allowing the bulb to be removed and disconnected from the terminal. Be careful not to touch the glass envelope of the bulb with the fingers. (Illustration, courtesy Ford Motor Co.)

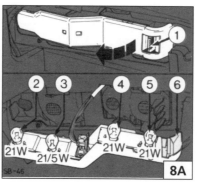

8A

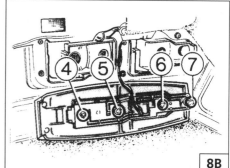

8B

☐ **Job 8. Rear lights and indicator bulbs.**

HATCHBACK MODELS UP TO 1987

8A. From inside the luggage compartment, press the locking tab as shown (1) and pull away the complete light assembly (6). Having identified the bulb concerned, push-and-turn anticlockwise to remove it. Fit the new bulb into the cluster and replace the unit, taking care to slide the outer end into the retainer and guiding the bulbs into their apertures, then press the assembly firmly back into place. (Illustration, courtesy Ford Motor Co.)

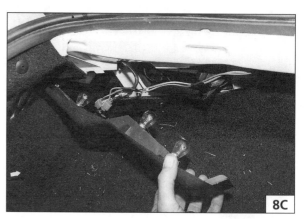

8C

(Key to bulb identification: 2 - Indicator; 3 - stop & tail light; 4 - reversing light; 5 - rear fog light).

HATCHBACK AND SALOON MODELS FROM 1987-ON

8B. The procedure is the same as for the previous **Job 8A**, but note the following difference in bulb positions within the cluster: 1 - stoplight; 2 - reverse light; 3 - tail light/rear fog light; 4 - direction indicator. (Illustration, courtesy Ford Motor Co.)

8C. Re-fit the cluster by engaging the outer end into its retainer, guide the bulbs through their apertures and push firmly home to engage the catch at the inner end.

8D

ESTATE MODELS (ALL YEARS)

8D. Open the tailgate and remove the trim cover from the relevant rear light unit. Release the tabs (1) & (2) at the top and bottom to withdraw the complete light assembly. Identify the bulb concerned and remove it by pressing inwards and turning anticlockwise. Make sure the light holder is clean and dry before fitting the bulb and refitting the assembly. BULB IDENTIFICATION: 4 - stoplight; 5 - tail light; 6 - direction indicator; 7 - reverse light; 8 - rear fog light. (Illustration, courtesy Ford Motor Co.)

P100 MODELS

8E. The rear light cluster is positioned in the rear body corners and protected by an outer metal plate; access to the light cluster is gained by removing the two crosshead screws and lifting away the plate, which reveals an inner dust cover secured by two 'wing-nut' type fasteners.

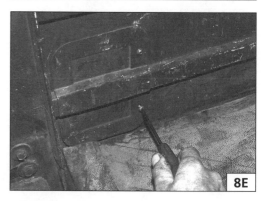

8E

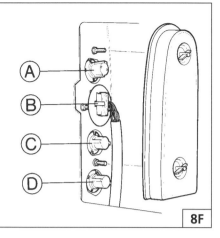

A. Direction indicators (12 volt, 21 watt)
B. Tail light/stop light (12 volt, 21 watt)
C. Reversing light (12 volt, 21 watt)
D. Rear fog light (12 volt, 21 watt)

8F

8F. Each bulb is retained by a holder which is removed by turning a quarter-turn anticlockwise. When removed, the bulb is released by pushing slightly, turning to the left and lifting out. (Illustration, courtesy Ford Motor Co.)

INSIDE INFORMATION : As mentioned above, earthing problems can arise on the rear light multi-bulb holder, mainly due to damp which causes corrosion of the metal 'tracks', or conductors, that connect each bulb to the wiring harness. To prevent this problem, smear petroleum jelly over the tracks and the edge connector terminals to protect them from the effects of moisture and air.

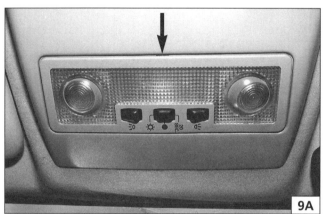

9A

☐ **Job 9. Interior light bulbs.**

9A. Prise the light cover away (position arrowed) with a screwdriver but take care not to damage the headlining/paintwork or the bulb holder. Unclip the bulb to remove it. Fit the bulb to the holder and press the assembly back into position.

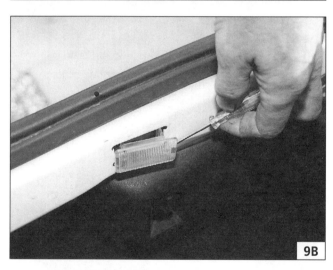

9B

9B. Luggage bay lights are removed in a similar fashion. The bulb holder and bulb are all-of-a-piece with the lens.

☐ **Job 10. Number plate light bulbs.**

ALL MODELS EXCEPT P100

10A. Gently lever the light assembly out of the bumper with a screwdriver.

10B. Turn the bulb socket anticlockwise and remove it from the light unit. The bulb is a push fit in the holder. Re-fit in the reverse order of removal.

10A

10B

P100 MODELS

10C. These lights are positioned one each end of the number plate. To remove a bulb, gently prise off the cover with a small screwdriver, press and turn the bulb to lift it away.

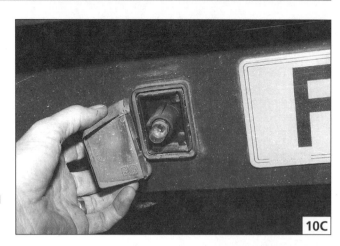

10C

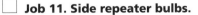
☐ Job 11. Side repeater bulbs.

11. Turn the complete light assembly in a clockwise direction and pull it out from the car body. Detach the housing from the bulb holder by turning it anticlockwise, then pull the bulb out of its holder. Make sure the bulb holder is clean and dry before fitting the bulb and re-fitting the assembly to the car.

☐ Job 12. Check horns.

12. Try the horn button. If the horn fails to work, examine the wiring to the horn's themselves - positioned beneath the radiator as shown - otherwise seek professional advice. (N.B. This view is from beneath the car.)

11

SPECIALIST SERVICE: Horn wiring and the connections are more complex than they appear at first. For instance, both terminals at the horn should be 'live'! If there is no obvious problem with the wiring connections, have the horn circuitry and switches checked over by a specialist.

☐ Job 13. Check windscreen wipers.

13A. Check the wiper blades for splitting, hardening of the rubber blade, and that no metal part of the blade carrier is contacting the screen, which will quickly score and ruin the glass - which is also a possible MoT failure. Wipe each blade with methylated spirit to remove traces of oil and dirt that would otherwise be smeared across the screen. Don't forget the rear tailgate wiper and/or headlight wipers if fitted to your model.

13B. Worn or damaged blades are easily replaced by squeezing this clip and pushing the blade towards the bottom of the arm, then lifting clear. Re-fit by placing the blade over the 'hook' of the arm and engaging the plastic clip. If new blades are being fitted, new clips also will be included. (Illustration, courtesy Ford Motor Co.)

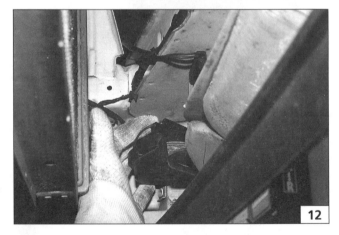

12

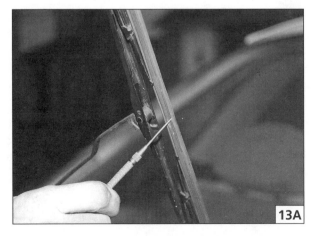

13A

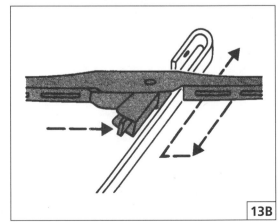

13B

☐ Job 14. Windscreen washers.

14A. The windscreen washer jets are adjustable, the direction of the jet 'aim' being altered by the use of a pin inserted in the jet nozzle. (Illustration, courtesy Ford Motor Co.)

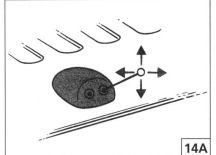

14A

14B. Make sure there is no build-up of dried polish or other debris which might obstruct the fine nozzles. If the spray from one of the jets seems uncertain or is non-existent, and you're sure the feed tube to the jet is secure, try poking the jet with a pin to clear possible blockage.

14C. Don't forget to check the rear screen washer (if fitted to your car); on some earlier models and all estates, the jet is positioned in the wiper arm 'hub' and is adjustable by use of a pin, as described above.

14D. Later hatchback models placed the washer jet at the top of the tailgate - adjustment is again made by use of a pin to 'aim' the jet at the centre of the screen.

14B

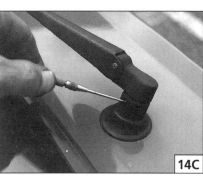

14C

14D

FACT FILE: FUSES

Fuse No:	Amps	Fuse Connections of Fuse Relay Box
1	20	LH Main Beam, LH Road Light
2	20	RH Main Beam, RH Road Light
3	10	LH Dip Beam
4	10	RH Dip Beam
5	10	LH Side Lights
6	10	RH Side Lights
7	15	Instrument Illum., Number Plate Light
8		Free
9	30	Headl. Clean.
10	20	Interior Lights, Clock, Door Locking, Power Mirror
11	20	Fuel Pump (Air Condition)
12	10	Hazard Flasher
13	30	Heated Seats, Cigar. Lighter
14	30	Horn
15	30	Wiper Motors, Washer Pump
16	30	Heat. Backlite, Heat. Mirror
17	20	Front Fog Lights, Dim Dip
18	30	Heater Blower
19		Rear Fog Light, on RHD Variants free
20	15	Flasher, Back up Lights
21	15	Stop Lights
22	10	Control Circuits, Indicators
23	20	Power Window
24	30	Fuel Pump

The fuse box on all models (also containing the relays) is found at the rear of the engine bay left-corner. Raise the lid of the box by lifting the forward end and disengaging the tab.

1,500 Miles - or Every Month, whichever comes first

Every 1,500 Miles - Around the Car

☐ **Job 15. Check tyres.**

See also *Chapter 7, Getting Through the MoT* for a more detailed explanation of tyre wear and problems likely to be encountered.

15A. Check the tyres for sufficient tread depth using a special depth gauge and note that, in the UK, the minimum legal tread depth is 1.6mm. However, tyres are not at their safest at that level, particularly in the wet, and you might want to replace them earlier. Measure the tread across the width of the tyre, at three or four places around the circumference. This will give early warning of any uneven wear pattern, perhaps caused by a steering or suspension fault, or a defect in the tyre itself.

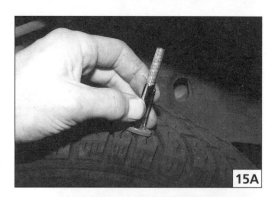
15A

15B. Check the inner and outer sidewalls for bulges and splits, also the wheel rims if kerbstones etc. have been driven over (accidentally, of course!). Raise each wheel off the ground, supporting the car on an axle stand, otherwise you won't be able to examine the inside wall of the tyre properly, nor will you be able to check that part of the tyre in contact with the ground. If you find any splits or other damage, the tyre(s) should be inspected immediately by a tyre specialist who will advise whether repair is possible or replacement is required.

☐ **Job 16. Check spare tyre.**

Don't forget the spare wheel - on all models it will be found beneath the boot floor covering. Check it as for the road wheels detailed previously, paying particular attention to the sidewalls which can be damaged if the tyre isn't fixed firmly in the wheel well. Check the tyre pressure too.

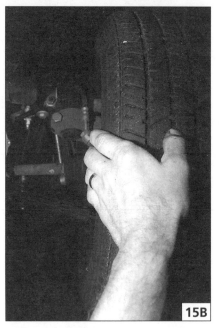
15B

 *making it easy!* *You should inflate the spare tyre to the maximum recommended for high speed or load running. Then, if you have a puncture while on a journey, you'll be okay. It's always easier to carry a tyre pressure gauge with you and let some air out than put some in.*

☐ **Job 17. Wash bodywork.**

INSIDE INFORMATION: Many people choose to wash their cars weekly, which is commendable, while others never seem to wash them at all! But there's no denying that regularly washed-and-waxed bodywork lasts longer and helps maintain a car's value. Getting into a regular car washing routine has the advantage that minor damage to the paintwork does not go unnoticed and can be quickly treated before serious corrosion gets a hold.

☐ **Job 18. Touch-up paintwork.**

18. Treat small areas of damage, like the stonechip shown here, as soon as possible, otherwise corrosion of the exposed metal will soon get a hold and prove difficult (and expensive) to repair. 'Touch-Up' type products are available from car accessory shops and garages in the form of paint 'pens' and even colour-matched film that is simply 'stuck' over the damaged area. These products may not give an invisible repair, but they do offer protection from road salt and water.

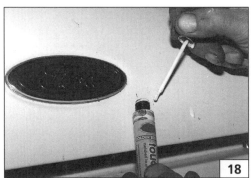
18

SAFETY FIRST!
Tyres that show uneven wear tell their own story, if only you know how to speak the language! If any tyre is worn more on one side than another, consult your main dealer or tyre specialist. It probably means that your suspension or steering is out of adjustment - probably a simple tracking job but conceivably symptomatic of suspension damage, so have it checked. If a tyre is worn more in the centre or on the edges, it could mean that your tyre pressures are wrong, but once again, have the car checked. Incorrectly inflated tyres wear rapidly, can cause the car's handling to become dangerous and can even cause the car to consume noticeably more fuel. When checking your tyres, don't forget to include the spare.

☐ Job 19. Radio aerial.

19. Clean each section of an extending aerial with a spray-on lubricant such as WD40 and work the aerial up and down a few times. With electrically-operated aerials it is especially important to keep the sections clean, otherwise the operating motor and/or gears will be over-stressed and quickly fail. Do not leave excess lubricating oil on the aerial sections as this will simply encourage the adherence of grit and dirt.

NOTE: Some models from 1989 onwards use the heated rear window element as an aerial also, so don't be confused if you can't find the aerial on a later car!

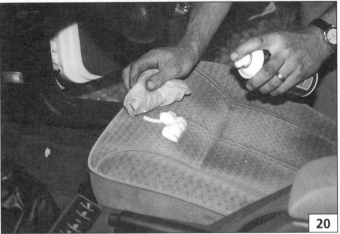

☐ Job 20. Valet interior.

20. Regularly vacuuming the seats and carpets will not only make the car more pleasant to drive, but will also remove a surprising amount of abrasive grit and dust, the main cause of worn patches. For stains and grease marks, use one of the many domestic upholstery cleaning materials. Some stains may only be effectively removed by the use of white spirit or methylated spirits - test these on an unseen area first though, to check for colour-fastness of the upholstery.

☐ Job 21. Improve visibility.

21. Use a proprietary glass cleaner to clean all the windows on the inside as well as the outside. Tar spots and dead insects can be removed with special cleaners available from garages and car accessory shops. 'Traffic film' can build up unnoticed and is a mixture of oil and grime thrown from the wheels of other vehicles, resulting in dangerous smearing of the windscreen in the wet, and which ordinary washer additives cannot shift. A proper traffic film remover is instantly effective however, and lasts well.

Every 1,500 Miles - Under the Car

☐ Job 22. Clean mud traps.

22. Use a water jet to clean underneath the wheel arches front and rear. If available, a high pressure washer is the most effective method but take care: on a powerful spray the pressure may blast away the underseal!

INSIDE INFORMATION: Even where the car is fitted with plastic 'inner' wheel arch linings, mud can build-up around the edges and will act like a sponge to salt- laden water thrown from the tyres. The result is bubbling and flaking of paint from around the edges of the wheelarches.

3,000 MILE SERVICE

3,000 Miles - or Every Three Months, whichever comes first

Every 3,000 Miles - The Engine Bay

☐ **Job 23. Generator drive belt.**

SAFETY FIRST!
Disconnect the battery before working on drive belts so that the engine cannot inadvertently be started or turned over, causing personal injury.

On all belts, look for signs of cracking, fraying or polishing on the inner face. Always replace if in doubt.

23A

23A. Check the tension of the alternator drive belt by deflecting it with firm finger or thumb pressure at a point halfway along the top 'run' of the belt. The amount of movement should be no more than 12mm (0.5in.). Also check the general condition of the belt, looking for signs of cracking and frayed edges.

23B. Tension the drivebelt (if necessary) by slackening all four bolts shown - loosen bolt 2 just sufficiently to allow movement of the alternator but maintaining a degree of 'grip'. On the V6 engine, the adjuster strap is beneath the alternator, rather than above it.

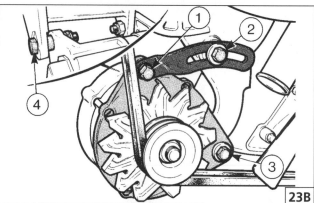
23B

making it easy! 23C. Use a length of wood (such as the handle of a hammer) to apply sideways pressure to the alternator body (as near to the drive end bracket as possible) moving it away from the engine against belt tension. Provided the alternator bracket bolt hasn't been loosened too much, the alternator should 'stay-put' while the adjuster stay nut and bolt are tightened. However, if you find this procedure difficult (it takes practice!) ask an assistant to hold the wood while you tighten the bolt.

23C

23D. On DOHC engines with power steering, an automatic belt tensioner is used which, as the name suggests, requires no manual adjustment; however, it is important to check the belt for general condition at this period.

23D

☐ **Job 24. Check brake/fuel lines.**

SAFETY FIRST! AND SPECIALIST SERVICE
Fuel injection systems remain pressurised even when the engine is switched off and this requires a special procedure to make it safe - UNDER NO CIRCUMSTANCES loosen or remove fuel pipes on a fuel injection system. If pipework requires repair, take the car immediately to a fuel injection specialist or Ford dealer.

As everyone is aware, petrol is highly flammable and only a small spark is necessary to ignite it, with potentially disastrous consequences. If a fuel leak, (however slight) is suspected or detected; don't smoke, switch off all car accessories (but don't disconnect the battery which often creates sparks as the terminals are removed) and mop-up any spilt or dripping fuel with rags which should by take immediately out of doors. Don't drive the car until professional advice is sought and the problem rectified.

24. Make a physical check of all the pipework and connections in the engine bay. Bend the flexible fuel lines in order to expose hairline cracks or deterioration which may not be immediately obvious. Look for signs of rust or tell-tale fluid marks on brake pipes and unions. Start the engine and check that there are no fuel leaks.

SAFETY FIRST!
Whenever you are dealing with diesel fuel, it's essential to protect your hands by wearing plastic gloves.

☐ **Job 25. Drain fuel filter.**

DIESEL ENGINES ONLY
Drain the diesel fuel filter to remove any water residue.

INSIDE INFORMATION: The fuel filter on diesel engines is designed so that any water which passes through it will collect at the bottom of the filter housing, immediately above the drain plug. This means that any water present will be drained first and the drain plug closed as soon as fuel begins to flow. Under normal conditions, the amount of water likely to be present is usually very small. However, the careful diesel owner may wish to check the filter every 3,000 miles.

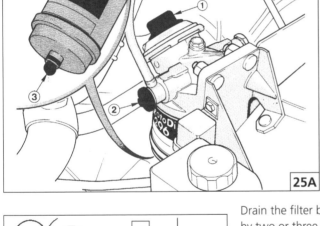

25A. The filter is located on the right-hand side of the engine bay sidewall adjacent to the suspension turret. Place a small container or wad of thick rags beneath the filter, to catch the fuel and any water contained in it when the valve is opened. Drain the filter by unscrewing the drain plug (3) fitted to the base of the filter unit by two or three turns; it may be necessary to open the bleed valve screw (2) a turn or two to allow the fuel to flow.

25B. If more than a very small amount of fuel is removed then it will be necessary to 'bleed' any air from the filter. This is done by operating the plunger (1) in 25A above, or, on pre-1987 models, the 'push-pull' plunger knob shown here. In both cases, make sure the drain plug is closed, but leave the bleed screw open two or three turns to allow any air to escape; when fuel begins to flow from the bleed screw, priming is complete and the screw can be closed.

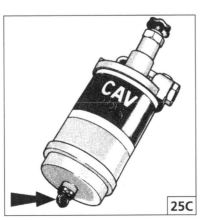

25C. The fuel filter and drain plug on pre-1987 models. (Illustrations, courtesy Ford Motor Co.)

Every 3,000 Miles - Around the Car

☐ Job 26. Check tightness of wheel nuts.

26. Check the tightness of all wheel nuts. The wheel brace supplied with the car is merely intended for use in an emergency and we strongly recommend the use of a torque wrench for this job. This will avoid over-tightening the nuts and avoids the danger of stripped threads or over-stressed studs.

To 'torque' the wheel nuts correctly, first slacken each nut and check that the threads aren't stiff or corroded, then tighten with the wrench to a torque of 9kg m (65 lb.ft).

26

☐ Job 27. Check brake/fuel lines.

27A. Carefully examine all the pipes under the car for signs of rust or weeping unions. Deep pitting indicates severe rusting and this, or even the slightest of leaks can render the car dangerous to drive. It must not be driven until the problem has been rectified.

27B. Bend all flexible hoses to show up signs of cracking rubber if any are found, the hose should be replaced as soon as possible. The hoses should also be free from bulges or chafing marks.

INSIDE INFORMATION: Bend the hoses double, and check visually near the union ends for any signs of wear or damage. Also, have an assistant press hard on the brake pedal while the hoses are checked for bulging. Any hose not in perfect condition should be replaced as soon as possible.

27A

☐ Job 28. Check handbrake adjustment.

28A. Apply the handbrake, without pressing the release knob at the end of the lever, and count the number of 'clicks' the lever goes through before the brake is firmly applied: the brake should lock at between 2 and 4 clicks. If more or less than these figures, the cable can be adjusted as follows.

Raise the rear of the vehicle sufficiently to allow the rear wheels to turn and to provide sufficient working clearance, and support the body on axle stands. Fully release the handbrake and apply the footbrake firmly several times to ensure the automatic adjusters on each wheel are fully 'set'.

27B

28B. The handbrake cable adjuster is located beneath the rear passenger-side floor and consists of two plastic 'hand-wheel' type nuts (A) & (B) threaded onto the outer casing of the cable, which abut a fixed bracket. Slacken locknut (B) and turn nut (A) to adjust the cable travel. Tightening (A) against the bracket reduces handbrake lever travel, while loosening (A) increases the travel. (Illustration, courtesy Ford Motor Co.)

SAFETY FIRST!
Don't work beneath a vehicle supported only on axle stands with someone else sitting inside trying the handbrake. It's too risky that their movements will cause the vehicle to fall off the axle stands. Make sure that you are well clear of the raised vehicle when someone is inside it. Read carefully the information at the start of this chapter on lifting and supporting the vehicle.

28A

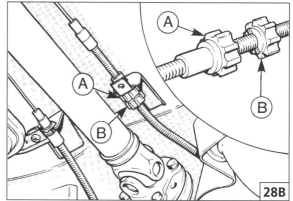
28B

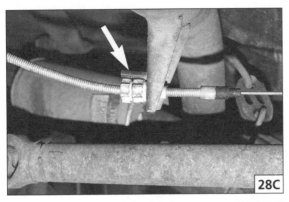

28C

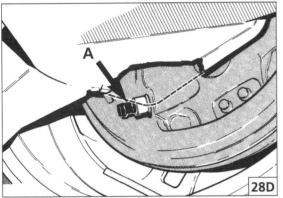

28D

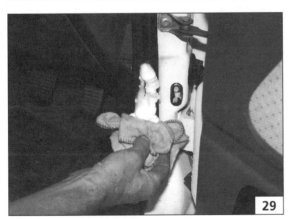

29

28C. Later models have a plastic 'pin' (arrowed) projecting from the bracket parallel with the nuts, whose purpose is to prevent both nuts turning together. The pin can be pushed slightly to one side to allow the adjusters to turn.

Adjustment is correct when, with the handbrake lever raised one 'click', the rear wheels are only just free to turn under firm hand pressure.

28D. On models fitted with drum brakes, confirm correct adjustment by pushing in the plungers (A) on each brake backplate the amount of movement should be 0.5 to 1.0mm. with the handbrake lever fully released. (Illustration, courtesy Ford Motor Co.)

On all models, apply the handbrake lever firmly several times to 'settle' the brake mechanisms and equalise the cables. Also, ensure the rear wheels are free to turn when the lever is fully released; a slight 'rubbing' sound from the brakes as the wheels are spun is permissible, provided there is no appreciable 'drag' affecting the wheels' freedom to turn.

When adjustment is correct, tighten the locking-nut (B) up to and against nut (A) ensuring the latter isn't disturbed, or turned in the process.

IMPORTANT: Make doubly sure the handbrake is applied firmly before lowering the car to the ground, to avoid the car rolling away with no-one inside!

INSIDE INFORMATION: If, during or after adjustment, braking effort on each side of the car seems unequal for a given number of 'clicks', or one side fails to work at all, there is a problem either with the cable to the wheel concerned (internal corrosion is the most common cause) or a fault with the handbrake mechanism contained within the drum or caliper. Refer to **Job 68** *or* **69** *(depending on model) for details of the rear brake internal mechanisms, or seek professional advice.*

☐ Job 29. Check door/tailgate seals.

29. To preserve the weather protection efficiency of door and tailgate (or bootlid) seals, they should be regularly cleaned and periodically treated with a proprietary 'conditioning' product. Also, if a sunroof is fitted to your car, treat the sunroof seal similarly.

☐ Job 30. Check windscreen.

30. Check the windscreen for chips and scratches which are a potential MoT failure point depending on their location and size see *Chapter 7, Getting Through the MoT,* for what is and is not acceptable according to UK regulations. Most small chips less than 10mm wide can be repaired by specialists, while light scoring can often be polished out by the same people. Kits are now available in most accessory stores for DIY repair. For larger chips - get out that insurance policy!

☐ Job 31. Rear view mirrors.

31. Check the rear view mirrors, both interior and exterior for cracking or other damage. Also ensure that the interior rear view mirror is securely fixed in place since they can work loose. When this happens, the vibration will not give a clear view of what is behind you.

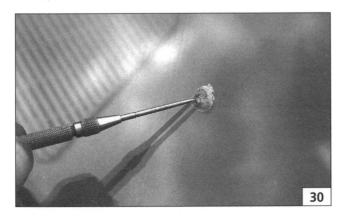

30

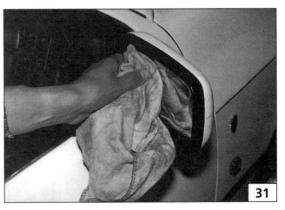

31

Every 3,000 Miles - Under the Car

☐ **Job 32. Check exhaust system for leaks/damage.**

32. Examine the silencers (as far as safe access will allow) for signs of corrosion, especially along seams and at the ends where the pipes are welded.

INSIDE INFORMATION: If you suspect a leak but its location isn't obvious, start the engine and try pressurising the system by holding a piece of board or similar so that it blocks off the tailpipe. Under pressure, the leak should be more noisy, enabling you to track down its position. Get an assistant to help you if you can, but remember an exhaust system can get very hot and touching the pipework can cause severe burns.

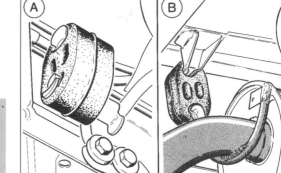

SAFETY FIRST!
Always run you car's engine out of doors and never in an enclosed space such as a garage. Exhaust gases can be toxic and an exhaust leak can allow gases into the car as you are driving along. Check the condition and security of the entire exhaust system, looking carefully for any signs of corrosion on the pipes and silencers, or leakage at the joints.

☐ **Job 33. Check exhaust system mountings.**

33A. If exhaust system mountings break, perish or come loose, the extra stresses on the exhaust system could cause the pipes or silencers to fracture. Always replace worn or damaged mountings before they break - it can save much hassle and expense later on. As well as a visual test, check the mountings by grasping the (cold) exhaust tailpipe with a piece of rag and 'shaking' it, listening for any rattles or bumps that indicate it is contacting the underside of the car - usually the result of weak or damaged mountings.

33B. These are the early V6-type of mountings.

☐ **Job 34. Check steering rack gaiters.**

SAFETY FIRST!
*This operation requires the steering to be moved from lock-to-lock so the use of axle stands is essential. Refer to **Raising the Car Safely**, at the beginning of this chapter for details of how to do this.*

The steering rack gaiters - also sometimes called 'boots' - are made of convoluted rubber, their purpose being to prevent dirt and grit getting inside the steering rack mechanism while keeping the lubricant inside it, and at the same time allowing the 'push-pull' motion of the steering arms as the steering wheel is turned.

A. Central insulators   B. Rear insulators

After a few years of continual movement plus attack from stones, grit and other road dirt, the gaiter can split leading to dirt and water entering so very soon and rack mechanism is prematurely worn out.

34A. With the steering turned on full lock (turned fully to the left or right) check the gaiter that is fully extended, looking for splits, chafing, perishing etc. Normally a split gaiter will allow grease to leak out, indicated by a tell-tale mark. Now turn the steering fully in the opposite direction and check the other gaiter in the same way.

34B. Make sure the gaiter securing clips are firm and doing their job. Clips can be metal bands either sprung or twisted into position, or plastic bands commonly known as 'cable-ties'.

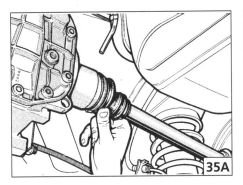

35A

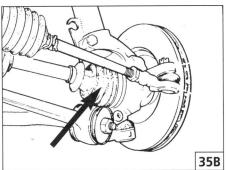

35B

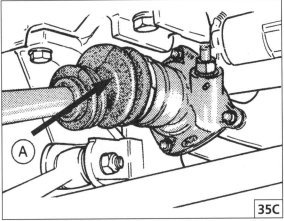

35C

36

Replacement of the gaiters involves removal of the track rod ends, a job beyond the scope of this book and a **SPECIALIST SERVICE** item. Driving with a split gaiter will very quickly ruin an expensive steering rack, so the most economical course of action is to get it renewed as soon as possible.

☐ Job 35. Check drive shaft gaiters.

35A. Gently flex each rubber gaiter, each side of the differential, and if any leaks or splits are found, **SPECIALIST SERVICE** - have them renewed.

Drive shaft gaiters perform a similar function to the steering rack gaiters i.e. keeping dirt out and lubricant in, while allowing articulating movement of the constant velocity joint within it.

4X4 ONLY

There are two gaiters to each drive shaft, - inner and outer, the latter being more prone to failure due to the larger range of movement necessary both for the steering and suspension movements.

35B. Turn the steering to full lock so that the outer driveshaft gaiter (arrowed) is put under tension, then slowly turn the road wheel and examine each gaiter around its circumference, checking for damage and signs of escaping grease. Also make sure the clips securing the gaiter at each end are secure.

35C. Check the inner gaiters (A) where the driveshaft enters the gearbox, in a similar fashion to the outer gaiters, but note there is no need to turn the steering onto full lock. (Illustration, courtesy Ford Motor Co.)

*INSIDE INFORMATION: On 4x4 cars, driveshaft gaiters play a vitally important part in keeping the joints correctly lubricated. If the gaiter is split or damaged, have the gaiter replaced as soon as possible and the joint checked for wear - both **SPECIALIST SERVICE** jobs.*

☐ Job 36. Check steering joints.

36. Steering joints, or 'track-rod-ends' provide the link between the steering arms and the road-wheels. A small rubber boot covers the steering joint and forms part of the assembly and it is vital to the life of the joint - any splits or cracks will allow the grease to escape and dirt to enter and ruin the joint.

making it easy! It's easier to check the joint if the front wheels are removed first. Refer to **Raising the Car Safely** at the beginning of this Chapter. Put the steering onto full lock so that each joint can be seen at the rear of the brake disc backplate. Check the condition and security of the protective boot on each track rod end. If split or damaged, the complete track rod end joint will have to be replaced. In theory you can fit a new boot, but it's false economy for the following reasons. i) Chances are that the old joint will be worn because the boot had a split in it and the resulting loss of lubricant, and ii), the joint will have to be removed from the steering arm in any case. This can be a difficult job so you might as well fit a relatively inexpensive new joint and have the wheel alignment checked at the same time.

SPECIALIST SERVICE: Fitting new track rod ends can be a difficult job for the inexperienced mechanic to carry out! A special ball-joint separating tool will be needed and the front wheel 'tracking' professionally adjusted afterwards.

☐ Job 37. Check suspension ball joints.

The suspension ball joints provide the link between the road-wheel/hub assembly and the lower track control arm. The ball joint allows the suspension to move up and down and the hub to swivel under the influence of the steering. The ball joint itself is protected by a small rubber boot similar to the steering joint, and it's condition is vital to the joint it protects.

3,000 MILE SERVICE

37A. Ideally, the road wheel should be removed to carry out the ball joint check so that the joint can be thoroughly examined for splits and/or cracking. If grease is evident on the outer surface of the rubber then the chances are there is a leak somewhere, but as the boot is in a somewhat 'squashed' and restricted position such a leak may not be readily obvious.

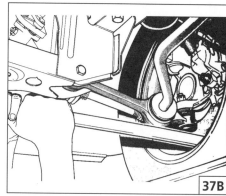

37B. The best way to check for joint wear is to place a lever between the wheel rim and the underside of the track control arm and lever up the arm - as shown. There should only be a just perceptible amount of free play in the joint. If there is more than this, the joint needs to be replaced. (Illustration, courtesy Ford Motor Co.)

SPECIALIST SERVICE: Replacing the joint is definitely a job for a garage or Ford dealer as the joint is an integral part of the track control arm which will need to be replaced as an assembly. Considerable dismantling of components is necessary.

☐ Job 38. Check rear springs.

P100 PICK-UP ONLY

The rear suspension on the P100 pick-up differs from the car version by having a leaf spring suspension and a solid live axle arrangement. To carry out the check, the rear of the vehicle will have to be raised and supported on axle stands - Refer to *Raising the Car Safely* at the beginning of this Chapter.

38. Check the main spring leaves carefully looking for signs of cracked leaves and other obvious visible damage. Check the tightness of the spring 'U'-bolt nuts where the springs are attached to the axle. At the rear of the springs, check the spring hanger rubber bushes for obvious wear also the securing nuts for tightness.

☐ Job 39. Check underside for leaks.

While you're under the car, look out for fluid leaks such as hydraulic fluid spotted on a tyre wall, oil dripping from beneath the engine or transmission or leaks from the fuel lines or tank. It is better to spot such leaks early before danger threatens or major expense is incurred.

Every 3,000 Miles - Road Test

☐ Job 40. Clean controls/check instruments.

40. Clean the door handles, controls and steering wheel: they may well have become covered in dirt and grease from your hands while you were carrying out the rest of the service work on your car. Start the engine while you are sitting in the driver's seat and check that all instruments and switches are functioning correctly.

☐ Job 41.Check brakes and steering.

SAFETY FIRST!
It's important that you check that the vehicle is fit to be driven before you take it on a public road. Ensure that all tools are removed from under, around and even under the bonnet after completing work. Choose a quiet stretch of road and pay particular attention to other road users, especially those behind you when testing your brakes! Only do so on a level, dry road, in daylight and away from other road users and pedestrians.

Only a proper brake testing facility at an MoT testing station will be able to check the operation of the brakes accurately enough for the MoT test, but you can check out one of the worst braking problems - pulling to one side - in the following way: drive along a clear stretch of road and, gripping the steering wheel lightly between the thumb and fingers of each hand, brake gently from a speed of about 40 mph. Ideally, the vehicle should pull up in a dead straight line without pulling to one side or another. If the car pulls very slightly to the left (while being driven on the left-hand side of the road) it could be due to the effects of the road camber that is causing the vehicle to pull over and not the brakes. If the vehicle pulls badly to the left or right, then try repeating the test on a stretch of road with little or no camber. If the brakes still pull to one side, check the tyre pressures first before seeking SPECIALIST SERVICE.

The second test is to check that the self-centring effect on the steering works correctly. If the steering stiffens up over a period of time, you can easily get so used to it that you don't notice that it isn't operating as it should. After going round a sharp bend, the steering should tend to move back to the straight-ahead position all by itself without having to be positively steering back to the straight-ahead position by the driver. This is because the swivel axis of the front wheels is set slightly ahead of the wheels' centre line so that the front wheels behave rather like those of a supermarket trolley. If the front suspension joints or mountings are stiff, or if the steering rack is worn or damaged then the steering will be stiff with little or no self-centring action.

Test this by driving round a sharp bend and, as the road straightens out, you should feel the steering wheel tend to turn itself back to the straight-ahead position. If it doesn't, check the tyre pressures before seeking a little more of that SPECIALIST SERVICE.

☐ Job 42. Check throttle pedal operation.

Check that the throttle pedal operates smoothly. If not, check the route of the cable inside the engine bay to see if it is bent sharply or damaged in some way.

Kinks in the outer casing or fraying of the cable ends, especially where the inner cable enters the outer casing can cause the cable to 'stick'. If you find any of these faults, fit a new cable. Ideally, the cable should follow a gentle curve for smooth operation.

Every 6,000 Miles - Or Every Six Months, whichever comes first

Every 6,000 Miles - The Engine Bay

Carry out the 3,000-mile/3-month service operations, plus the following:

SAFETY FIRST!
Refer to the section on ENGINE OILS in Chapter 1, Safety First before carrying out the following work. It is essential to wear rubber or plastic gloves since used engine oil can be carcinogenic. Oil drain plugs are often overtightened. i) Take care that the spanner does not slip causing injury to hand or head. (Use a socket or ring spanner - never an open-ended spanner - with as little offset as possible, so that the spanner is near to the line of the bolt.) ii) Ensure that your spanner is positioned so that you pull downwards, if at all possible. Take great care that the effort needed to undo the drain plug does not cause the vehicle to fall on you or to slide off ramps - remember those wheel chocks. iii) Refer to the information at the start of this Chapter on Raising a Car Safely!

☐ Job 43. Change engine oil.

making it easy! Apart from small differences in location of the oil filter and the sump drain plug, the procedure is the same for all models. Before draining the sump, run the engine (if cold) for around five minutes to warm the oil slightly, so that it will drain more freely - but not so hot that it will scald.

Use an oil drainage container to catch the oil as it drains from the sump - note that the oil will fall in an arc away from the drain hole, so position the container to allow for this. Spread newspaper on the floor beneath the engine bay to protect it from oil spills and drips.

Probably the one service operation on which most DIY motorists will 'cut their teeth' is an engine oil change - that is emptying the old oil out through the sump drain plug situated beneath the engine and, eventually, pouring in a specified quantity of new oil through the oil filler, found on the valve cover at the top of the engine. And no matter how technically complex the engine, an oil change still remains basically a simple operation.

43A. This is the location of the oil drain plug on the great majority of Sierra engines, viewed from under the car. As we stated previously, the plug will often be tight and require some force to move initially, when it may suddenly 'give' and offer little or no resistance - be careful not to rap your knuckles! Rubber or plastic gloves can compromise your grip on the spanner, so it may be wise to leave them off for the initial 'tug', but remember to don them immediately the plug has been slackened.

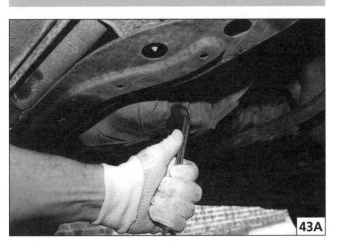
43A

43B. The sump plug on CVH engines (being pointed out here with a long screwdriver) is located on the opposite side of the sump to other models, that is facing towards the left as you look towards the rear of the car.

Once the plug has started to move in its thread it can be undone with the (gloved) fingers; remember to hold onto the plug when fully unscrewed. Be ready to reposition your bowl - the angle of 'spurt' changes as the oil flows out of the sump!

making it easy! It is not necessary to use excessive force when tightening the sump drain plug. Simply grip the spanner so that the thumb rests upon the spanner head, thereby limiting the amount of leverage that can be applied to it, applying 'firm' pressure only.

43C. The drain plug has a copper or nylon sealing washer - examine the latter for signs of distortion or splitting, renewing it if in doubt. New ones are obtainable from most accessory shops and it is a good idea to buy a new copper one with the oil and filter. They are designed to crush when the plug is tightened and are not meant to be re-used.

OIL CARE FOLLOW THE CODE

Also, see page 4.

Before re-fitting the sump drain plug, wipe around the drain hole with a piece of clean cloth to remove any dirt and check that the sealing washer is fitted.

43D. Pour the recommended amount of fresh oil into the engine (quantities are given in *Chapter 8, Facts & Figures*) at a steady rate - too much too soon will cause it to overflow as the air displaced from inside the engine tries to escape. It's a good idea to place a cloth around the oil filler anyway to catch the inevitable spillage.

making it easy! Before undoing the drain plug, take off the oil filler cap: this relieves any partial vacuum in the system - the faster the oil can drain from the sump the more debris it will drag out with it.

43E. Check the oil level on the dipstick after the approximate measured amount has been poured in. Note that the level is likely to be above the MAX mark because the engine hasn't been started and the new filter is still empty. The level should be checked again after running the engine for a short time and topped up if required.

SAFETY FIRST!
DON'T pour the old oil down the drain - it's both illegal and irresponsible. Your local council waste disposal site will have special facilities for disposing of it safely. Moreover, don't mix anything else with it, as this will prevent it from being recycled. See page 4.

☐ Job 44. Change engine oil filter.

44A. The oil filter on petrol engines (and Turbo Diesel) is located on the left-hand side of the engine block, as you look to the rear of the car, beneath the exhaust manifold.

SAFETY FIRST!
Ensure the manifold is cool before attempting to remove the filter.

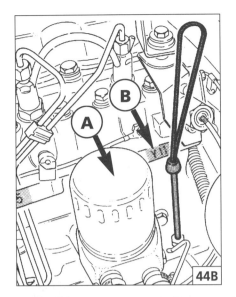

44B

44C

44B. The diesel engine oil filter (A) on non-turbo models is situated under the air cleaner housing, which has to be removed in order to change the filter. Shown at (B) is the engine oil dipstick. (Illustration, courtesy Ford Motor Co.)

making it easy! 44C. Oil filter removal tools are numerous to cope with various engine types, but this simple chain wrench will fit all Sierra engines and is available cheaply from car accessory shops. You'll need this tool as it is almost impossible to unscrew the old filter by hand.

44D

44D. One full turn of the filter using the wrench is usually enough to get it started, after which it can be unscrewed by hand. Note that some oil loss will occur, so position an oil tray or container under the engine to catch it. It's also a good idea to place a cloth round the filter when unscrewing it to prevent the oil dribbling over your hand. Clean the filter sealing face on the engine.

44E. Make sure the rubber sealing ring is properly fitted to the new filter, then apply a smear of clean engine oil to the ring to prevent it buckling as the filter is screwed home.

44E

44F. Screw the new filter onto the threaded stub, taking care to avoid cross-threading. Most filters have tightening instructions printed in the casing, but essentially all filters are fitted by screwing on by hand only. When the sealing ring contacts the face on the engine, tighten it a further three-quarters of a turn and leave it - there's no need to tighten it any further as this will only distort the sealing ring and make it difficult to remove the filter next time.

☐ **Job 45. Check/adjust spark plugs.**

PETROL ENGINES ONLY

INSIDE INFORMATION: It is recommended that spark plugs be renewed at 12,000 mile intervals - this is easily arranged by changing them at every alternate 6,000 service.

45A. Numbered spark plug leads (traditionally called 'H.T.' or 'High Tension' leads) are standard on Sierras, the numbers being printed into the leads themselves. Note that the numbering starts from the radiator end of the engine.

44F

45A

INSIDE INFORMATION: If the lead numbers are ineligible or non-original leads fitted, mark them with a spot of paint - typists' correction fluid is used by many mechanics as it is easy to apply and dries very quickly. Mark them from the radiator end of the engine in the sequence one, two, three and four 'dots'.

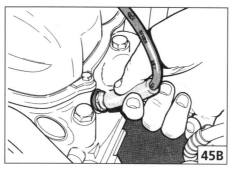

IMPORTANT NOTE: Identification of the plug leads is important as if incorrectly replaced, the engine will not run!

45B. When you have numbered the leads, the plug caps can be pulled off. Be careful not to tug on the lead itself as you may pull it from the cap, which will remain on the plug! (Illustration, courtesy Ford Motor Co.)

45C. Using a suitably long spark plug spanner or socket extension, unscrew the spark plugs. Take care to keep the plug spanner or socket in line with the plug body, otherwise the porcelain insulator of the plug can break.

INSIDE INFORMATION: If you are trying to remove a plug which gets ever tighter as you turn it, there's every possibility that it is cross threaded. Tighten it up again and take the car to a Ford Dealer or specialist who may be able to clean up the threads with a purpose-made tool. If this can't be done, he will have to add a thread insert to your cylinder head. It pays to take great care when removing and fitting spark plugs, especially when dealing with aluminium cylinder heads!

45D. Clean the plug electrodes by vigorous use of a wire brush to remove any carbon deposits. If the electrodes of the plug look 'rounded' and worn (compare them to a new plug) they should be replaced.

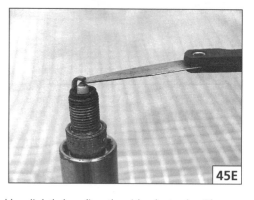

45E. If using a flat feeler gauge select the 'blade' of the correct thickness (see **Chapter 8, Facts and Figures**) and slide it between the electrodes as shown. The gap between the two electrodes should provide a sliding fit, with no 'slack'. If necessary, adjust the gap using a pair of snipe-nosed (thin, pointed jaws) pliers, carefully bending the curved side-electrode towards or away from the tip of the centre electrode, until the feeler gauge fits the gap as described. The gap is adjusted by slightly bending the side electrode either closer or further-away from the centre electrode. With a special gapping tool, this is easy and carries little risk of damaging the plug, which can occur if the electrode is moved by use of a screwdriver or pliers.

Replace the plugs when the gaps are correct, adding just a slight smear of copper grease to the threads to make future removal easier. There is no need to screw the plugs down with great force just tighten them firmly. Before replacing the plug leads, clean them by use of a maintenance spray and a piece of rag or tissue. Also clean the exterior of the distributor cap (into which the plug leads fit) using the same method.

☐ **Job 46. Check ignition timing.**

OHC PETROL ENGINES UP TO 1987 ONLY

making it easy! Leave the spark plug in the socket spanner while using the wire brush - this is kinder on the fingers and lessens the risk of dropping the plug and breaking it.

OPTIONAL: The ignition timing is set with great accuracy during manufacture and the distributor clamp bolt is 'sealed' with a blob of blue compound over the bolt head and clamp; if the seal is intact then there is no need to check the timing. Ford do not include this check in their routine servicing schedules, but we describe the procedure for checking the timing for those owners who have acquired a used car and wish to confirm the timing is correct during a 'fresh-start' service. However, some owners may prefer to have this check carried out professionally by a garage or tuning specialist.

STROBOSCOPIC TIMING

46A. Because of the type of electronic ignition systems used on Sierras, the only way of checking the ignition timing is dynamically, using a stroboscopic test light such as the Gunson's model shown here. The test light enables you to see the timing mark on the crankshaft pulley as the engine is running, and thus automatically takes into account any wear and slackness in the ignition timing mechanisms.

If you don't already possess a strobe light, your accessory shop will stock various models at an affordable price. The easiest to use are those with a xenon light (brighter than neon) and an inductive pick-up that simply clamps over the plug's HT lead. Most are simply powered via clip-on leads to the car battery, although there are models that use their own internal batteries.

making it easy! It is a good idea to apply a spot of white paint, chalk or typists' correction fluid to the marks, as we have here, to make them stand out in the brief flashes of the timing light.

46B. The timing marks will be found at the front of the engine (as you look towards the rear of the car), one a series of embossed lines on the rim of the crankshaft pulley, the other a pointer fixed to the engine 'block'. The marks on the pulley are arranged in degrees before-top-dead-centre, each line representing four degrees; therefore, reading left-to-right the lines represent 0, 4, 8, 12, and 16 degrees advance. Check *Chapter 8, Facts & Figures* - for the correct advance mark for your car.

46C. Connect the timing light to the No. 1 plug lead as shown in the maker's instructions. Start the engine and allow it to settle to an even tickover - check the idle speed for your engine in *Chapter 8, Facts & Figures*, and ensure it has reached operating temperature. Aim the timing light at the marks: If the (correct) notch and pointer are aligned at tick-over speed, the timing is correct but if not, the timing will require adjustment.

*INSIDE INFORMATION: Adjusting the ignition timing is not a job we would recommend to owners with little previous mechanical experience: As stated in **SAFETY FIRST!** above, very high voltages are present among the ignition components i.e. distributor, coil and H.T. leads, voltages that are quite capable of passing through their insulation to any 'earth' connection that presents itself - such as the human body! Merely brushing the hand against the distributor cap or an H.T. lead can induce a severe electric shock; coupled with the close proximity of the cooling fan and the natural reaction of quickly withdrawing a hand, severe injury is a very real possibility. The method for adjusting the timing is described below for those owners who feel competent and are aware of the dangers, otherwise the job is a **SPECIALIST SERVICE** for a Ford dealer or tuning specialist.*

making it easy! 46D. (Or at least, this makes it a little easier!) Switch off the engine and slacken the distributor clamp bolt as shown, just enough to enable the distributor to move under firm pressure. Turn the distributor clockwise to 'retard' the timing, or anti-clockwise to 'advance' it. For example, if the specified timing for your model is given as 10 degrees B.T.D.C but the timing light shows the 4 degree mark next to the pointer, the distributor will need to be rotated anti-clockwise, to advance the timing by 6 degrees and bring the 10 deg. mark to align with the pointer. Note that only half the required movement (in degrees) is required at the distributor body, due to the gearing of its drive-chain.

DO NOT try to adjust the distributor with the engine running; make an adjustment, start the engine and check with the timing light to see if further movement is necessary. If so, stop the engine, adjust, and start up again. When the timing is correct, stop the engine and tighten the distributor clamp bolt, taking care not to alter the position of the distributor while doing so. Make a final check on the timing before disconnecting the 'light.

6,000 MILE SERVICE

☐ Job 47. Lubricate throttle controls.

47A

47A. Lubricate the accelerator control linkage at the injection system or carburettor in the engine bay. Also lubricate the throttle pedal pivot in the footwell recess. Use a spray lubricant like Castrol DWF or white silicone grease in the footwell, so as not to spoil your shoes with dripping oil - it stains leather!

47B. Grease cable ends, where you can get at them...

47B

47C. ...and any springs and cams within reach.

47D. There are rather more lubrication points on a carburettor. With air filter removed, oil every spring, moving part and joint in the linkages.

47C

☐ Job 48. Check coolant radiator matrix.

48. It is worth checking there is no build-up of leaves or other debris in the radiator matrix, that could restrict airflow through it. Use a soft brush and hose, if necessary. Look out for the tell-tale staining which indicates a leak.

47D

48

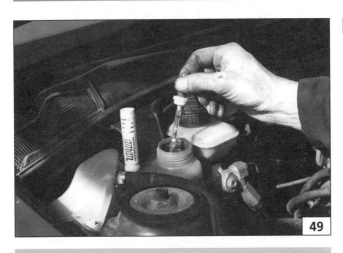

49.

Job 49. Check engine coolant.

49. Use a hydrometer to check the specific gravity of the coolant which in turn indicates the strength and effectiveness of the antifreeze content. The tester shown is readily available from accessory shops and is acceptably accurate. In use, a small quantity of coolant is drawn into the glass 'dropper' and an indication of the strength of antifreeze is given by the number of beads that float in the tube.

It is important that all engines have the correct proportion of antifreeze in the coolant. This not only helps prevent freezing in the winter, but also overheating in the summer temperatures. In addition, antifreeze also helps prevent internal engine corrosion and is particularly necessary in those engines fitted with alloy cylinder heads.

Job 50. Check water pump for leaks.

The water pump on all engines is situated at the front of the engine (as you look to the rear of the car). It is driven by the generator drive belt except on CVH engines where it is driven by the camshaft drive belt.

SAFETY FIRST!
i) The coolant level should only be checked WHEN THE SYSTEM IS COLD. If you remove the pressure cap when the engine is hot, the release of pressure can cause the water in the cooling system to boil and spurt several feet in the air with the risk of severe scalding. ii) Take precautions to prevent antifreeze being swallowed or coming in contact with the skin or eyes. If this should happen, rinse immediately with plenty of water. Seek immediate medical help if necessary. Keep antifreeze away from children and pets.

While conducting these other checks it is worth visually examining the engine block around the water pump mountings for any sign of a leak.

50. Leaks are characterised by a white, or greeny-white, powdery deposit, sometimes tinged with the colour of antifreeze, that can be seen in 'runs' down the side of the block. If any evidence of such a leak is present, first make sure that the coolant hoses, connections and thermostat housing are not the cause, otherwise the car should be taken to a competent garage for investigation.

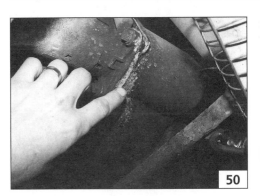

50.

IMPORTANT NOTE: Two of the following three jobs are, of course, carried out 'Under the Car' but since they fall naturally at this stage, **Jobs 51** and **53** have been placed deliberately out of position. You may wish to carry them out after you have finished with the Engine Bay.

Job 51. Check manual gearbox oil.

MANUAL TRANSMISSION ONLY

ALL MODELS EXCEPT 4X4

51A. The gearbox filler/level plug will be found on the left-side of the gearbox, looking forwards from underneath. Remove the plug using a suitable size spanner or Allen key, turned anticlockwise. If oil drips from the hole as the plug is removed then the level is correct, and the plug can be replaced. If no oil is evident however, topping-up isn't necessarily required as there is an allowance for the level to be up to 5mm below the hole on some models; to measure this requires a hook-shaped piece of wire that can be inserted through the hole and pointed downwards into the oil. We recommend: play safe and top-up to the hole, while you're under there!

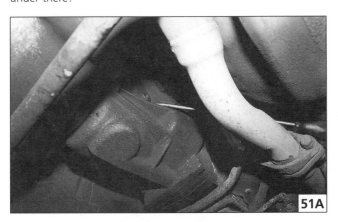

51A.

SAFETY FIRST!
This job requires the vehicle not only to be raised but also level to the ground, in order for the operation to be effective. Therefore two sets of axle stands and a trolley jack will be required - see the Raising the Car Safely section at the beginning of this chapter for how to do this safely. The level/drain plug is likely to be tight so take care not to apply 'sideways' pressure to the spanner which could make the supported car unstable - pull or push the spanner in a down-or-upwards direction.

6,000 MILE SERVICE

TOPPING-UP. If topping-up is required, use a 'squeezeable' bottle with a flexible spout (eg. Castrol Syntax Universal gearbox oil) that can be inserted into the hole, as space is severely limited beneath the car! When oil begins to issue from the hole, replace the plug and wipe any spilt or excess oil from the gearbox casing.

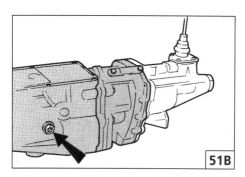

51B

51C

4X4 MODELS ONLY, GEARBOX, TRANSFER BOX & FRONT AXLE

51B. The main gearbox oil level is checked and topped-up as described in **Job 51A** above. However, the 4WD transfer box is fitted to the rear of the gearbox and this requires the level to be checked at similar intervals, as follows:

IMPORTANT NOTE: The transfer box uses automatic transmission fluid and not gearbox oil; mixing the two inadvertently can damage the components of the 'box. See *Appendix 1, Recommended Castrol Lubricants.* (Illustration, courtesy Ford Motor Co.)

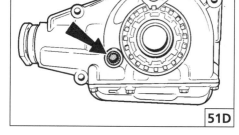

51D

51C. The transfer box is positioned at the rear of the normal gearbox, the filler plug located in the lower right-hand corner, facing rearwards. It is undone using a 17mm spanner and, as before, the level is correct when the fluid is in line with the bottom of the filler hole. Top up with Castrol Dexron RIII automatic transmission fluid. (Illustration, courtesy Ford Motor Co.)

51D. The front axle oil level/filler plug is located just behind the driveshaft output point on the right-hand side of the engine, looking forwards. Check the level as in **Job 51A** above, but note that a 10mm Allen key will be required for removing the drain plug; top-up (if necessary) with Castrol Syntrax Universal gearbox oil. (Illustration, courtesy Ford Motor Co.)

☐ Job 52. Automatic transmission fluid.

AUTOMATIC TRANSMISSION ONLY

INSIDE INFORMATION: The auto. transmission fluid is checked with the engine running at normal operating temperature and the drive selector in the 'P' or PARK position. Normal operating temperature is only reached after ten to fifteen miles driving, so allowing the car to 'warm-up' for five or ten minutes is not enough to warm the fluid sufficiently.

IMPORTANT NOTE: Absolute cleanliness is essential when dealing with the automatic transmission as even tiny particles of dirt or grit can have an adverse, and expensive, effect on the delicate precision components within it.

IMMEDIATELY before checking the level, apply the handbrake and footbrake, then move the gear selector lever through all positions (i.e. 'P' to '1') three times; place the lever in PARK and allow the engine to idle for a further minute. Check the fluid level WITH ENGINE RUNNING.

52. The transmission fluid dipstick is positioned on the left-hand rear of the engine (as you look to the rear of the car). Withdraw the dipstick, wipe it clean and replace it, pushing fully home up to the handle. Withdraw it again and note the reading on the side of the dipstick.

☐ Job 53. Check rear axle oil level.

INSIDE INFORMATION: Although, as we said earlier, this is not strictly in sequence, this job is more conveniently checked now, when the vehicle is raised and level!

ALL MODELS EXCEPT P100

53A. The rear axle (differential) oil level is checked by removing the level/filler plug located in the rear axle casing, and facing to the rear of the car. Top-up if the level is below the bottom of the filler hole. (Illustration, courtesy Ford Motor Co.)

making it easy! Fluid is added by pouring into the mouth of the dipstick tube. Make sure you buy the transmission fluid that is sold in bottles with a small spout, especially for this purpose.

52

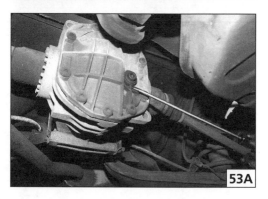

53A

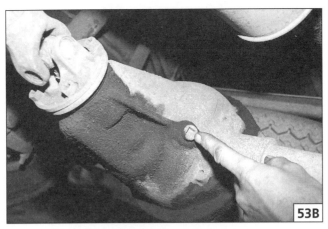

53B

P100 MODELS ONLY

53B. The level/filler plug is positioned on the front of the differential casing, as shown. Before removal, clean around the plug with a wire brush and rag, to remove any dirt or grime that might otherwise find its way into the axle.

☐ Job 54. Check power steering fluid level (if fitted).

If your car is fitted with power steering, check the fluid level in the reservoir.

54A. On early Sierra models the fluid reservoir is an integral part of the power steering pump and is situated on the front nearside of the engine.

54A

54B. Remove the cap by turning anticlockwise, wipe the small dipstick fixed to the underside of the cap and replace it - then withdraw it again and note the fluid level. With the engine at operating temperature the fluid level should be at the FULL mark, while on a cold engine the level shouldn't fall below the ADD mark.

54C. Later models have a remote see-through reservoir mounted on the offside of the engine bay. The fluid level should normally be between the MAX and MIN marks with the engine at normal operating temperature.

Top up using the correct Castrol fluid as specified in *Appendix 1, Recommended Castrol Lubricants.*

☐ Job 55. Check valve clearances.

OHV DIESEL ENGINE ONLY

The valve clearances should be checked with the engine cold - that is, the engine should not have been run for several hours beforehand. Note that the cylinders are numbered from the rear of the engine, so that No.1 cylinder is at the radiator end.

Incorrect valve clearances not only make the engine sound noisy and maybe to idle badly, but they also affect engine performance and lead to increased fuel consumption.

55A. Undo the mounting bolts (arrowed) and remove the air cleaner housing.

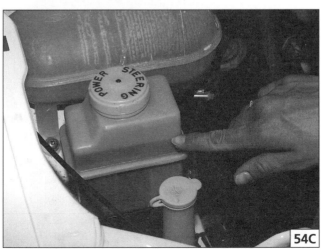

54B

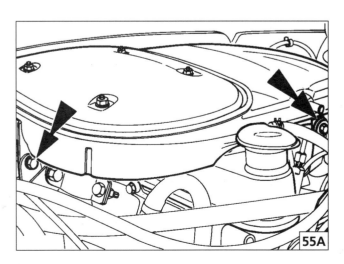

54C

55A

55B. The valve rocker cover must be removed first to 'get at' the valve mechanism. Remove the air cleaner ancillaries and undo the screws along the top of the cover (arrowed) before removing it.

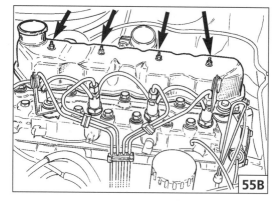

55C. Using a spanner on the crankshaft pulley bolt (arrowed), turn the engine in the normal (clockwise) direction of rotation to the point where No. 1 cylinder valves are overlapping. In other words, the inlet and exhaust valve rockers are moving in opposite directions.

55D. The valves on No.4 cylinder at the radiator end can now be checked and adjusted. Check the clearance by inserting a feeler gauge blade of the specified clearance between the valve stem and rocker arm. If the clearance requires adjustment, slacken the adjuster locknut on the rocker arm with a spanner (as shown) then use a screwdriver to turn the adjuster screw until the feeler gauge blade is a neat sliding fit. Hold the adjuster screw in this position and retighten the locknut with the spanner. Recheck the adjustment before going on to the next valve.

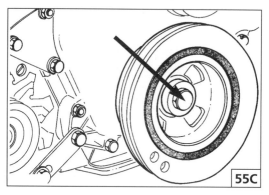

When you've completed the adjustment on No.4 cylinder valves, turn the crankshaft further in a clockwise direction to the point where No.3 cylinder valves are overlapping. In this position, check and adjust the valves on No.2 cylinder as detailed previously. Continue in the sequence described, checking No.1 cylinder when the valves overlap on No.4, then checking No.3 cylinder when the valves overlap on cylinder No.2.

making it easy! To make the sequence easier to remember, note that the number of the cylinder being checked, when added to the number of the cylinder in 'overlap', always comes to 5. This is useful to remember for those times when you are half-way through checking the clearances and get called away or distracted!

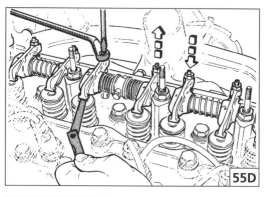

Fit a new gasket to the rocker cover before re-fitting the cover and air cleaner assembly.

V6 ENGINE ONLY

55E. The cylinders on the V6 engine are numbered from the front (radiator) end of the engine with Nos 1, 2 and 3 on the left-hand (driver's side) and Nos. 4, 5 and 6 on the right.

55F. Remove the air cleaner assembly (carburettor models) or intake ducting (fuel injection) to provide access to the valve rocker covers.

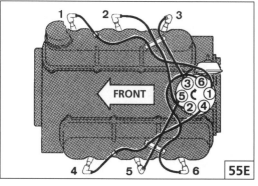

55G. Note that the valve rocker covers are secured by seven 10mm screws and 'stiffener' plates of two types - see illustration for type and positioning.

Using a suitable spanner on the crankshaft pulley bolt, turn the engine clockwise until the timing notch on the crankshaft pulley is aligned with the TDC (Top Dead Centre) mark on the engine timing cover. Now turn the crankshaft a few degrees either side of the TDC position and check whether the valves on either No.1 or No.5 cylinders are overlapping. In other words the inlet and exhaust valve rockers on that particular cylinder are moving in opposite directions.

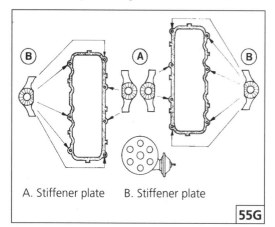

A. Stiffener plate   B. Stiffener plate

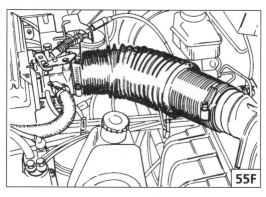

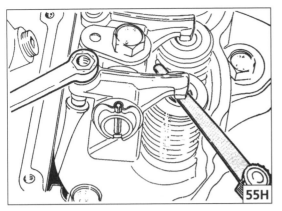

55H. If the valves on No.1 cylinder are overlapping, adjust the valves on cylinder No.5, or vice-versa. Using a feeler gauge of the specified thickness, check the clearance between the valve and rocker. The gauge should be a neat sliding fit. If the clearance is incorrect, slacken the adjuster locknut with a spanner and turn the adjuster screw until the correct clearance is obtained. Hold the adjuster screw in position while the locknut is tightened, then recheck the clearance. Repeat the adjustment procedure on the other valve.

After completing the adjustments to the first cylinder, turn the crankshaft slowly in the normal (clockwise) direction of rotation until the valves on either No.4 or No.3 cylinders are overlapping, depending on the cylinder you first adjusted. Now carry out the valve adjustments detailed previously in the order shown below.

Valves overlapping	Valves to adjust
Cylinder No.	Cylinder No.
No. 5	No. 1
No. 3	No. 4
No. 6	No. 2
No. 1	No. 5
No. 4	No. 3
No. 2	No. 6

When all the valves have been checked and adjusted, fit a new gasket to each rocker cover (see 55G above for gasket shape and orientation) before re-fitting, followed by replacement of the air cleaner assembly/injection air trunking. (Illustration, courtesy Ford Motor Co.)

☐ Job 56. Check steering column coupling.

56. Check the rubber coupling on the steering column - it can be seen by looking down into the engine bay, positioned beneath the brake master cylinder. The coupling allows movement between upper and lower column in the manner of a 'universal' joint. Check the rubber disc for signs of splitting, chaffing and perishing and have the coupling renewed if any damage is evident.

☐ Job 57. Check fuel injection pipes and sensor wires.

SAFETY FIRST!
Fuel injection systems remain pressurised even when the engine is switched off and require special procedures to make them safe to work on. Take great care when slackening or disconnecting a fuel pipe and take precautions to minimise fuel loss. Always place a cloth around a pipe union first and always slacken the nut gently to slowly relieve the fuel pressure.

SAFETY FIRST!
As everyone is aware, petrol is highly flammable and only a small leak is necessary to ignite it with potentially disastrous consequences. If a fuel leak, however slight, is suspected or detected, don't smoke, switch off all car accessories but don't disconnect the battery as this in itself could cause a spark as the terminal is disconnected.

57. Carry out a visual check of all fuel pipes and unions in the engine bay, looking for any signs of unsecured pipes. Start the engine (taking the usual precautions) and check that there are no fuel leaks.

Check the wiring and plug connections to the various components on the engine. Make sure all plugs are securely fitted and clean. Check that the wiring is properly secured away from any potential damage source such as exhaust pipes or cooling fan.

☐ Job 58. Check exhaust emission.

Exhaust emissions became part of the British MoT test in 1991 and are always likely to be the subject of change, so check for the latest requirements. See also, *Chapter 7, Getting through the MoT*.

> **SAFETY FIRST!**
> *Carbon monoxide is extremely poisonous and can kill within minutes - even when a catalytic converter is fitted. ALWAYS carry out emission testing in the open - NEVER in your garage or other confined space.*

58. At present there are no DIY machines capable of measuring diesel smoke emissions, but the Gunson's Gastester MKII, shown in use here and also in *Chapter 9, Tools and Equipment*, can measure petrol engine CO (Carbon Monoxide) levels very accurately. It comes with comprehensive instructions and data for most vehicles including of course, the Sierra! Otherwise, its a **SPECIALIST SERVICE** job.

☐ Job 59. Adjust idle speed and mixture setting.

CARBURETTOR MODELS ONLY

INSIDE INFORMATION: i) This Job requires the use of gas testing equipment and a tachometer to check the idle speed, if any meaningful results are to be obtained. Indeed, attempting to 'tune' a carburettor without this equipment is likely to result in increased fuel consumption and poor performance, except in the hands of experienced mechanics although, it has to be said, even they tend to use them anyway, for speed of use and accuracy! ii) The carburettor should be the last part of the engine tune-up procedure, as the general settings will be affected by the condition and efficiency of other engine components such as the ignition system.

59A. In order to 'get at' the carburettor, you'll have to remove the air filter assembly first, disconnecting it from the air intake. On some engines, you need to unclip the top cover first and unscrew nuts to remove the unit from the carburettor. On other models, you only have to remove three or four screws to detach the air filter.

Before proceeding further it's a good idea to familiarise yourself with the carburettor fitted to your car. It will be one of four types: Ford VV, Weber 32/36 DGAV, Pierburg 2E3 or Solex 35 EEIT (see *Chapter 8 - Facts & Figures* for precise applications). You will also need to know the location of the idle speed and 'mixture' adjusting screws. Use the accompanying diagrams to determine where the screws are positioned.

As mentioned previously, adjustments will be made without air filter housing in place: here's what the various carburettors look like with the air filter removed. Also, make sure you have a screwdriver of a length suitable for working in the confined space most adjustments are made in.

59B. These are the Idle Speed (A) and mixture (B) adjustment screws on the Ford VV carburettor. Note: Later versions used an extended idle screw (A).

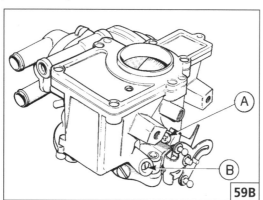

> **SAFETY FIRST!**
> *Carburettor adjustment has to be carried out with a warm, running engine. Therefore: i) Watch out for rotating cooling fan and belt and do not wear loose clothing or jewellery and tie back long hair. ii) Take care that you do not burn yourself on the hot engine parts and/or exhaust manifolds. iii) Always work out of doors. DO NOT perform this check in your garage or any confined space - exhaust gases are highly poisonous and can kill within minutes! iv) Apply a strict No Smoking! rule whenever you are servicing your fuel system. Remember, it's not just the petrol that's inflammable, it's the fumes as well. Overall, if you're not (justifiably) confident, give the job to someone who is fully competent. Some manufacturers recommend that only trained mechanics should carry out work on a vehicle's fuel system. Read Chapter 1, Safety First!.*

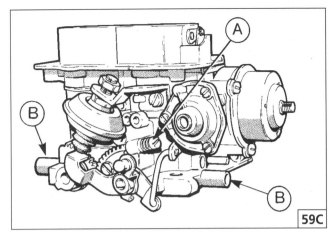

59C. The idle speed (A) and mixture (B) screws on the Weber 2V carburettor. NOTE: Later versions have no idle speed screw - controlled electronically.

59D. Idle speed (B) and mixture screw (A) on the Solex carburettor.

59E. Idle speed (A) and mixture (B) screws on the Pierburg 2E3 carburettor. (Illustrations, courtesy Ford Motor Co.)

INSIDE INFORMATION: Tamper proof caps may be fitted to the adjusting screws - remove them either with a pair of pliers or sharp instrument, depending on the type of seal. In the UK it isn't necessary to replace the seals, but in certain EC countries it is a legal requirement that they are replaced after adjustment.

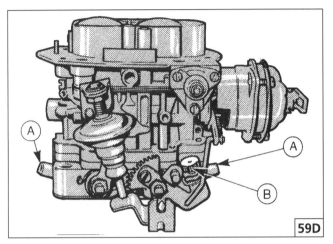

Before connecting up the gas analyser and tachometer the engine needs to be at operating temperature, so take the car for a short drive (five miles will do) or allow it to run at a fast idle speed for fifteen minutes or so. It is important that the engine is at working temperature, not only for the accuracy of the gas analyser but also to make sure the choke control is off and the many fine tolerances found in the engine and its components are at their operating norm.

Once the engine is thoroughly warmed, connect up the gas analyser and tachometer according to the makers' instructions, making sure all electrical accessories are switched off and, if an automatic transmission is fitted, that the drive selector is in the 'P' or 'PARK' position.

First check the idle speed on the tachometer - *Chapter 8, Facts and Figures* for your model - and adjust the idle-speed screw if necessary. Turning the screw clockwise increases the speed, anti-clockwise reduces it.

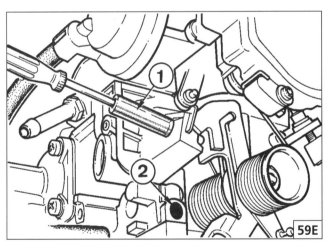

Next, read the gas analyser to check for CO level and adjust the mixture screw if the reading is above or below the specification.

59F. Turning the screw 'in' or clockwise weakens the mixture and lowers the CO, while turning it 'out' richens and increases the CO reading. Only small movements of the screw are normally necessary, so turn it a quarter-turn at a time and check the readings, allowing the effects of each adjustment to register on the analyser - around thirty seconds may be necessary.

making it easy! Generally, the newer the car the more accurately this can be set, but with older cars it may be necessary to allow an increase in the CO setting to ensure the engine runs smoothly in use. For instance, the specified CO level of 2.5% or 3% in order for it to run smoothly and efficiently. Some trial and error may be necessary to balance the lowest desirable CO content with smooth running. See *Chapter 7, Getting Through the MoT,* for the maximum allowable CO readings.

If a reading within the 'legal' range proves difficult or impossible to achieve consistent with smooth running, some other factor may be affecting the combustion process of the engine such as air leaks, poor valve condition, choked or leaking exhaust. Have the car checked by a reputable garage or Ford dealer if necessary.

IMPORTANT NOTE: Running the engine for any length of time on a 'weak' mixture (very low CO reading) is likely to lead to internal engine damage, while driving it on a 'rich' or 'high' reading is illegal, environmentally un-friendly and a waste of expensive fuel!

Once the desired richness level/CO setting has been obtained, you will invariably have to readjust the tick-over speed as it will have been affected by the change in mixture.

When all adjustments have been made, disconnect the gas analyser and tachometer and take the car for test drive, checking that it doesn't stall, pulls smoothly and doesn't overheat.

FUEL INJECTION PETROL ENGINES ONLY

SPECIALIST SERVICE: Due to the need for an accurate tachometer to check idle speed, and an exhaust gas analyser to check the mixture (and the knowledge to use them and interpret the readings) it is recommended that these checks be carried out by a specialist tuning firm or reputable garage. However, for the keen DIY mechanic these items of equipment are available from Gunson's (see *Chapter 9, Tool & Equipment*) together with full instructions and data.

☐ **Job 60. Replace fuel filter.**

DIESEL MODELS ONLY

The diesel fuel filter is located on the nearside inner wing panel of the engine bay, just ahead of the suspension turret. Before proceeding, make sure a container is at hand in which to catch the fuel contained in the filter, together with a quantity of absorbent rag to mop up any spillages. A one-litre container will be sufficient. Always wear plastic gloves.

60A. Position the container beneath the filter housing and open the bleed screw (A) on the end of the fuel outlet union to speed up draining.

60B. Holding a hand underneath the unit to support it, unscrew and remove the long bolt (arrowed) then carefully detach the filter unit from the upper body.

60C. Detach the filter bowl (D) from the filter and discard the filter element (C). Fit the new sealing rings and O-ring supplied with the new filter and assemble the filter to the filter bowl. Then offer up the filter to the underside of the housing and secure it with the long bolt. Tighten the bolt firmly but do not overtighten it.

Refer back to the drawing in **Job 60A**. Slacken the bleed screw (A) and unscrew the hand pump plunger (B). Pump the plunger up and down to draw fuel through from the tank and to purge air from the pipes. Continue to pump until clean fuel is seen to come through the bleed tube, catching any excess fuel in a piece of rag.

Tighten the bleed screw, screw down the plunger and run the engine for a few minutes to check around the filter for leaks. (Illustrations, courtesy Ford Motor Co.)

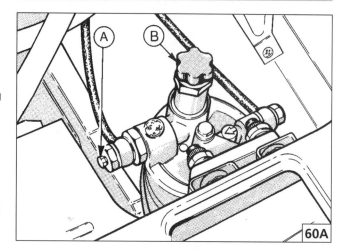

60A

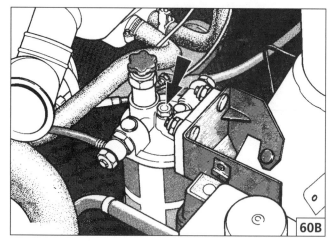

60B

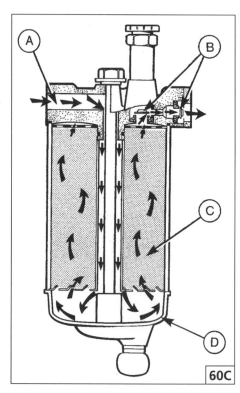

60C

61A

Job 61. Check ignition components.

It's a good idea to inspect the ignition system components perlodically. It takes only a few minutes and guards against some of the most frequent causes of breakdowns. Check the wires to the distributor are clean and that the connections are tight. Follow by checking the plug leads, making sure they are all clean and free from oil and dirt - a frequent reason for rough running and bad starting in wet weather. Examine the high and low tension wires and connections the distributor, paying particular attention to the terminal ends of the HT leads.

OHC ENGINES ONLY

61A. On OHC engines, remove the distributor cap by releasing the two spring clips; this can usually be done with the fingers, but a screwdriver may be needed if the clips are stiff.

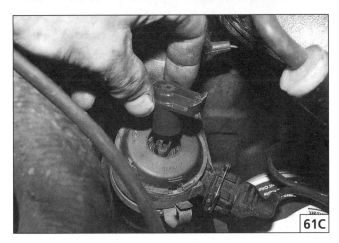

61B

61B. With the cap removed, clean any dirt from the inside and outside with a clean cloth. A small toothbrush is an ideal tool to clean between the high tension turrets on the outside of the cap. If there is a small carbon brush inside the cap at the top, as shown here, it should be free to slide up and down; otherwise there may be a spring contact on top of the rotor arm which bears on a fixed carbon brush in the cap. Check the cap carefully for hairline cracks or other damage, which will allow the H.T. current to track to earth and cause poor starting in damp conditions; have the cap replaced if in doubt.

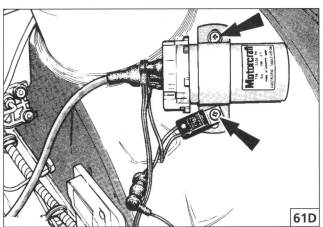

61C

61C. Remove the rotor arm from the distributor shaft by pulling upwards; check it for cracks and other damage, and clean the contact area in the centre of the arm which bears against the sprung carbon brush on the inside of the cap.

61D. Finally, check the ignition coil, making sure it is fixed firmly to its mounting bracket (arrowed). Check the high and low tension wires and clean them with a maintenance spray. Also clean all dirt from the top of the ignition coil and make sure the terminals are also clean. (Illustration, courtesy Ford Motor Co.)

Every 6,000 Miles - Around the Car

Job 62. Check seat belts.

Make sure the seat belts are clean and are not showing any signs of fraying or other damage. Ensure that if you pull slowly, the belt unreels smoothly; but also make sure that if you pull sharply the belt locks up. Check the buckles latch securely and that the reel mounting is secure.

61D

☐ **Job 63. Lubricate locks and hinges.**

OIL CAN LUBE

It doesn't always figure highly, if at all, in service schedules, but there are a fair few moving parts on the motor car which would benefit from occasional oil-can lubrication. They will then work more smoothly, probably more quietly, and will certainly last longer. Here are just a few examples - but if you get into the habit of regularly 'carrying the can' around your car, you'll probably spot a few more!

63A

63B

63A. Door hinges are a prime area of neglect - the hinge-pins of Sierra doors are solid and not easy to penetrate with oil, so the use of a thin oil like Castrol Everyman is recommended; start with the top hinge....

63B. ...then the bottom, applying plenty of oil to the 'joints' of the hinge and working the door to-and-fro to help it penetrate. Mop-up any excess with a rag afterwards.

INSIDE INFORMATION: On older, or previously neglected door hinges, it could be beneficial to first douse them with penetrating fluid,

63C

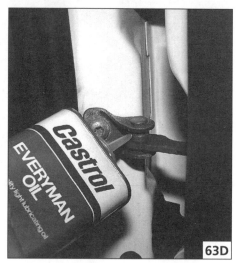
63D

following up with the oil-can a little later, when the penetrating stuff has done its work.

63C. Don't forget the door check strap, which if left unlubricated, dries out, rusts up, and not only retards smooth door opening and closing, but also causes those strident 'graunching' noises which are always an embarrassment - particularly in your drive-way late at night! An occasional smear of grease works wonders too.

63D. Remember to oil the checkstrap pivot too.

63E. Castrol's easing fluid, using the can's slim 'accessory tube', is handy for penetrating stiff lock mechanisms or door lock push-buttons.

63F. Estate and hatchback tailgate hinges will benefit from a drop or two of oil as well. Be careful not to put too much oil on the hinges, as it could seep past the seal and stain the headlining.

63E

63G. Don't forget the various lock and latch mechanisms such as the tailgate latch shown here which, if a remote release is fitted to your car, will keep it operating smoothly.

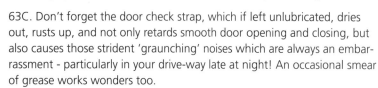

63F

63G

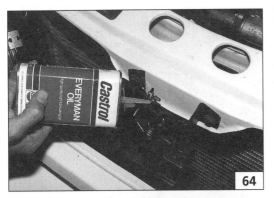

☐ Job 64. Lubricate bonnet release mechanism.

64. While you've got the oil can in your hand, go back under the bonnet. If the bonnet latch is not kept lubricated one day you may find you can't, in fact, get under the bonnet, because the latch has rusted and seized. There are possible 'emergencies' that could arise from this, but even more horrific is when a bonnet that has not closed securely flies open when you are driving! Lubricate the bonnet hinges too.

☐ Job 65. Check seats.

65. Check the condition and security of the seats. The front ones should slide smoothly on their runners and latch securely as well as being securely mounted. Clean the runners of any dirt or grit that might have built up.

☐ Job 66. Test suspension shock absorbers.

66. Press down on each corner of the car in turn in order to check the efficiency of the shock absorbers. The car body should rebound once and then come to rest. If the body continues to bounce a second time, the shock absorber mechanism inside the 'shock absorbers' is worn. Worn shock absorbers should be replaced in pairs, 'across' the car. Efficient shock absorbers can make an enormous difference to your car's safety and handling. If one or more shock absorbers appears to be leaking, no matter how slight, have the shock absorbers checked by a specialist or Ford dealer as soon as possible.

Every 6,000 Miles - Under the Car

☐ Job 67. Check/replace front disc brake pads.

GENERAL INFORMATION: All Sierra models are fitted with disc brakes at the front. These brakes adjust themselves automatically as the pads wear down and so manual adjustment is not required or, indeed, possible. Wear on the pads is the reason why the brake fluid level will go down slightly between services, even when there's no sign of brake fluid leakage.

Two types of front caliper have been fitted to Sierras depending on model and year, the main differences concerning the method of securing the caliper to the bracket, and the shape and surface area of the pads used. Checking the pad thickness is identical, while pad renewal for each type is described separately below.

SAFETY FIRST! AND SPECIALIST SERVICE
Obviously, your car's brakes are among its most important safety related items. Do NOT dismantle or attempt to perform any work on the braking system unless you are fully competent to do so. If you have not been trained in this work, but wish to carry it out, we strongly recommend that you have a garage or qualified mechanic check your work before using the car on the road. See also the section on BRAKES AND ASBESTOS in Chapter 1, Safety First! for further information. Always start by washing the brakes with a proprietary brand of brake cleaner - brake drums removed, where appropriate - never use compressed air to clean off brake dust. Always replace the disc pads and/or shoes in sets of four - never replace the pads/shoes on one wheel only. After fitting new brake shoes or pads, avoid heavy braking - except in an emergency - for the first 150 to 200 miles (250 to 300 km).

CHECK PAD THICKNESS (ALL MODELS)

Slacken the wheel nuts before jacking-up the car, then make sure it is safely supported - **see Raising The Car Safely** at the beginning of this chapter. After the wheel is removed, the front brake caliper and disc are exposed. The thickness of the pad friction-lining material will be clearly visible.

67A. It's important to ensure there is sufficient friction material left on the pads. This can be seen looking down into the caliper with the wheel removed, the example shown here is the later 'Teves' types caliper - the earlier Girling caliper is checked similarly.

INSIDE INFORMATION: The manufacturer's recommend a minimum permissible brake pad thickness is 7mm (including the steel backing-plate) but you should allow for the fact that you won't be checking the brakes again for a further 6,000 miles or six months. Also bear in mind that it is common for one pad to wear down more quickly than the other and you should always take the thickness of the most worn-out pad as your guide. As ever with your braking system, replace sooner rather than later.

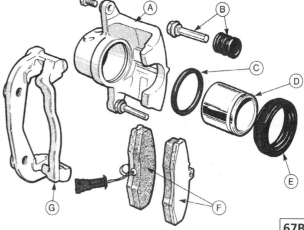
67A

REPLACING FRONT DISC PADS

1.3 AND EARLY 1.6 MODELS ONLY

67B. This is an exploded drawing of the Girling caliper used on these cars.

A. Piston housing
B. Guide pin and dust cover
C. Piston seal
D. Piston
E. Dust cover
F. Brake pads
G. Anchor bracket

67B

67C. Disconnect the pad wear warning sensor wiring (if fitted); thoroughly flush away all traces of brake dust with brake cleaner to prevent it becoming airborn. Use an open-ended spanner to hold the upper guide pin while undoing the guide pin bolt securing the caliper to the carrier bracket.

67D. There is no need to remove the lower guide pin bolt; simply swing the caliper forwards and down until there is sufficient room to lift out the pads. If the pads stick in their seatings, gently lever them away with a screwdriver but never lever against the disk itself.

Thoroughly clean the caliper, using brake cleaner and a wire brush, paying particular attention to the pad seatings in the carrier bracket.

67E. The piston has to be retracted into the caliper so that it will pass over the increased width of the new pads. The Ford service tool is shown in use here to illustrate the principle, but you could use a large pair of grips (as in 67R below), or improvised G-cramp. (Illustration, courtesy Ford Motor Co.)

making it easy! As the piston is forced into its bore, the brake fluid it displaces will cause the master cylinder reservoir level to rise, possibly to the point of overflowing. Raise the bonnet so that the master cylinder can be observed as the piston is pushed home - it may be necessary to syphon a small quantity of fluid from the reservoir, for which purpose an old battery hydrometer is particularly useful to draw fluid from the reservoir, a little at a time.

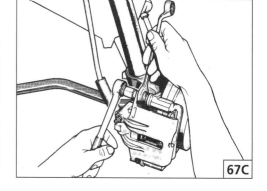
67C

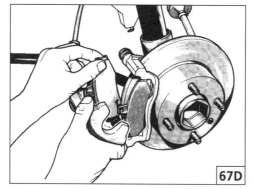
67D

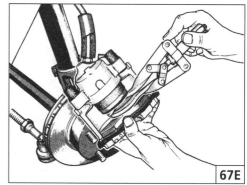
67E

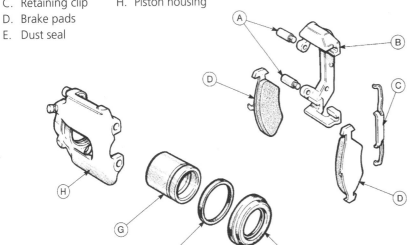

A. Retaining bolts
B. Anchor bracket
C. Retaining clip
D. Brake pads
E. Dust seal
F. Piston seal
G. Piston
H. Piston housing

67F.

LATER 1.6 AND ALL 1.8, 2.0, V6 AND DIESEL MODELS

67F. This is an exploded view of the Teves caliper type fitted to these models. (Illustration, courtesy Ford Motor Co.)

67G. *INSIDE INFORMATION: A 7mm Allen key like this will be needed to unscrew the often very-tight Teves type caliper retaining bolts and you will also need some form of tool to retract the caliper piston into its bore. The latter can be improvised using a woodworking G-cramp or valve spring compressor tool and one of the old brake pads. ALWAYS replace disc pads in sets of four across the car: that is, both front wheels or both rear wheels at the same time. Failure to do this will result in unequal and dangerous braking, due to the imbalance in efficiency.*

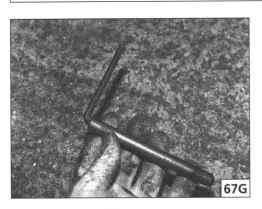

67G.

67H. First disconnect the brake wear indicator wiring, if fitted to your car, by pulling the connector (A) apart. The caliper is retained by two hollow bolts (B) for which the Allen key referred to above is required, either of the socket-adapter type shown at (C)...

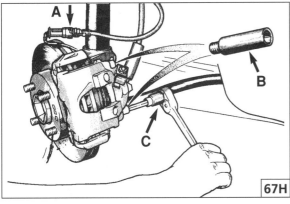

67H.

67I. ...or the type referred to in 67G and as shown here. Note - later models have plastic caps fitted to the bolt dust-excluding tubes which surround the bolts - remove them first. The bolts themselves are likely to be very stiff to turn initially, but take care as they often release quite suddenly, 'skinning' the knuckles of the unwary!

67J. Remove both bolts completely, but don't remove the caliper until...

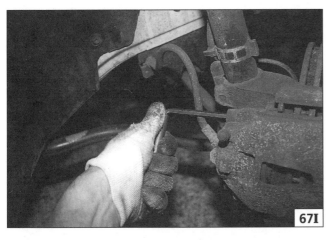

67I.

67J.

6,000 MILE SERVICE

67K. ...the caliper assembly has been doused with brake cleaner to prevent brake dust being disturbed into the atmosphere.

67L. This pad retaining spring is found on models from 1989-on; detach it by levering-out one end of the spring to release the tension, when it can be lifted away.

67M. The caliper assembly can now be pulled forwards over the disc. Note that the outer pad may remain with the carrier bracket and require a sharp tap or two from a hammer to free it.

67N. If a wear-ridge is present on the outer edge of the disc you may find it necessary to lever the caliper carefully against the disc to retract the piston slightly. Use a screwdriver as shown, or refer to 67P if a large pair of grips are available.

67O. INSIDE INFORMATION: The inner pad has a three-legged spring retaining it to the hollow piston - the pad usually comes away easily, but might need a tap from a hammer to free it if corroded.

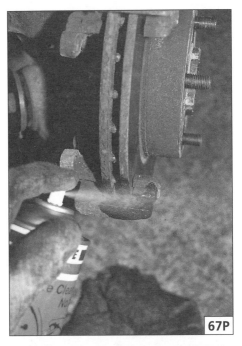

67P. Spray brake cleaner over the carrier bracket, paying particular attention to the pad seatings and those areas not accessible when the pads are fitted.

67Q. Wire brush the pad seatings on the bracket, removing any hard scale or rust by scraping with an old screwdriver or chisel.

67R. Retracting the piston is necessary when fitting new pads. This can be done earlier in the sequence when the caliper is still attached to the carrier, or now before cleaning. See the note after **Job 67E** regarding fluid level in the master cylinder reservoir.

SAFETY FIRST!
67S. NEVER allow the caliper to hang by the flexible brake hose: Unseen damage can occur to the hose that may not materialise until later, possibly when the brakes are needed in an emergency. Improvise a simple 'hook' from stout wire and suspend the caliper from the shock absorber/spring seat.

6,000 MILE SERVICE

67T. Check the piston dust-excluder seal for splits, chafing or perishing. If any sign of brake fluid is present a leak is indicated, you should have the affected caliper inspected by a qualified specialist or Ford dealer immediately.

Reassemble the new pads to their seats, fit the caliper and bolts, replace the pad retaining spring (if fitted) and reconnect the wear indicator wiring. Do not over-tighten the caliper bolts tighten with a torque wrench to the recommended figure off 15 to 18 lb.ft. (20 to 25 Nm).

SPECIALIST SERVICE: Consult your Ford dealer and have them examine the disc and measure it with a micrometer if deep scoring is evident.

Badly scored or ridged discs will seriously reduce braking efficiency even with fully bedded-in pads. New pads would take for ever to bed-in on them and meanwhile braking efficiency could be virtually nil!

67T

SAFETY FIRST!
If you are in any doubt as to the condition of the disc or discs, seek professional advice immediately. Corroded or pitted areas of the disc's working surface indicates a possible problem with the caliper, which may be partially seized. Additionally, deep scoring causes the pad friction material to contract only onto the 'peaks' of the ridges, thereby drastically reducing the area of contact and subsequent braking efficiency.

☐ **Job 68. Check/replace rear disc pads.**

MODELS WITH ABS ONLY

If you're not sure whether or not your car is fitted with ABS (anti-lock) brakes, ask your dealer.

Rear pads - inspection

Slacken the wheel nuts before jacking up the car, then make sure it is safely supported - see *Raising The Car Safely* at the beginning of this chapter.

68A. After the wheel is removed the disc pads can be inspected through the top of the caliper; a small torch may be needed to see 'inside' the caliper window and by the spring clip.

68A

INSIDE INFORMATION: Just as with the front brakes, it is important to ensure that there is sufficient depth of friction material on the rear pads, which tend to wear at a lesser rate than the front pads. The recommended minimum permissible brake pad thickness is 7mm (including the steel backing plate) but you should allow for the fact that you won't be checking the brakes again for another 6,000 miles or six months. As brake pads very rarely wear evenly, you should take the thickness of the most worn pad as your guide.

Rear brake pad replacement

The rear caliper is very similar to the front caliper in operation, except for the inclusion of the handbrake mechanism within the caliper itself. This requires a special tool to retract the piston, which has to be 'wound' back into its bore, rather than simply pushed in. However, pad replacement is straightforward and follows the procedure described in **Job 67A**-onwards, so a brief outline of the job follows which should be considered as additional to that described above.

SAFETY FIRST! AND SPECIALIST SERVICE.
*Obviously, your car's brakes are among its most important safety related items. Do NOT dismantle or attempt to perform any work on the braking system unless you are fully competent to do so. If you have not been trained in this work, but wish carry it out. we strongly recommend that you have a garage or qualified mechanic check your work before using the car on the road. See also the section on BRAKES AND ASBESTOS in **Chapter 1, Safety First!** for further information. Always start by washing the brakes with a proprietary brand of brake cleaner never use compressed air to clean off brake dust. Always replace the disc pads in sets of four - never replace the pads on one wheel only. After fitting new pads, avoid heavy breaking - except in an emergency - for the first 150 - 200 miles (250 to 300 km).*

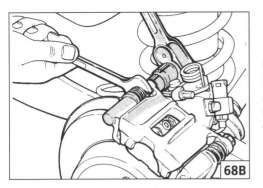

68B. It is strictly only necessary to remove the front caliper retaining bolt for pad replacement, although we recommend both bolts are removed and the caliper and bracket thoroughly cleaned. Steady the caliper-bolt sleeve with a 17mm spanner while the bolt itself is undone. Disconnect the brake wear indicator wires, if fitted to your car. (Illustration, courtesy Ford Motor Co.)

68C. Remove the two caliper retaining bolts completely.

68D. To allow movement of the caliper, unclip the handbrake cable from the lower suspension arm by bending the clip upwards slightly and freeing the cable.

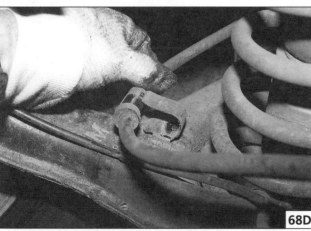

68E. Swing the caliper upwards so that the pads can be removed sideways - a sharp tap from a hammer may be needed to free the pads if corroded.

68F. The piston is 'screwed' into its bore by this tool, the head of which engages with the slotted segments in the piston face...

68G. ...while the bored carrier plate pushes against the outer caliper 'arms'.

68H. Once retracted, check the piston dust excluder for splitting and other damage.

68I. Scrape any rust or scale from the pad seatings in each end of the bracket with a screwdriver. This is important to ensure free movement of the pads.

68J. If the existing pads are to be re-fitted, clean them all over with a wire brush to remove any rust.

Re-assemble by fitting the pads to the carrier bracket, replacing the caliper over the pads and fitting the bolt. Retighten with a torque wrench to 23 to 26 lb.ft (31 to 35 Nm). Don't forget to replace the handbrake cable in its clip on the lower suspension arm, bending the tab over the cable after fitting.

68K. Apply a dab of grease to the handbrake cable and operating arm - a copper-based grease has been used here.

You can learn a lot about the condition of an engine from looking at the spark plugs. The following information and photographs, reproduced here with grateful thanks to NGK, show you what to look out for.

1. Good Condition

If the firing end of a spark plug is brown or light grey, the condition can be judged to be good and the spark plug is functioning at its best.

4. Overheating

When having been overheated, the insulator tip can become glazed or glossy, and deposits which have accumulated on the insulator tip may have melted. Sometimes these deposits have blistered on the insulator's tip.

6. Abnormal Wear

Abnormal electrode erosion is caused by the effects of corrosion, oxidation, reaction with lead, all resulting in abnormal gap growth.

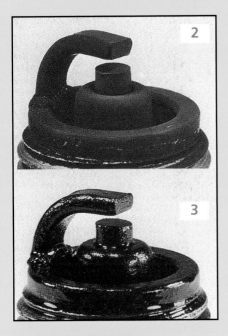

2. Carbon Fouling

Black, dry, sooty deposits, which will eventually cause misfiring and can be caused by an over-rich fuel mixture. Check all carburettor settings, choke operation and air filter cleanliness. Clean plugs vigorously with a brass bristled wire brush.

3. Oil Fouling

Oily, wet-looking deposits. This is particularly prone to causing poor starting and even misfiring. Caused by a severely worn engine but do not confuse with wet plugs removed from the engine when it won't start. If the "wetness" evaporates away, it's not oil fouling.

5. Normal Wear

A worn spark plug not only wastes fuel but also strains the whole ignition system because the expanded gap requires higher voltage. As a result, a worn spark plug will result in damage to the engine itself, and will also increase air pollution. The normal rate of gap growth is usually around 'half-a-thou.' or 0.0006 in. every 5,000 miles (0.01 mm. every 5,000 km.).

7. Breakage

Insulator damage is self-evident and can be caused by rapid heating or cooling of the plug whilst out of the car or by clumsy use of gap setting tools. Burned away electrodes are indicative of an ignition system that is grossly out of adjustment. Do not use the car until this has been put right.

6,000 MILE SERVICE

68L. Push the thin 'probe' that comes with each can of Castrol DWF lubricant into the rubber sleeve at the end of the handbrake cable, to help prevent it seizing.

68M. Finally, check the condition of the flexible brake hose that connects the caliper to the axle bracket, looking for signs of cracking and chafing.

☐ **Job 69. Check/adjust/renew rear drum brakes.**

NOT ABS MODELS

Check lining thickness

69A. A simple method of checking the lining thickness is provided by way of an aperture in the brake backplate through which the linings can be seen. A rubber plug is fitted to exclude water. The minimum lining thickness is 1mm, but you should consider replacing the shoes when the thickness approaches 2 - 3mm on grounds of safety and general efficiency. (Illustration, courtesy Ford Motor Co.)

Check or replace linings

Although it is possible to check lining thickness without removing the brake drum, as described above, it is recommended that the drums be removed periodically to enable any build-up of brake dust to be removed (often the cause of brake 'squeal') and to allow the hydraulic wheel cylinders to be checked for leaks.

69B. With the rear of the car raised and the wheel removed, undo the single drum retaining screw, release the handbrake and pull the drum off. (Illustration, courtesy Ford Motor Co.)

Place a rag beneath and use a proprietary brake cleaning spray to 'flood' away all loose dust and dirt. Do the same with the inner surfaces of the drum.

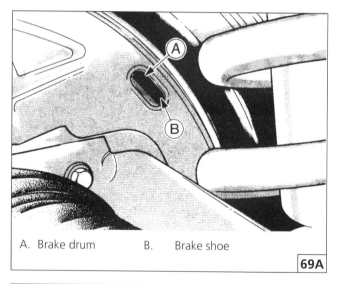

A. Brake drum   B.   Brake shoe

SAFETY FIRST! AND SPECIALIST SERVICE.
Obviously, your car's brakes are among its most important safety related items. Do NOT dismantle or attempt to perform any work on the braking system unless you are fully competent to do so. If you have not been trained in this work, but wish carry it out. we strongly recommend that you have a garage or qualified mechanic check your work before using the car on the road. See also the section on BRAKES AND ASBESTOS in Chapter 1, Safety First! for further information. Always start by washing the brakes with a proprietary brand of brake cleaner - brake drums removed, where appropriate -never use compressed air to clean off brake dust. Always replace the disc pads and/or shoes in sets of four - never replace the pads/shoes on one wheel only. After fitting new brake shoes or pads, avoid heavy breaking - except in an emergency - for the first 150 - 200 miles (250 to 300 km).

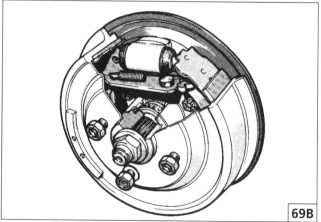

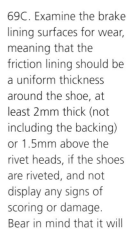

69C. Examine the brake lining surfaces for wear, meaning that the friction lining should be a uniform thickness around the shoe, at least 2mm thick (not including the backing) or 1.5mm above the rivet heads, if the shoes are riveted, and not display any signs of scoring or damage. Bear in mind that it will be another 9,000 miles before you check again, so err on the cautious side. Check also for traces of oil, grease or brake fluid - if present the shoes will need replacement.

69D. Examine the hydraulic wheel cylinder, in particularly the rubber gaiters at each end. Pull each gaiter back slightly and check for any sign of dampness, which would indicate the internal seals of the cylinder are worn and require urgent replacement - seek professional help immediately.

BRAKE SHOE REPLACEMENT

A. Leading shoe
B. Cylinder dust cover
C. Piston
D. Piston seal
E. Spring
F. Wheel cylinder housing
G. Mounting bolts

H. Hold down pin
J. Carrier plate
K. Adjustment plunger
L. Trailing shoe and handbrake lever
M. Auto adjuster
N. Hold down spring and clip

69E

making it easy!

69E. Before dismantling brake shoes, but after the drum has been removed, make a careful record of where everything goes, especially brake shoe return springs. Make a careful sketch, take a couple of photographs (a Polaroid would be ideal) or 'video' the assembly - it could turn out to be a life saver - literally! Also, only work on one side at a time, so that you've always got the other one to refer to. If necessary, refer to the exploded diagram here.

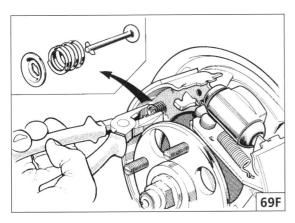

69F. Release the spring clips on the shoe steady pins by holding the pin at the rear of the brake backplate and pushing against the spring with pliers - with the spring compressed, turn it through 90 degrees and allow it to pass over the holding-pin head.

69G. Release the top of the forward-facing (leading) shoe by unhooking the spring - use a strong pair of snipe-nosed pliers for this, as the spring is under some tension. Next, lever the bottom of the shoe from its seat and unhook the lower spring.

69H. The rear shoe will now be free, although the automatic adjusting mechanism will be attached to it; swing the shoe backwards to clear the backplate. Unhook the handbrake cable from the operating arm on the brake shoe.

69I. These are the shoe contact points on the backplate - it is important these be clean and free from rust in order for the shoes to slide easily over them. Clean thoroughly with brake cleaner and rag, removing any rust spots with abrasive paper. Apply a very thin smear of special brake grease to the contact points, but ensure no grease will get onto the shoes when fitted. (Illustration, courtesy Ford Motor Co.)

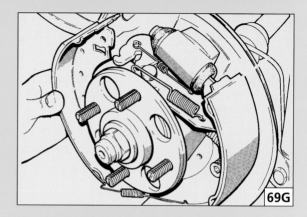

69G

If new shoes are to be fitted, note the way the adjuster mechanism is attached to the rear shoe and the location of the spring, and transfer the adjuster over to the new shoe.

INSIDE INFORMATION: Try to remove the shoe in as near 'assembled' state as possible, to aid renewal. Place the assembly flat on the ground and build-up the new shoes a step at a time, transferring springs and adjuster in sequence. In this way you will avoid any confusion as to what part goes where, and can clean each part as it is dealt with.

69J. As soon as the shoes are lifted away, tie a loop of wire or cord around the hydraulic cylinder to prevent the pistons popping out of their bores, which would require the brakes to be bled.

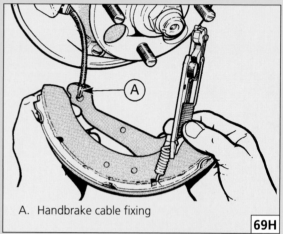

A. Handbrake cable fixing

69H

Clean the backplate and cylinder with spray and a rag before fitting the new shoes. Remember to attach the handbrake cable connector to the respective shoe before assembling the components; otherwise the installation operation is a reversal of the above procedure. Take care not to allow oil or grease to contaminate the new shoes!

On completion, operate the handbrake several times, followed by the foot brake, to centralise the shoes and allow the automatic adjuster to take up any slack.

☐ Job 70. Check brake proportioning valve.

This component is fitted to the rear underside of the car, its purpose being to control the flow of hydraulic fluid to the rear brakes, depending on the load carried by the vehicle. It does this by a connection to the bodywork in the form of a sprung arm which is deflected at varying angles depending on the load - the greater the load, the more fluid is allowed to pass and therefore the greater breaking effort applied to the rear wheels.

69I

SPECIALIST SERVICE: Have this component checked by a reputable garage or Ford dealer.

Every 6,000 Miles - Under the Car

Please note that the only two jobs in the 'Under the Car' category at this mileage fit more neatly in an earlier section. See Jobs 51 and 53.

69J

12,000 Miles or Every Twelve Months, whichever comes first

Every 12,000 miles - The Engine Bay

As for 6,000 mile service plus the following additional items.

In 1992, Ford changed their recommended servicing intervals from 6,000 and 12,000 mile periods to 10,000 and 20,000 miles respectively. This does not make any difference to the servicing items we cover and we leave it up to you to decide which servicing period is more convenient for you.

IMPORTANT NOTE: Renewal of the spark plugs is recommended at this interval - see Job 45 for details of removal and replacement.

☐ Job 71. Check camshaft timing belt and condition.

NOT DOHC, V6 OR DIESEL

INSIDE INFORMATION: The camshaft drivebelt, or 'cambelt' is driven by the crankshaft and transmits power to the camshaft and water

pump by way of toothed pulleys (the cambelt itself being 'toothed'). As such the belt plays a vital part in the operation of the engine, for without it the engine cannot run. It is obviously important that the belt be in good condition at all times, especially as a breakage of the belt while the engine is running can cause serious damage to the pistons and/or valve gear, as well as stopping the vehicle.

SPECIALIST SERVICE: Ford recommend changing the belt every three years or 36,000 miles, whichever comes first. There is no recommended period of inspection, but many owners prefer to have a tension and overall condition of the belt checked at 12,000 miles or every two years, if only for peace of mind. Most reputable garages will be happy to carry out these checks for a small charge. Special tools are required to change and tension the cambelt, as well as strict procedure, so we recommend the job be undertaken by a proficient mechanic or Ford agent.

☐ Job 72. Emission control equipment.

SIERRAS FROM 1992 ONLY

72. Check the condition of all breather pipes, looking for signs of splitting, perishing etc and also check that connections are tight.

SPECIALIST SERVICE: The emission control systems fitted to cars from 1991 form part of the engine management systems and to test them requires special Ford test instruments and a procedure that takes into account numerous other components, many of which cannot be tested individually. We therefore recommend that the emission control equipment is tested by a Ford agent or dealer.

☐ Job 73. Renew air filter element.

CARBURETTOR MODELS ONLY

73A. The air filter cover is secured by a series of clips around the edge as shown and three or four crosshead screws, depending on the model. Release the clips and undo the screws.

73B. Lift the air cleaner cover away to reveal the filter element, which can be removed and discarded.

Remove any dust or debris (leaves, flies etc.) from the lower casing, taking care that none enters the carburettor intake situated in the centre of the housing - a vacuum cleaner with hose and nozzle is deal for this task, if available.

73C. Carefully place the new filter in position, making sure the lower seal of the element fits snugly around the raised portion of the filter housing. Replace the cover, screws and clips.

73D. Check the condition of the air trunking that connects between air filter housing and the intake beside the radiator - that shown here has split and requires replacement.

73E. Check the air-flap vacuum tube and connectors between the carburettor and intake capsule on the air cleaner housing. Test the capsule by sucking on the tube from the carburettor end - the flap should be drawn upwards and close-off the fresh-air duct when the engine is cold.

☐ Job 74. Renew air filter element.

FUEL INJECTION MODELS ONLY

Although there may be minor positional differences between models, the procedure is the same for all.

74A. The air filter cover is secured by spring clips. Release the clips, using a screwdriver if they prove too stiff for the fingers!

74B. Lift the top cover as far as the air intake hose will allow, and as much as is necessary to remove the old filter.

Clean the lower housing of debris, with a vacuum cleaner hose and nozzle if possible.

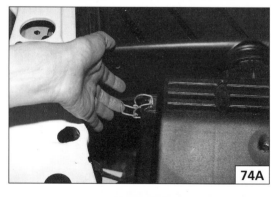

74C. Place the new filter in position, ensuring the latex seal on the upper edge of the filter seats properly in the groove on the lower housing - the upper casing will not fit properly if the filter is misplaced. Re-fit the top cover and secure with the clips.

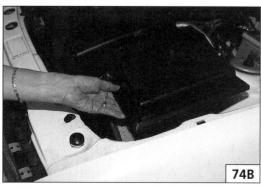

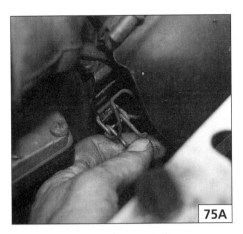

75A.

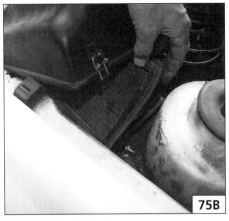

75B.

76.

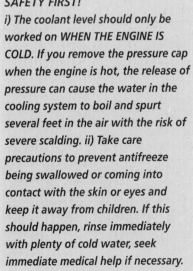

77A.

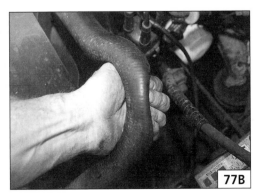

77B.

Job 75. Renew air filter element.

DIESEL ENGINES ONLY

75A. The air filter housing on diesel engines is situated on the nearside of the engine bay adjacent to the suspension turret. To remove the filter, release the clips around the filter assembly, The cover can now be lifted off to expose the paper element type filter.

75B. Remove the old filter element and clean all dirt and dust from the filter housing. Fit the new filter and re-fit the cover and secure with the clips.

Job 76. Check/renew fuel filter.

SAFETY FIRST!
Only a small amount of fuel is likely to be lost with this job, so position a suitable container or large rag under the unit to catch whatever fuel is lost.

EARLY FUEL INJECTION MODELS ONLY

76. The fuel in-line filter is located on the right-hand side of the engine bay, beneath the air cleaner housing. Slacken the fuel pipe unions slowly, and have a large rag handy to catch the fuel spillage that will occur. Slacken the filter clamp screw and remove the filter unit from the car.

Fit the new filter ensuring that the arrows embossed on the filter casing point in the direction of fuel flow. Tighten the clamp screw and reconnect the fuel pipe unions.

LATER FUEL INJECTION MODELS

SPECIALIST SERVICE: Fuel injection systems remain pressurised even when the engine is switched off and require special procedures to make them safe - UNDER NO CIRCUMSTANCES loosen or remove fuel pipes on a fuel injection system without taking appropriate steps to contain the fuel that will issue under pressure. If pipework requires repair, take the car immediately to a fuel injection specialist or your Ford dealer.

Job 77. Check coolant hoses.

77A. Certainly once a year, before adding antifreeze as described shortly, check the condition of all coolant hoses and the security of their clips. But beware of tightening a clip on a leaking elderly hose - renewing both hose and clip is the wiser option.

77B. Examine the hoses for signs of cracking (carefully bending the straights and straightening the bends) and squeeze them to feel for any softening, perhaps caused by oil contamination. Don't overlook minor hoses, such as a feed to a water-heated inlet manifold.

Arguably, once your cooling system contains anti-freeze your car is protected for ever more from the dangers of freezing up, since it is widely held that the strength of the antifreezing element in the mixture will never

SAFETY FIRST!
i) The coolant level should only be worked on WHEN THE ENGINE IS COLD. If you remove the pressure cap when the engine is hot, the release of pressure can cause the water in the cooling system to boil and spurt several feet in the air with the risk of severe scalding. ii) Take care precautions to prevent antifreeze being swallowed or coming into contact with the skin or eyes and keep it away from children. If this should happen, rinse immediately with plenty of cold water, seek immediate medical help if necessary.

wane. However, whether this is entirely true or not, there is the danger, that over a long period casual topping-up of the coolant with plain water will have weakened the mixture. On top of that, we are told that while the antifreeze constituents live on, the beneficial 'all the year round' anti-corrosion inhibitors built into the mixture do not.

☐ Job 78. Check power steering and hoses.

78A.The power steering rack is located underneath and to the front of the engine. Carefully trace the high pressure pipes from the pump to the rack, checking for any sign of leaks, including the unions and pipe connectors. If a leak is suspected, have the car checked by a reputable garage as soon as possible.

78B. Check the low-pressure return-hose and connections between the rack and reservoir, ensuring clips are secure.

☐ Job 79. Check air conditioning operation (if fitted).

Check all connections to the air conditioning compressor and look for signs of corrosion and leaks. However, the first sign of something amiss (for most owner!) is when the system fails.

SPECIALIST SERVICE: Problems with air conditioning equipment must be referred to a Ford dealer or specialist, due to the equipment needed to test it and the precautions necessary in handling the ozone-damaging gas with which it is filled. Under no circumstances should you attempt to disconnect pipework or components.

☐ Job 80. Battery terminals.

Provided the battery is kept clean and dry and is not topped-up over generously, its terminals should also remain clean and sound unless a generator fault is causing it to be over-charged, with consequent heavy ' gassing ' from the cells. Generally speaking, it is electrolyte spillage or this excess vapour which leads to the 'fungal growth' noted on the terminals of neglected batteries. It is a condition which, as well as the highly corrosive effect on nearby metals, such as the battery clamp and the battery tray, also poor electrical contact. In the extreme, the starter may fail to operate, or all electrics may apparently fail.

80A. If you have inherited a secondhand vehicle suffering from this problem, simply pouring hot water (or a mixture of hot water and domestic soda) over the terminals and any other affected parts, such as the battery strap or clamp, and the battery tray, will usually prove remarkably effective. Take care that you don't pour the hot water into the battery cells or onto nearby vulnerable components.

---

making it easy! Old hoses referred to in 77A and 77B become very set in their ways, and should you need to renew one you may find that, even with its clips fully slackened off, it will be reluctant to budge.

Rather than employ too much force, particularly on a radiator, where there's a high risk of fracturing the hose stub, simply slide the clip out of the way and use a strong, sharp knife to slit the hose until you can open it up and peel it off the stub.

However careful you are, there is always a danger of contaminating the new linings with oil or grease from dirty fingers. Cover the linings with masking tape before you start and you won't have to worry about it! Remove the tape once the new shoes are in place.

Thoroughly clean the stubs, carefully using a file and emery cloth if necessary, to remove the lumpy corrosion often found on elderly alloy cooling system components.

Position new clips (preferably of flat, 'worm-drive' type) on the new hose, ensuring their tightening screws are best placed for easy screwdriver access when the hose is fitted. A smear of washing-up fluid will help the hose slide fully home on the stubs. Tighten the clips firmly, but don't 'bury' them in the hose.

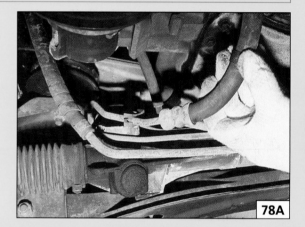

78A

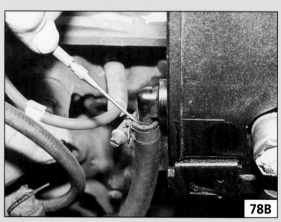

78B

80A

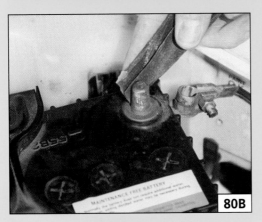

80B. If necessary, the hot water treatment can be followed by use of a wire brush and/or emery cloth to bring the battery lead connectors and the battery terminal posts back to clean and bright condition. A slim knife blade or half-round file can be useful to clean inside the lead connectors. (A typical cause of accidental short-circuit is the bristles of a wire brush touching a battery terminal and a battery strap at the same time, or, similarly, a spanner being used to tighten a terminal nut also touching this strap or the car bodywork.)

SAFETY FIRST!
Be very careful to guard against ' short circuits' when working on battery terminals. The gas ensuing from the cells, particularly when the battery is being charged, is extremely explosive and ignition by a careless spark can cause a truly horrific battery explosion.

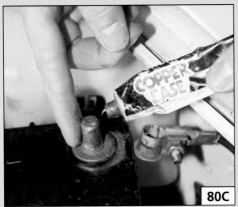

80C. Once all connections are clean and dry, a smear of petroleum jelly (such as 'Vaseline') or a copper-based grease, will guard against further corrosion and help to maintain good electrical contact. Badly affected metals should be treated with a rust killer and re-painted.

80D. Finally, terminal connections should be tight but not 'murdered' to the point of distortion!

☐ Job 81. Check and clean glow plugs.

DIESEL ENGINES ONLY

Rarely will you see any mention of the glow plugs or pre-heating system made on service schedules. This is because manufacturers regard the cold-starting system as one that either works or doesn't ...and if it doesn't, you can probably set things right by renewing all the glow plugs.

However, as a keen DIY-er you'll no doubt want to keep an eye on the condition of the plugs, which can be a handy indicator of injector problems. Our recommendation is that you remove all glow plugs at each major service (typically the annual service), wipe the soot from them, check there's no erosion, and refit them. It's best to catch worn-out plugs before you start experiencing starting difficulties.

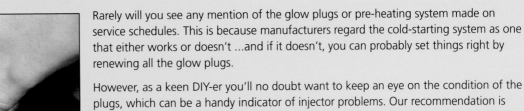

GLOW PLUG REMOVAL

81. Before removing a glow plug from the cylinder head, disconnect the battery earth lead, and remove the air filter assembly and intake trunking. Next, disconnect the wire or connecting strap from each plug and unscrew it from the cylinder head by just a couple of turns using a ring spanner or socket. Clean away dirt from around the plug so that none finds its way into the engine once the plug is removed, then fully unscrew the plug (and its sealing washer, if fitted). It's a good idea to blank off the plug hole with a piece of cloth to prevent dirt from entering.

Re-fitting is a reversal of the above, but take car not to overtighten the plugs, and ensure the electrical connections are bright and clean.

☐ Job 82. Check visible electrical wiring for security.

It's a good idea to check the wiring in the engine bay from time to time if only to clean off any dirt from the terminals. Also check the wiring loom for security, especially where it is adjacent to vulnerable areas like the exhaust and cooling fan.

12,000 MILE SERVICE

Every 12,000 Miles - Around the Car

☐ Job 83. Toolkit and jack.

Inspect the toolkit, wipe tools with oily rag to stop them rusting and lubricate the jack, checking that it works smoothly. Also, check that the spare wheel retaining bolt hasn't rusted solid. Remove it and lubricate the threads with a dab of grease.

☐ Job 84. Check wheel bearings.

Although the wheel bearings on the Sierra are of no-maintenance type, it is a good idea to check the bearings for wear periodically. For this, each wheel should be raised clear of the ground in turn and the wheel slowly rotated by hand to detect and roughness in the bearing. Detecting a worn wheel bearing can be difficult and this job is probably best left to a garage or Ford dealer if you are not an experienced mechanic.

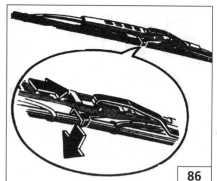

86

☐ Job 85. Check headlight alignment.

It is possible to adjust your own headlights but not with sufficient accuracy. Badly adjusted headlights can be very dangerous if they don't provide you, the driver, with a proper view of the road ahead or they dazzle oncoming drivers. Older drivers and those with poor eyesight can become disorientated when confronted with maladjusted headlights.

SPECIALIST SERVICE: Have the work carried out for you by a garage with beam measuring equipment. Any MoT testing station in the UK will be properly equipped.

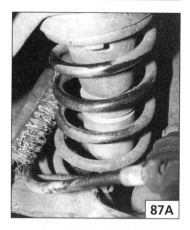

87A

☐ Job 86. Check/replace wiper blades.

Wiper blades don't last for ever, even though some people seem to think they do! It's a good policy to change them every year at least, not only on safety grounds but because a clear screen makes driving, especially at night, so much more comfortable. Refer to **Job 13** for details of how to change them.

86. A more economical way is to change just the rubber blades, as shown (full instructions will accompany the new blades).

☐ Job 87. Check steering and suspension.

Although most of the 'running' checks (that is, those that tend to wear) have been covered in the earlier 3,000 mile service schedule, there area few other components that are worthy of attention at less frequent intervals, mainly to check tightness and security. Test the steering column by grasping the steering wheel and rocking it up-and-down and sideways. Excessive play needs to be investigated - seek professional advice.

87B

87A. Check the front spring/shock absorber units (correctly termed 'MacPherson struts') looking for badly corroded or broken springs. (Give them a good cleaning off it they're caked in mud.) Make sure the drain holes in the lower spring seat-pan are clean and clear. Check the shock absorber inside the spring for signs of oil staining, indicating a failed unit - have it investigated and always renew shock absorbers in pairs, one each side of the car.

Check the rear unit in a similar way, but note the springs are separate. Grasp each shock absorber and try to rock it - there should be little or no free play, but if some is present, check the mounting bolts are secure, otherwise seek professional help.

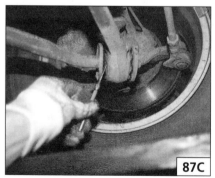

87C

87B. Check also the mounting bushes, looking for signs of damage or perishing of the rubber; try to rock the shock absorber and look for any excessive movement of the bush.

87C. Check the anti-roll bar mounting bushes for damage, either mechanical damage such as splitting, or chemical damage caused by oil contamination. Check here, at the road wheel...

87D. ...and at the body mountings.

☐ Job 88. Replace alarm remote batteries.

If an alarm is fitted to your car, replace the battery in each alarm sender unit. Otherwise, it is all too easy to be banished from your own car, if the battery 'dies' at an inopportune moment.

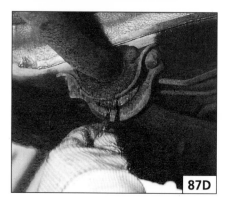

87D

Every 12,000 miles - Under the Car

☐ Job 89. Inspect underside and clear drain holes.

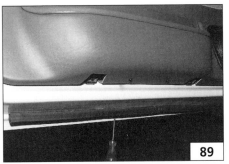

89

When dry inspect the underside of the car for rust and damage. Renew paint, underbody sealant and wax coating locally as necessary. Old-fashioned bitumen type underseal goes brittle and comes loose anyway, this only makes the problem worse. Water will soon penetrate this area and form a breeding ground for corrosion. Scrape off any such loose underseal and paint on wax coating in its place, when dry.

Use an old screwdriver or light hammer to test for unsound and corroded areas of bodywork beneath the car, including the inner panels of the boot and engine bay. Investigate areas of loose paint and flaking rusty metal.

89. Check and clear drain holes in doors, sills, boot etc. Use a thin probe to poke the holes clear, although for a lasting job a vacuum and nozzle will clear most debris. Check also the bulkhead well at the rear of the engine bay, especially for leaves in winter - your vacuum cleaner is possibly the only thing that will shift them!

☐ Job 90. Check prop shaft U.J.s & driveshafts.

90A

CONVENTIONAL AND 4X4 CARS

90A. Grasp the propeller shaft and 'twist' it while holding the axle input flange, to test for any play or slackness in the joints of which there should be none. Also examine the rubber coupling for signs of damage, splitting or perishing. Have them replaced if in any doubt.

90B

90C

90B. Check the rear driveshaft joints, both inner and outer, at the axle and wheel respectively. Check the condition of the rubber gaiters, looking for splits, chafing etc or other leak. Grasp the driveshaft and check for excessive play and noise (clunks!) by rocking and rotating it. If in doubt about the condition of these components, seek professional advice.

90C. Examine the intermediate prop-shaft rubber coupling for damage, looking for signs of splitting, softening, chafing and perishing. If the coupling is damaged, it's a **SPECIALIST SERVICE** replacement job.

Every 24,000 Miles - or Every Two Years, whichever comes first

☐ Job 91. Replace brake fluid.

SPECIALIST SERVICE: Although Ford recommend that the brake fluid is changed every three years, we would recommend that this is done every two years. This is best done by a garage or Ford agent, who will have the necessary facilities and equipment to carry out the work quickly.

☐ Job 92. Check brake discs/drums and calipers.

SPECIALIST SERVICE: Although a check on the general condition of the discs/drums and calipers has been covered in the 6,000 mile service schedule, it is advisable to have a specialist or Ford dealer inspect them at this longer period, where they can be tested for run-out (a slight wobble of the disc), ovality (excessive wear in the drums can leave them slightly oval) and sticking pistons in the calipers. The specified minimum dimensions for discs and/or drums can also be measured with great accuracy.

☐ Job 93. Replace crankcase emission valve.

V6 ENGINE ONLY

The emission valve controls the amount of normal crankcase fumes entering the inlet manifold to be burnt inside the combustion chambers. The valve is located on the side of the engine block and is easy to replace.

Disconnect the hose from the emission valve and pull the valve from its housing in the engine and discard it. Check that the rubber sealing ring is correctly fitted then press the new valve into position. Reconnect the hose.

☐ Job 94. Clean/replace engine oil filler cap.

DIESEL ENGINE ONLY

The oil filler cap on the diesel engine is an integral part of the crankcase ventilation system and should be cleaned periodically to remove any dirt which might prevent the engine from breathing-in fresh air.

The cap should be washed in a suitable solvent such as paraffin to remove any build up of oil sludge and general dirt. Shake the cap dry afterwards and re-fit it to the engine.

94. Diesel models from 1987-on feature a revised ventilation arrangement, see illustration. Check the condition of the pipes and replace the valve annually.

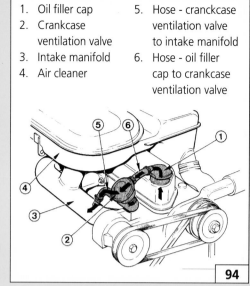

1. Oil filler cap
2. Crankcase ventilation valve
3. Intake manifold
4. Air cleaner
5. Hose - cranckcase ventilation valve to intake manifold
6. Hose - oil filler cap to crankcase ventilation valve

94

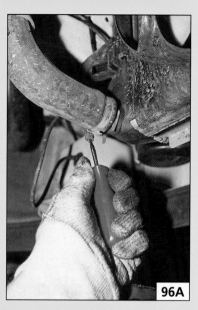

96A

☐ Job 95. Adjust brake bands.

AUTOMATIC TRANSMISSION ONLY

SPECIALIST SERVICE: Apart from checking and topping up the fluid level, any other maintenance work on an automatic transmission should be done by a transmission specialist or Ford dealer who will have the tools and knowledge to do the job correctly. Ford do not consider changing the transmission fluid is necessary, and no provision is provided for doing so.

☐ Job 96. Change engine coolant.

96B

96A. Antifreeze also prevents internal corrosion - but only if it's changed regularly. Probably the quickest and most effective way to drain the coolant is to disconnect the bottom radiator hose, after positioning a container beneath it. When the coolant has drained, reconnect the hose and tighten the clip.

96B. Pour the fresh antifreeze into the coolant header or expansion tank to give a 50-50 dilution; refer to *Chapter 8, Facts & Figures* for the capacity of your car's cooling system. Finally, add the required amount of fresh water, then start the engine and check for leaks. After running the engine for a few minutes, switch off, leave to cool down and top up again. Do so again after the first time you use the car.

Every 36,000 MILES - or Every Three Years, whichever comes first

☐ Job 97. Replace camshaft drive belt.

SPECIALIST SERVICE & INSIDE INFORMATION: Ford recommend the cam belt be changed at 36,000 miles or THREE years for all 4-cylinder single overhead camshaft engines (not the DOHC unit). A cam belt breaks without warning and, if it does so, an engine can be very severely damaged as pistons hit valves. This job is best entrusted to a reputable garage or Ford agent.

☐ Job 98. Renew HT leads.

Modern HT leads are made of a low-resistance material that helps reduce radio and TV interference. However, it is possible for the conductor and insulator to deteriorate over a period of time, with the result that starting and general performance are affected.

Renew the leads one at a time, taking care to ensure each new lead is positioned identically to the old one. Also ensure that the contact terminals at the distributor and coil ends of the leads are fully pushed 'home'. Make sure that the new leads are neatly gathered together and that there is no danger of a lead coming into contact with any moving or hot part of the engine.

☐ Job 99. Rustproofing.

Corrosion costs car owners far more than mechanical wear. Completely rustproofing your car every three years can save you a small fortune - see *Chapter 5, Rustproofing*.

CHAPTER 4 - BODYWORK

In this Chapter, we show you how to make your car look its best. First, we demonstrate that your car's appearance can be improved beyond recognition by a couple of hours of work on a Sunday morning. Then, just in case a passing gate post should leap out at you, we explain how to carry out simple bodywork repairs at home.

PART I: THE BODY BEAUTIFUL

Have you ever looked in amazement at the condition of cars on a dealer's forecourt and wondered why your car doesn't look like that? Well, it can! It's all a matter of know-how and a bit of hard work - and using the techniques described in this Chapter, you'll find that your car can be made to look almost like new again, without using too many cans of elbow grease!

☐ I.2 Weekend trips in your car are likely to be cursed by the 'bugs on the bumper' syndrome, as well as black tar on the bodywork. Soak all the bug-splatted areas with soapy water first, while you wash the rest of the car, then come back later, when they've been softened. Rub off with cloth, rather than a sponge. Use a proprietary brand of tar remover to wipe off tar splash.

☐ I.1 Apply a thin coat of modern car polish, to give a far longer-lasting shine than old-fashioned waxes (though we've yet to find one that lasts as long as claimed!). Cover just one section of the car at a time and then, as soon as the wax dries to a haze, buff off for a superb shine. You'll see the dull paint and oxides come off on the cloth as you buff.

I.1

SOFT-TOP SPORTS CARS: If your vinyl soft-top has ingrained dirt, scrub it gently all over with a nail brush and soapy water. When dry, apply a good quality vinyl cleaner to bring the appearance back like new. Fabric soft-tops should only be washed, not scrubbed, but can be hosed off to shift the dirt.

I.2

making it easy! • As you polish, keep turning the cloth, always presenting a clean face to the surface of the paint - that's the secret of obtaining a clear shine with no rub marks. You'll need several clean cloths for polishing a whole car!

• Try removing a bug splat with a kitchen abrasive pad - the gentler sort made for non-stick pans - but only on glass and chrome; it'll ruin the shine on paintwork.

☐ I.3 It's easy to forget that around a fifth of your car's 'bodywork' is in fact glass. Use purpose-made glass cleaner, or a clean wash leather, for sparkling results. Clouding on the inside (said to be the vapour from upholstery plastics!) cleans off in the same way.

I.3

BODYWORK

☐ I.4 Tyres are one of the most 'visual' parts of your car. There are proprietary tyre polishes and paints available, but be warned that the improvement in appearance goes the first time you drive on a wet road! A good cleaning with the wash sponge - *after* you've washed the rest of the car - is usually enough. Alloy wheels need a spray-on alloy wheel cleaner to shift stuck-on brake dust.

I.4

☐ *I.5 INSIDE INFORMATION: Many people just don't know what to do about dull plastic bumpers. Use a colourless trim cleaner and you'll find that just wiping it on will bring about a magical improvement. Several coats may be needed. (The old, black-coloured bumper polish makes a real mess of your hands, by the way!)*

☐ I.6 Even when an engine bay is clean, it often looks dirty. Use a spray-on cleaner to remove the heavy dirt and grease - best if you let it soak in to the worst areas. Use an old paintbrush in nooks and crannies. A vinyl protectant will then bring up a wonderful sheen to all of your hoses and pipes as well as all underbonnet paintwork.

making it easy! If your engine is very oily, ask a local garage with a steam cleaner to hose off the worst of the 'grunge' before starting to clean up the engine bay. Paint any bare metal exposed by the steam cleaning, before it starts to rust.

☐ I.7 Choose a vinyl cleaner designed to put back the suppleness into vinyl and protect it from fading, as well as to remove dirt and grime and restore the appearance. If you hate the 'tacky' high gloss shine produced by some of them, look out for the low-gloss variety, giving a more natural finish.

I.5

INSIDE INFORMATION: If you can't get hold of low-gloss vinyl cleaner, try wiping over with a damp cloth before the cleaner has fully dried. This also 'wipes' away the worst of the gloss.

Rubber seals will last far longer if they are protected against the elements, by regular treatments with vinyl and rubber protectant. Scrape out dirt and grit from around the lower door seals then treat them all with several coats.

☐ I.8 Fabric seats and carpets will certainly benefit from cleaning with a proprietary brand of spray-on car upholstery cleaner - or a household upholstery cleaner. Follow the instructions carefully, take care not to soak cloth trim (it could cause shrinking) and the result will be carpets and cloth seats that look like new.

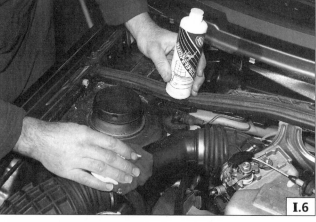

I.6

You can make leather more supple, and keep it cleaner and longer lasting by using a purpose-made brand of leather care. After use, the leather will feel soft and supple, because of the lanolin and moisturisers that you will have added. At first, you may be surprised to see the colour of your leather go much darker but don't worry; that will pass as the leather cleaner dries out naturally.

I.7

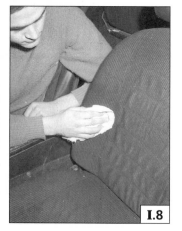

I.8

PART II: REPAIRING BODYWORK BLEMISHES

However well you look after your car, there will always be the risk of car park accident damage - or even worse! The smallest paint chips are best touched up with paint purchased from your local auto. accessory shop. If your colour of paint is not available, some auto. accessory shops offer a mixing scheme (including aerosols, in some cases) or you could look for a local paint factor in Yellow Pages. Take your car along to the paint factor and have them match the colour and mix the smallest quantity of cellulose paint that they will supply you with. Larger body blemishes will need the use of body filler.

SAFETY FIRST!
Always wear plastic gloves when working with body filler, before it has set. Always wear a face mask when sanding filler and wear goggles when using a power sander.

☐ II.1 The rear of this car's bodywork has sustained a nasty gash, the sort of damage for which you will certainly need to use body filler. The first stage is to mask off. Try to find "natural" edges such as body mouldings or styling stripes and wherever you can, mask off body trim rather than having to remove it.

☐ II.2 Remove all paint from the damaged area and for about 25mm (1 in.) around the damaged area. Roughen the bare metal or surface with coarse abrasive paper - a power sander is best. Wipe over the area with white spirit (mineral spirit) and then wash off with washing-up liquid in water - *not* car wash detergent.

INSIDE INFORMATION: Rub the surrounding paintwork with cutting compound so that the new paint has a better chance of matching the old.

☐ II.3 Mix the filler and hardener, following the instructions on the can. It's best to use a piece of plastic or metal rather than cardboard because otherwise, the filler will pick up fibres from the surface of the card. Mix thoroughly until the colour is consistent and no traces of hardener can be discerned.

☐ II.4 You can now spread the filler evenly over the repair. If the damage is particularly deep, apply the paste in two or more layers, allowing the filler to harden before adding the next layer. The final layer should be just proud of the level required, but do not overfill as this wastes paste and will require more time to sand down.

☐ II.5 It is essential when sanding down that you wrap the sanding paper around a flat block. You can see from the scratch marks that this repair has been sanded diagonally in alternate directions until the filler has become level with the surrounding panel, but you have to take care not to go deeply into the edges of the paint around the repair.

INSIDE INFORMATION: There will invariably be small pin holes even if the right amount of filler was applied first time. Use a tiny amount of filler scraped very thin over the whole repair, filling in deep scratches and pin holes and then sanding off with a very fine grade of sand paper - preferably dry paper rather than wet-or-dry because you don't want to get water on to the bare filler.

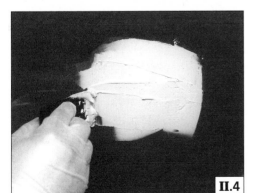

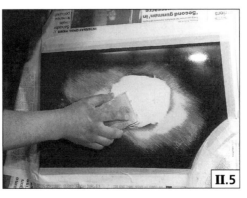

BODYWORK

☐ II.6 You can now use an aerosol primer to spray over the whole area of the repair but preferably not right up to the edges of the masking tape...

☐ II.7 ...and now use wet-or-dry paper, again on a sanding block, to sand the primer paint.

INSIDE INFORMATION: Don't sand fresh primer paint - leave it up to a day to harden off.

The filler is now protected from the water by the paint. If you do apply paint right up to the edge of the tape, be sure to 'feather' the edges of the primer, so that the edges blend in smoothly to the surrounding surface, with no ridges.

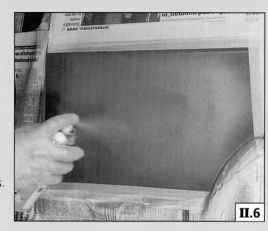

II.6

SAFETY FIRST!
Always wear an efficient mask when spraying aerosol paint and only work in a well-ventilated area, well away from any source of ignition, because spray paint vapour, even that given off by an aerosol, is highly flammable. Ensure that you have doors and windows open to the outside when using aerosol paint but in cool or damp weather, close them when the vapour has dispersed, otherwise the surface of the paint will "bloom", or take on a milky appearance. In fact, you may find it difficult to obtain a satisfactory finish in cold or damp weather.

II.7

☐ II.8 Before starting to spray, ensure that the nozzle is clear. Note that the can must be held with the index finger well back on the aerosol button. If you let your finger overhang the front of the button, a paint drip can form and throw itself on to the work area as a paint blob.

making it easy! • One of the secrets of spraying paint which doesn't run, is to put a very light coat of spray paint on to the panel first, followed by several more coats, allowing time between each coat for the bulk of the solvent to evaporate.

• Alternate coats should go on horizontally, followed by vertical coats as shown on the inset diagram.

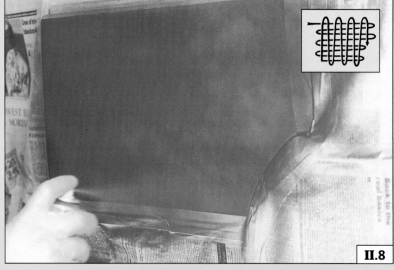

II.8

☐ II.9 After allowing about a week for the paint to dry, you will be able to polish it with a light cutting compound, blending the edges of the repair into the surrounding paintwork.

*INSIDE INFORMATION: Do note that if your repairs don't work out first time and you have to apply more paint on top of the fresh paint that you have already used, allow a week to elapse otherwise there is a strong risk of pickling or other reactions to take place. Also note that a prime cause of paint failure is the existence of silicones on the surface of the old paint before you start work. These come from most types of polish and are not all that easy to remove - they **won't** sand off!. Thoroughly wipe the panel down with white spirit before starting work and wash off with warm water and washing-up liquid to remove any further traces of the polish and the white spirit - but don't use the sponge or bucket that you normally use for washing the car otherwise you will simply introduce more silicones onto the surface!*

II.9

CHAPTER 5 - RUSTPROOFING

When mechanical components deteriorate, they can cost you a lot of money to replace. But when your car's bodywork deteriorates, it can cost you the car, if corrosion goes beyond the point where repairs are economical to carry out. Rust prevention should be regarded as a regular maintenance job, one which enables you to extend the life of your car by many years - and that will save you *real* money!

If you want to prolong its life, you'll have to inject rustproofing fluid into all the enclosed box sections and 'chassis' sections on your car. In many cases, you'll find holes already in place; in others, you'll be able to take off a cover, a piece or trim or a door lock in order to gain access. But in quite a few cases, you'll need to drill holes to gain an entry.

Don't be a drip!

*INSIDE INFORMATION: i) Place **lots** of newspaper beneath the car to catch the inevitable drips. ii) Some seat belts retract into a cavity that you will want to spray with fluid. Pull each belt out and hold it there until you have finished spraying the fluid. iii) All electric motors should be covered up with plastic bags so that none of the rust-proofing fluid gets in and all windows should be fully wound up. iv) Ensure that all drain channels are clear so that any excess rustproofing fluid can drain out and also check once again that they are clear after you have finished carrying out the work to ensure that your application of the fluid has not caused them to be clogged up, otherwise water will become trapped, negating much of the good work you have carried out.*

making it easy! Decide on your drill size with reference to the size of the injector nozzle and the size of grommets that you can obtain for blanking the holes off again afterwards. You'll feel a bit foolish if you drill first, only to find that they don't make grommets to fit the holes you've drilled!

Choose Your Weapon

Those hand pump injectors that you can buy from DIY shops are often worse than useless. They don't usually make a proper spray, but simply squirt a jet of fluid that does nothing to give the all-over cover required. Make a dummy 'box section' out of a cardboard box - cut it and fold to make it about 10 or 15 cm square - and try a dummy run. Open up and see if it has worked. If you haven't obtained full misting of the fluid, you could be making the problem worse.

INSIDE INFORMATION: Rust strikes even harder in those areas that aren't properly covered!

Consider taking your car to a garage with suitable equipment and having them do the work for you. Full, professional injection equipment, as shown in the following picture sequence, will make the fluid reach much further and deeper than amateur equipment, and if you enlist the services of the best experts as featured here, you'll be able to benefit from their experience.

SAFETY FIRST!
*Before using rustproofer, read the manufacturer's safety notes. Keep rustproofing fluid off the exhaust or any other components where it could be ignited. Keep it away from brake components, covering them up with plastic bags before starting work. Follow **Chapter 1, Safety First!**, and advice at the start of **Chapter 3, Servicing Your Car** especially with regard to safe working beneath a car raised off the ground. Rustproofers all contain solvents. In a confined space, such as a garage, solvents can build up, creating both a health and a fire hazard. Wear an efficient face mask so that you don't inhale vapour and work out of doors, keeping out of confined spaces. Wear gloves and goggles, but if you do get any fluid in your eyes, wash out with copious amounts of water and immediately seek medical advice if necessary. If any welding has to be carried out on the vehicle within a few months of rust-proofing being carried out, you must inform those who are carrying out the work because of the fire risk.*

Our thanks are due to Dinol Ltd for carrying out the work shown here, using Dinitrol rustproofing fluid.

RUSTPROOFING

☐ Job 1. Clean underbody.

You will have to hose off the underside of the body, paying particular attention to the undersides of the wings and wheel arches, before you can start to apply new rustproofing. Scrape off any hard, thick deposits of mud, and any old flaking body sealant under the car. One of the quickest ways to do the job is to use a power washer with a long lance. Many garages have this equipment for customer use in a wash bay and this is a very efficient way of doing the job. You will, however, still have to go underneath with a scraper afterwards as even a power jet won't take off flaking body sealant. You will also have to wait up to a week for the underside of the car to dry thoroughly (in warm, dry weather) before applying new rustproofing.

☐ Job 2. Equipment.

2. Gather together all the materials you need to do the job before you start. You will also need lifting equipment and axle stands.

making it easy! A compressor-driven gun of this type won't break the bank - try your local motor trade parts factors - but you'll need to buy or hire a compressor. Results will be perfect.

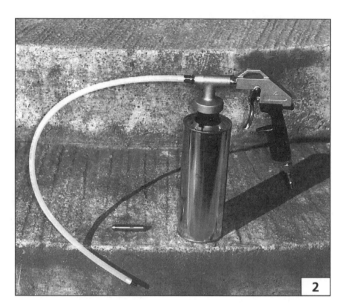

Bear in mind the safety equipment you will need - referred to in *Safety First!* - see page 81. You will need copious amounts of newspaper to spread on the floor because quite a lot of rust-proofing fluid will run out of the box sections and other areas under the car and you may have to park your car over newspaper for a couple of days after carrying out this treatment. Remember that the vapour given off by the materials will continue for several days, so park your car in the open for a week or so if you can, rather than in an enclosed garage.

INSIDE INFORMATION: Tip from Dinol, the manufacturers of Dinitrol: Except in a heat wave, it is essential to stand the container of rustproofer in a tub of hot water to keep it fluid. Top up the tub from time to time with more hot water while you are working. Not only will warm rustproofer penetrate seams better, it will flow through the applicator better and not clog so easily. Some people thin the rustproofer with white spirit, but warming it is better. Wash the gun and lances out with white spirit afterwards. If you let the rustproofer set, it is almost impossible to clean them.

Around the Car

☐ Job 3. Chrome trim and seams.

Some rustproofing fluids in aerosol cans are thin enough for injecting behind chromium trim strips and badges but some people find that they are inclined to leave a stain on the paintwork around the trim. As an alternative to a rustproofing fluid, you can use a water dispersant or a thin oil.

☐ Job 4. Doors.

4. Remove the trim panel and carefully "peel" away the clear plastic membrane that covers the door inner cavity. Insert the nozzle to cover all the inside of the door, making sure you get plenty of 'creeping' fluid into the steel joints, where water could collect and corrosion could occur. Naturally, the main problem is that moisture collects in the bottom of the doors and rots them out from the inside - use plenty of fluid here. If you don't want to remove the door trims, then fluid can be sprayed through the lower drain slots, but note that this will only provide protection for the lower surfaces and seams.

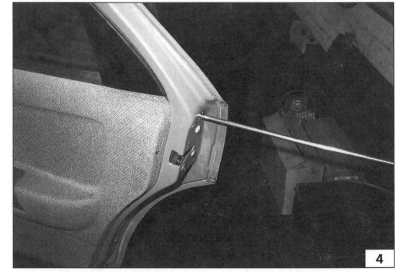

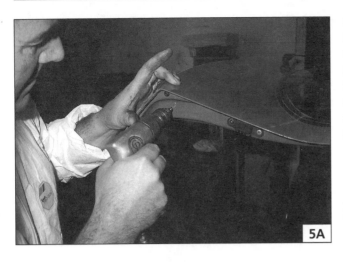

INSIDE INFORMATION: Think carefully before drilling holes to insert rustproofing fluid, especially in the "chassis", where there are numerous holes already. If you do drill a hole in steel, make sure that you file off the rough burrs and then apply an anti-rusting agent, followed by a coating of paint followed by a layer of wax. Make sure the area you drill into is indeed hollow and not the inside of the car or luggage bay! Spend time looking out for wires or pipes. Disconnect the car's battery.

☐ **Job 5. Tailgate or boot lid.**

5A. When you have drilled an access hole each side...

5B. ...inject the rustproofing fluid in all the double-skinned areas of the tailgate or boot lid. You can do this with a lance or the plastic pipe of the applicator.

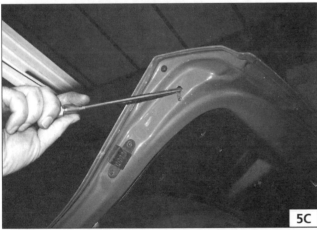

5C. It is a good idea to cover the floor of the boot or rear luggage compartment with paper in case fluid runs out of the tailgate or boot lid and spoils the carpet. Ensure that you cover all nooks and crannies and reach up into all box sections, especially on Sapphires with their hollow ribbing sections.

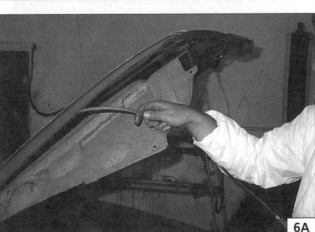

☐ **Job 6. Bonnet.**

6A. Put a generous helping of rustproofer in the box sections of the bonnet. It was necessary to remove the insulation material from the underside of the bonnet on this Sierra. It is held on by some screws and some clips that were gently levered out with a screwdriver. When you have finished, carefully press back the clips to hold the insulation in place.

RUSTPROOFING

6B. Pay special attention to the front edges, using existing holes in all cases.

☐ Job 7. Sills.

7A. Drill holes in the sills to make it possible to inject the fluid all the way to the front and back of the sill cavities.

7B. Use a long pipe or lance, push it all the way in each direction then inject the fluid as you withdraw the pipe. Make especially sure that the fluid penetrates the areas around the jacking points. Rusty sills can contribute to an MOT failure so protect them well.

☐ Job 8. Door pillars.

8A. As with the rest of the car, the door pillars are best injected through existing holes wherever you can find them. The rigid nozzle was used here and the cranked end turned every which way so that the fluid went in all directions.

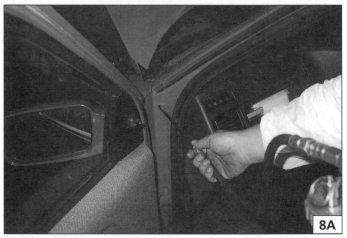

8B

 *8B. The door-operated courtesy light switches can be removed, providing excellent access to the A-post (the front one) and, on 4-door and 5-door cars, the B-post (the middle one).*

8C. Where you must drill, you must! This is the box-section extension at the bottom of the B-post.

8D. Be sure to use a long, flexible lance to reach all the way to the top and bottom of all three pillars. Ensure, when injecting the C-post shown here, that you don't inadvertently extend the lance into the boot on non-Sapphire models!

☐ Job 9. Top of the front wings.

9. The area of the round suspension turret and its surroundings must take the strain of the front suspension and this is always checked carefully in the MoT test. The mounting hinges of the bonnet are also in the vicinity. A short lance with a hooked end was used for this job to achieve the maximum coverage inside the pressings. Complement this work with a thorough coat under the wheel arches.

Under the Car

Dinol recommend the use of two fluids, a thinner fluid which is capable of 'creeping' deep into seams and joints, to arrest any rust that is present and a thicker one to withstand the 'pressure washing' that the underside of the car is subjected to and keep out the elements.

☐ Job 10. Wheel arches.

10. After applying thinner fluid to seams and the underside of the suspension towers, apply a good coat of the thicker rust preventer under all the wheel arches making sure that all the flanges are thoroughly treated. This is where careful preparation and meticulous scraping out of the awkward corners will pay dividends. The upper areas near the suspension mountings must also be well prepared even though access is not easy. Mind you, access is well-nigh impossible with the wheels still on, as this shot demonstrates. If you can't be bothered to take the wheels off, you can't properly protect the brakes - and you really shouldn't be doing the job!

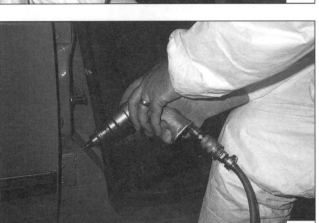

8C

8D

9

10

☐ Job 11. Under-floor box sections.

11. Use the flexible pipe to go all the way to the ends of the box sections, injecting as you withdraw the pipe. The box sections run across as well as along the car and help to provide some of the car's basic strength. You'll need a fair amount of sleuthing work to work out where each nook ends and a cranny begins.

☐ Job 12. Underside of the floor panels.

12. Finally, make sure there is no old loose or flaking underseal on the floor panels. Put a thorough coat of the thinner 'creeping' rustproofer on all the seams, and then spray the thicker stuff over the whole surface, protecting the panels and preventing the thinner stuff from being washed away. Unlike Dinol's man, you really *should* wear goggles when carrying out this work.

Get yourself prepared for this job! Disposable overalls or old clothes are a necessity and none more so than some form of headgear to protect your hair. Gloves and a face-mask are also essential.

First of all, the thinner, 'creeping' type of fluid is sprayed into and onto every seam. (This would wash away if not covered over.) Then, it's time to cover the entire surface with the tougher type of protectant. For this process the thicker, black underbody fluid is used - note that this needs to be warmed by standing it in a bucket of very hot water for twenty minutes or so before use. Make doubly sure that the car is safely raised and stable - this is no time to take chances - and ensure any floor protection is in place and secure. (See the start of *Chapter 3, Servicing Your Car.*) Spray the fluid while it is still warm and 'thin', taking care to ensure an even coverage with no gaps. When spraying over fuel and brake pipes make at least two passes with the spraygun, at different angles, so that the fluid isn't masked by the pipes which would leave an unprotected 'shadow' behind them. Start at the front of the car and work backwards, ending with the boot underside and spare wheel well.

It is advisable to park the car outside for a few days after the rustproofing treatment. This is because the fluid contains a solvent which will take time to evaporate. If the car is parked in an enclosed space, the smell might take longer to go. If you can, put the car in the shade. The sun could make the fluid run out of those nooks and crannies. Once the fluid is set, however, it will not run again.

☐ Job 13. Fit grommets to holes.

13. Fit grommets to all of the holes you have drilled, dipping each one in rustproofing fluid first, so that the edges of the holes are protected.

CHAPTER 6 - FAULT FINDING

This Chapter aims to help you to overcome the main faults that can affect the mobility or safety of your vehicle. It also helps you to overcome the problem that has affected most mechanics - amateur and professional - at one time or another... Blind Spot Syndrome!

It goes like this: the vehicle refuses to start one damp Sunday morning. You decide that there must be no fuel getting through. By the time you've stripped the fuel pump and fuel lines and "unblocked" the fuel tank, it's time for bed. And the next day, the local garage finds that your main HT lead has dropped out of the coil! Something like that has happened to most of us!

Don't jump to conclusions: if your engine won't start or runs badly, if electrical components fail, follow the logical sequence of checks listed here and detailed overleaf, eliminating each "check" (by testing, not by "hunch") before moving on to the next. And remember that the great majority of failures are caused by electrical or ignition faults: only a minor proportion of engine failures come from the fuel system. Follow the sequences shown here - and you'll have a better chance of success in finding that fault. Before carrying out any of the work described in this Chapter please read carefully *Chapter 1, Safety First!*

Engine won't start.

1. Starter motor doesn't turn.

2. Is battery okay?

3. Check battery connections for cleanliness/tightness.

4. Have battery 'drop' test carried out by specialist.

5. Test battery with voltmeter or, preferable, with a hydrometer.

6. Can engine be rotated by hand?

7. If engine cannot be rotated by hand, check for mechanical seizure of power unit, or pinion gear jammed in mesh with flywheel - 'rock' car backwards and forwards until free, or apply spanner to square drive at front end of starter motor.

8. If engine can be rotated by hand, check for loose electrical connections at starter, faulty solenoid, or defective starter motor.

9. Starter motor turns slowly.

10. Battery low on charge or defective - re-charge and have 'drop' test carried out by specialist.

11. Internal fault within starter motor - e.g. worn brushes.

12. Starter motor noisy or harsh.

13. Drive teeth on ring gear or starter pinion worn/broken.

14. Main drive spring broken.

15. Starter motor securing bolts loose.

16. Starter motor turns engine but car will not start. See 'Ignition System' box.

Ignition system.

> **SAFETY FIRST!**
> It is essential that you read **Chapter 1, Safety First!, The Ignition System** before carrying out work on this part of the car.

(Carry out the following checks as appropriate. For example, some vehicles have contact breaker ignition while the majority of modern cars have electronic ignition. Only Step 17 can be carried out on cars with electronic ignition. If any faults are found - SPECIALIST SERVICE.)

17. Check for spark at plug (remove plug and prop it with threads resting on bare metal of cylinder block). Do not touch plug or lead while operating starter.

MODELS WITHOUT ELECTRONIC IGNITION ONLY

18. If no spark present at plug, check for spark at contact breaker points when 'flicked' open (ignition 'on'). Double-check to ensure that points are clean and correctly gapped, and try again.

19. If spark present at contact breaker points, check for spark at central high tension lead from

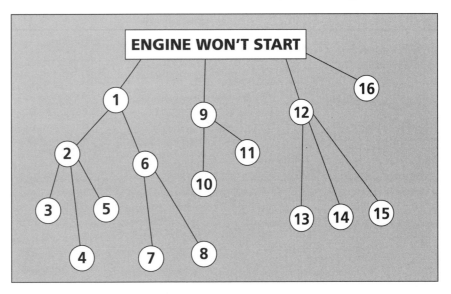

coil. NOTE: Don't carry out this check with electronic ignition systems. An uncontrolled spark can, in some cases, seriously damage the ECU (Electronic Control Unit).

20. If spark present at central high tension lead from coil, check distributor cap and rotor arm; replace if cracked or contacts badly worn.

21. If distributor cap and rotor arm are okay, check high tension leads and connections - replace leads if they are old, carbon core type suppressed variety.

22. If high tension leads are sound but dirty or damp, clean/dry them.

23. If high tension leads okay, check/clean/dry/re-gap sparking plugs.

24. Damp conditions? Apply water dispellant spray to ignition system.

25. If no spark present at contact breaker points (cars without electronic ignition only), examine connections of low tension leads between ignition switch and coil, and from coil to contact breaker (including short low-tension lead within distributor).

26. If low tension circuit connections okay, examine wiring.

27. If low tension wiring is sound, is capacitor okay? If in doubt, fit new capacitor.

28. If capacitor is okay, check for spark at central high tension lead from coil. NOTE: DON'T carry out this check with electronic ignition systems. An uncontrolled spark can, in some cases, seriously damage the ECU (Electronic Control Unit).

29. If no spark present at central high tension lead from coil, check for poor high tension lead connections.

30. If high tension lead connections okay, is coil okay? If in doubt, fit new coil.

31. If spark present at plug, is it powerful or weak? If weak, see '27' (non-electronic ignition models only).

32. If spark is healthy, check ignition timing.

33. If ignition timing is okay, see 'Fuel System' box.

Fuel system.

FUEL INJECTED ENGINES ONLY

34. Do not disconnect fuel pipes to check fuel flow, as system is pressurised; check fuel pump operation by listening for "buzz" when ignition is switched on - buzz should last no more than 1 or 2 seconds; if longer, suspect fuel pump. If no buzz, suspect fuel pump relay - seek professional help.

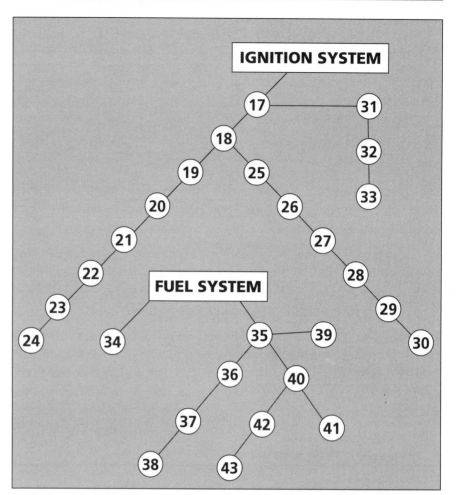

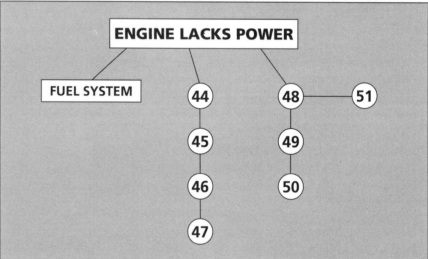

NON FUEL INJECTED ENGINES ONLY

35. Check briefly for fuel at feed pipe to carb. See 36. If no fuel present at feed pipe, is petrol tank empty? (Rock car and listen for 'sloshing' in tank, as well as looking at gauge).

SAFETY FIRST! Before working on the fuel system, read Chapter 1, Safety First! Take special care to 1) only work out of doors, 2) wear suitable gloves and goggles and keep fuel out of eyes and away from skin: 3) if fuel does come into contact with skin, wash off straight away, 4) if fuel gets into your eyes, wash out with copious amounts of clean, cold water. Seek medical advice if necessary, 5) when testing for fuel flow, pump into a sufficiently large container, minimising splashes, 6) don't smoke, work near flames or sparks or work when the engine or exhaust are hot.

36. Check for a defective fuel pump. With outlet pipe disconnected AND AIMED AWAY FROM HOT EXHAUST COMPONENTS, ETC. as well as your eyes and clothes, and into a suitable container, turn the engine over (manual

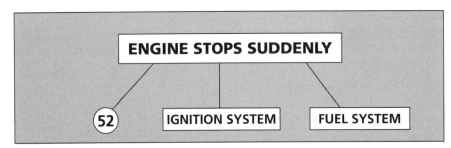

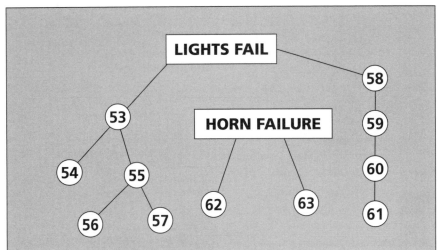

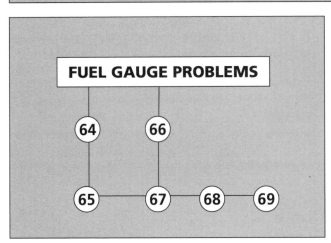

47. If oil level okay, check for slipping fan belt, cylinder head gasket 'blown', partial mechanical seizure of engine, blocked or damaged exhaust system.

48. If engine temperature is normal, check cylinder compressions.

49. If cylinder compression readings low, add a couple of teaspoons of engine oil to each cylinder in turn, and repeat test. If readings don't improve, suspect burnt valves/seats.

50. If compression readings improve after adding oil as described, suspect worn cylinder bores, pistons and rings.

51. If compression readings are normal, checkfor mechanical problems, for example, binding brakes, slipping clutch, partially seized transmission, etc.

Engine stops suddenly.

52. Check for sudden ingress of water/snow onto ignition components, in adverse weather conditions. Sudden failure is almost always because of an ignition fault. Check for simple wiring and connection breakdowns.

Lights fail.

53. Sudden failure - check fuses.

54. If all lamps affected, check switch and main wiring feeds.

55. If not all lamps are affected, check bulbs on lamps concerned.

56. If bulbs appear to be okay, check bulb holder(s), local wiring and connections.

57. If bulb(s) blown, replace!

58. Intermittent operation, flickering or poor light output.

59. Check earth (ground) connections(s).

60. If earth(s) okay, check switch.

61. If switch okay, check wiring and connections.

Horn failure.

62. If horn does not operate, check fuse, all connections (particularly earths/grounds) and cables. Remove horn connections and check/clean. Use 12v test lamp to ascertain power getting to horn.

63. If horn will not stop(!), disconnect the horn and check for earthing of cable between button and horn unit and the wiring and contacts in the horn switch housing. SPECIALIST SERVICE. Horn wiring and connections are more complex than they appear at first. If necessary, have them checked by a specialist.

40. If fuel is present at carburettor feed pipe, remove spark plugs and check whether wet with unburnt fuel.

41. If the spark plugs are fuel-soaked, check that the choke is operating as it should and is not jammed 'shut'. Other possibilities include float needle valve(s) sticking 'open' or leaking, float punctured, carburettor incorrectly adjusted or air filter totally blocked. Clean plugs before replacing.

42. If the spark plugs are dry, check whether the float needle valve is jammed 'shut'.

43. Check for severe air leak at inlet manifold gasket or carburettor gasket. Incorrectly set valve clearances.

Engine lacks power.

44. Engine overheating. Check oil temperature gauge (where fitted). Low oil pressure light may come on.

45. Air cleaner intake thermostat not opening/closing at the correct temperatures. Replace or free-off as necessary.

46. If thermostat okay, check oil level. BEWARE - DIPSTICK AND OIL MAY BE VERY HOT.

pump) or switch on ignition (electric pump) and fuel should issue from pump outlet.

37. If pump is okay, check for blocked fuel filter or pipe, or major leak in pipe between tank and pump, or between pump and carb.

38. If the filter is clean and the pump operates, suspect blocked carburettor jet(s) or damaged/sticking float, or incorrectly adjusted carburettor.

39. If there is petrol in the tank but none issues from the feed pipe from pump to carburettor, check that the small vent hole in the fuel filler cap is not blocked and causing a vacuum. NOTE: On some cars there is no vent hole in the filler cap. Other arrangements are made for venting the tank. There are many systems - SPECIALIST SERVICE.

Fuel gauge problems.

64. Gauge reads 'empty' - check for fuel in tank!

65. If fuel is present in tank, check for earthing of wiring from tank to gauge, and for wiring disconnections.

66. Gauge permanently reads 'full', regardless of tank contents. Check wiring and connections as in '65'.

67. If wiring and connections all okay, sender unit/fuel gauge defective.

68. With wiring disconnected, check for continuity between fuel gauge terminals. Do

NOT test gauge by short-circuiting to earth. Replace unit if faulty.

69. If gauge is okay, disconnect wiring from tank sender unit and check for continuity between terminal and case. Replace sender unit if faulty.

FACT FILE: EMERGENCY STARTING

Pushing or Towing

NOTE: This is not possible for vehicles with automatic transmission. Diesel engines: only attempt in warm weather or with a warm engine.

Turn off all unnecessary electrical load; switch on ignition and depress the clutch pedal. Select second or third gear; release the clutch when the car reaches a person's running speed.

Starting with Jump Leads

Safety First!
This process can be dangerous and the following instructions must be followed to the letter. Also see Chapter One, Safety First! and the relevant part of Chapter 3 for information on safe handling of car batteries.

Ensure that the battery providing the jump start has the same voltage (12 volt) as the battery fitted to your car.

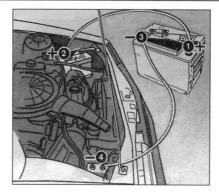

Do not lean over the battery during jump starting.

Switch off all unnecessary electrical loads and apply the hand brake. Auto. Transmission: Place gear selector in 'P'. Manual Transmission: Place gear shift lever in neutral.

Note that on some batteries and on battery connections, '+' (positive) terminals are coloured red and '-' (negative) terminals are coloured blue or black.

Run the engine of the vehicle providing the jump start (if battery fitted to vehicle).

(The following instruction numbers refer to the numbers on the drawing.)

1. Connect one end of the jump lead to the positive ('+') terminal of the battery providing the jump start.

2. Connect the other end of the same lead to the positive terminal on the car being started.

3. Connect one end of the other jump lead to the negative ('-') terminal on the 'slave' battery...

4. ...and the other end to the negative battery lead on the car, or to some bare metal in the car's engine bay.

Now try to start the car as quickly as is reasonably possible.

IT IS IMPORTANT that the leads are removed in the exact reverse sequence to that shown above. Keep hands, hair and loose clothing away from moving parts in both engine bays.

Supplementary information - diesel engines

The following fault finding chart covers only those parts of the system that can be checked at home. If a simple solution is not found, it will be necessary to call on the services of a main dealer or diesel injection specialist.

1. No fuel. *If the tank is allowed to run dry, the system will have to be bled.*

2. Fuel blockages from the tank to the pump can be checked at home. *However, see Safety First! below...*

SAFETY FIRST!
It is most important that any checks on the fuel system from the pump to the engine are carried out by a specialist. The high pressure means that a blockage is unlikely but also means that there is a safety hazard involved in working on this part of the system. Very high pressure can remain in the system even when the engine is not running.

3. Air in fuel system. *Bleed as described in Chapter 3, Servicing Your Car.*

4. Glow plugs (cold engine). These only fail after a very high mileage and usually one at a time. The usual symptom is an engine which starts, misfires and smokes badly until warmed up. *Proper checking is usually a SPECIALIST SERVICE job.*

5. Slow cranking speed. *Can be caused by bad electrical connections or a flat battery.*

6. Worn bores will affect a diesel engine more severely than a petrol engine. *A worn out engine is less likely to start or run properly.*

7. Stop control faulty. *Check that the solenoid in the stop control "clicks" when the solenoid is switched on or off, in which case you can assume it is*

working. If a manually-controlled valve is fitted, check that the valve at the pump operates when the knob is moved. Otherwise this is also a SPECIALIST SERVICE job.

8. Injection pump faulty. *SPECIALIST SERVICE*

9. Injector faulty. *SPECIALIST SERVICE*

10. Injector feed pipe leaking. *SPECIALIST SERVICE*

	1	2	3	4	5	6	7	8	9	10
Engine will not start	✓	✓	✓	✓	✓	✓	✓	✓		
Engine will not stop							✓			
Engine misfires	✓					✓		✓	✓	✓
Excessive (black) smoke from exhaust								✓	✓	

CHAPTER 7
GETTING THROUGH THE MOT

This Chapter is for owners in Britain whose vehicles need to pass the 'MoT' test. The Test was first established in 1961 by the then Ministry of Transport and it attempts to ensure that vehicles using British roads reach minimum standards of safety. Approximately 40 per cent of vehicles submitted for the test fail it, but many of these failures could be avoided by knowing what the vehicle might 'fall down on', and by taking appropriate remedial action before the test 'proper' is carried out.

It is true that the scope of the test has been considerably enlarged in the past few years, with the result that it is correspondingly more difficult to be sure that your vehicle will reach the required standards. In truth, however, a careful examination of the relevant areas, perhaps a month or so before the current certificate expires, will highlight components which require attention, and enable any obvious faults to be rectified before you take the vehicle for the test.

Getting Ahead

It is also worth noting that a vehicle can be submitted for a test up to a month before the current certificate expires - if the vehicle passes, the new certificate will be valid for one year from the day of expiry of the old one, provided that the old certificate is produced at the time of the test.

PART I: THE BACKGROUND

Keeping Up To Date

Alterations are being made to the Test on a regular basis - almost always making it tougher than it was before. It is MOST IMPORTANT that UK owners find out for themselves about any changes in the requirements that might have been made since this book was written. Your local MoT Testing Station should be able to help - if not, take your custom elsewhere! Also, non-UK owners should obtain information on the legal requirements in their own territory - and act accordingly.

Making A Good Impression

If your vehicle is muddy or particularly dirty (especially underneath) it would be worth giving it a thorough clean a day or two before carrying out the inspection so that it has ample time to dry. Do the same before the real MoT test. A clean vehicle makes a better impression on the examiner, who can refuse to test a vehicle which is particularly dirty underneath.

On the other hand, a clean vehicle makes a better impression and it will help the examiner to see what he is supposed to be examining. Generally, this will work in the owner's favour. For example, if a component or an area of underbody or chassis is particularly difficult to examine due to a build-up of oily dirt etc., and if the examiner is in doubt about its condition, he is entitled to fail that component because it was not possible for him to conclude that it reached the required standard. Had it been clean, it might well have been tested, and passed!

MoT testers do not dismantle assemblies during the test but you may wish to do so during your pretest check-up for a better view of certain wearing parts, such as the rear brake

SAFETY FIRST!
*The MoT tester will follow a set procedure and we will cover the ground in a similar way, starting inside the vehicle, then continuing outside, under the bonnet, underneath the vehicle, etc. When preparing to go underneath the vehicle, do ensure that it is jacked on firm level ground and then supported on axle stands or ramps which are adequate for the task. Wheels which remain on the ground should have chocks in front of and behind them, and while the rear wheels remain on the ground, the hand brake should be firmly ON. For most repair and replacement jobs under your vehicle these normal precautions will suffice. However, the vehicle needs to be even more stable than usual when carrying out these checks. There must be no risk of it toppling off its stands while suspension and steering components are being pushed and pulled in order to test them. Read carefully **Chapter 1, Safety First!** and the first part of Chapter 3, Servicing Your Car for further important information on raising and supporting a vehicle above the ground.*

shoes for example. See *Chapter 3, Servicing Your Car* for information on how to check the brakes.

Buying And Selling

This chapter provides a procedure for checking your vehicle's condition prior to its official MoT test. The same procedure could be equally useful to UK and non-UK owners alike when examining vehicles prior to purchase (or sale for that matter). However, it must be emphasised that the official MoT certificate should not be regarded as any guarantee of the condition of a vehicle. All it proves is that the vehicle reached the required standards, in the opinion of a particular examiner, at the time and date it was tested.

Pass The MoT!

The aim of this chapter is to explain what is actually tested on a vehicle and (if it is not obvious) how the test is done. This should enable you to identify and eliminate problems before they undermine the safety or diminish the performance of your vehicle and long before they cause the expense and inconvenience of a test failure.

Tool Box

Dismantling apart, few tools are needed for testing. A light hammer is useful for tapping panels underneath the vehicle when looking for rust. If this produces a bright metallic noise, then the area being tapped is solid metal. If the noise produced is dull, the area contains rust or filler. When tapping sills and box sections, listen also for the sound of debris (that is, rust flakes) on the inside of the panel. Use a screwdriver to prod weak parts of panels. This may produce holes of course, but if the panels have rusted to that extent, you really ought to know about it. A strong lever (such as a tyre lever) can be useful for applying the required force to suspension joints etc. when assessing whether there is any wear in them.

You will need an assistant to operate controls and perhaps to wobble the road wheels while you inspect components under the vehicle.

Age Related Checks

Two more brief explanations are required before you start your informal test. Firstly, the age of the vehicle determines exactly which lights, seat belts and other items it should have. Frequently in the next few pages you will come across the phrase "Cars first used ..." followed by a date. A vehicle's "first used" date is either its date of first registration, or the date six months after it was manufactured, whichever was earlier. Or, if the vehicle was originally used without being registered (such as a vehicle which has been imported to the U.K. or an ex-H.M. Forces model, etc.) the "first used" date is the date of manufacture.

Rust And Load Bearing Areas

Secondly, there must not be excessive rust, serious distortion or any fractures affecting certain prescribed areas of the bodywork. These prescribed areas are load-bearing parts of the bodywork within 30 cm (12 in.) of anchorages or mounting points associated with testable items such as seat belts, brake pedal assemblies, master cylinders, servos, suspension and

steering components and also body mountings. Keep this rule in mind while inspecting the vehicle, but remember also that even if such damage occurs outside a prescribed area, it can cause failure of the test. Failure will occur if the damage is judged to reduce the continuity or strength of a main load-bearing part of the bodywork sufficiently to have an adverse effect on the braking or steering.

The following notes are necessarily abbreviated, and are for assistance only. They are not a definitive guide to all the MoT regulations. It is also worth mentioning that the varying degrees of discretion of individual MoT testers can mean that there are variations between the standards as applied. However, the following points should help to make you aware of the aspects which will be examined. Now, if you have your clipboard, checklist and pencil handy, let's make a start...

The 'Easy' Bits

Checking these items is straightforward and should not take more than a few minutes - and could avoid an embarrassingly simple failure...

Lights

Within the scope of the test are headlights, side and tail lights, brake lights, direction indicators, and number plate lights (plus rear fog lights on all cars first used on or after 1 April, 1980, and any earlier cars subsequently so equipped, and also hazard warning lights on any vehicle so fitted). All must operate, must be clean and not significantly damaged; flickering is also not permitted. The switches should also all work properly. Pairs of lights should give approximately the same intensity of light output, and operation of one set of lights should not affect the working of another - such trouble is usually due to bad earthing.

Front fog and spot lights are not part of the MoT test (although their use is covered by *Construction and Use* regulations so that, for instance, spot lights should go out when headlights are turned off main beam) and won't be tested, provided they're not a physical hazard. Rear fog lights are part of the Test however. See later in this Chapter for details.

Indicators should flash at between 60 and 120 times per minute. 'Rev' the engine to encourage them, if a little slow (although the examiner might not let you get away with it!) Otherwise, renew the (inexpensive) flasher unit and check all wiring and earth connections.

Interior 'tell-tale' lights, such as for indicators, rear fog lights and hazard warning lights should all operate in unison with their respective exterior lights.

Headlight aim must be correct - in particular, the lights should not dazzle other road users. An approximate guide can be obtained by shining the lights against a vertical wall, but final adjustment may be necessary by reference to the beam checking machine at the MoT station. Most testers will be happy to make slight adjustments where necessary but only if the adjusters work. Make sure before you take the vehicle in that they are not seized solid!

Reflectors must be unbroken, clean, and not obscured - for example, by stickers.

Wheels And Tyres

Check the wheels for loose nuts, cracks, and damaged rims. Missing wheel nuts or studs are also failure points, naturally enough!

There is no excuse for running on illegal tyres. The legal requirement is that there must be at least 1.6 mm of tread depth remaining, over the 'central' three-quarters of the width of the tyre all the way around. From this it can be deduced that there is no legal requirement to have 1.6 mm (1/16 in.) of tread on the 'shoulders' of the tyre, but in practice, most MoT stations will be reluctant to pass a tyre in this condition. In any case, for optimum safety - especially 'wet grip' - you would be well advised to change tyres when they wear down to around 3 mm (1/8 in.) or so depth of remaining tread.

Visible 'tread wear indicator bars', found approximately every nine inches around the tread of the tyre, are highlighted when the tread reaches the critical 1.6 mm point.

Tyres should not show signs of cuts or bulges, rubbing on the bodywork or running gear, and the valves should be in sound condition, and correctly aligned.

Old-fashioned cross-ply and radial-ply tyre types must not be mixed on the same axle, and if pairs of cross-ply and radial-ply tyres are fitted, the radials must be on the rear axle.

Windscreen

The screen must not be damaged (by cracks, chips, etc.) or obscured so that the driver does not have a clear view of the road. Permissible size of damage points depends on where they occur. Within an area 290 mm (nearly 12 in.) wide, ahead of the driver, and up to the top of the wiper arc, any damage must be confined within a circle less than 10 mm (approx. 0.4 in.) in diameter. This is increased to 40 mm (just over 1.5 in.) for damage within the rest of the screen area swept by the wipers.

Washers And Wipers

The wipers must clear an area big enough to give the driver a clear view forwards and to the side of the vehicle. The wiper blades must be securely attached and sound, with no cracks or 'missing' sections. The wiper switch should also work properly. The screen washers must supply the screen with sufficient liquid to keep it clean, in conjunction with the use of the wipers.

Mirrors

Your vehicle must have at least two, one of which must be on the driver's side. The mirrors must be visible from the driver's seat, and not be damaged or obscured so that the view to the rear is affected. Therefore cracks, chips and discolouration can mean failure.

Horn

The horn must emit a uniform note which is loud enough to give adequate warning of approach, and the switch must operate correctly. Multi-tone horns playing 'in sequence' are not permitted, but two tones sounding together are fine.

Seat Security

The seats must be securely mounted, and the sub-frames should be sound.

Seat Belts

Seat belts must be in good condition (i.e. not frayed or otherwise damaged), and the buckles and catches should also operate correctly. Inertia reel types, where fitted, should retract properly.

Belt mountings must be secure, with no structural damage or corrosion within 30 cm (12 in.) of them.

Number (Registration) Plates

Both front and rear number plates must be present, and in good condition, with no breaks or missing numbers or letters. The plates must not be obscured, and the digits must not be repositioned (to form names, for instance).

Vehicle Identification Numbers (VIN)

Vehicles first used on or after 1 August, 1980 have to have a clearly displayed VIN - Vehicle Identification Number (or old-fashioned 'chassis numbers' for older cars) which is plainly legible. See *Chapter 2, Buying Guide* for the correct location on your vehicle.

Exhaust System

The entire system must be present, properly mounted, free of leaks and should not be noisy - which can happen when the internal baffles fail. 'Proper' repairs by welding, or exhaust cement, or bandage are acceptable, as long as no gas leaks are evident. Then again, common sense, if not the MoT, dictates that exhaust bandage should only be a very short-term emergency measure. For safety's sake, fit a new exhaust if yours is reduced to this!

PART II: THE CHECKLIST

You've checked the easy bits - now it's time for the detail! Some of the 'easy bits' referred to above are included here, but this is intended as a more complete check list to give your vehicle the best possible chance of gaining a First Class Honours, MoT Pass!

Inside The Vehicle

1. The steering wheel should be examined for cracks and for damage which might interfere with its use, or injure the driver's hands. It should also be pushed and pulled along the column axis, and also up and down, at 90 degrees to it. This will highlight any deficiencies in the wheel and upper column mounting/bearing, and also any excessive end float, and movement between the column shaft and the wheel. Look, too, for movement in the steering column couplings and fasteners (including the universal joint if applicable), and visually check their condition and security. They must be sound, and properly tightened.

In the case of cars (the majority) with steering racks, rotate the steering wheel in both directions to test for free play at the wheel rim - this shouldn't exceed approximately 13 mm. (0.5 in.), assuming a 380 mm. (15 in.) diameter steering wheel.

In the case of the smaller number of cars with steering boxes, free play at the wheel rim shouldn't exceed approximately 75 mm (3.0 in.), assuming a 380 mm (15 in.) diameter steering wheel.

In both cases where the steering wheel is larger or smaller the amount of permissible free play should be raised or lowered accordingly.

☐ 2. Check that the switches for headlights, sidelights, rear fog lights direction indicators, hazard warning lights, wipers, washers and horn, appear to be in good working order and check that the tell-tale lights or audible warnings are working where applicable.

☐ 3. Make sure that the windscreen wipers operate effectively with blades that are secure and in good condition. The windscreen washer should provide sufficient liquid to clear the screen in conjunction with the wipers.

☐ 4. Check for windscreen damage, especially in the area swept by the wipers. From the MoT tester's point of view, Zone A is part of this area, 290 mm (11.5 in.) wide and centred on the centre of the steering wheel. Damage to the screen within this area should be capable of fitting into a 10 mm (approx. 0.4 in.) diameter circle and the cumulative effect of more minor damage should not seriously restrict the driver's view. Windscreen stickers or other obstructions should not encroach more than 10 mm (approx 0.4 in.) into this area. In the remainder of the swept area the maximum diameter of damage or degree of encroachment by obstructions is 40 mm (approx. 1.6 in.) and there is no ruling regarding cumulative

multi-tone horns (which alternate between two or more notes) are not permitted at all. On cars first used after 1 August 1973, the horn should produce a constant, continuous or uniform note which is neither harsh nor grating.

☐ 6. There must be one exterior mirror on the driver's side of the vehicle and one other mirror - either an exterior mirror fitted to the passenger's side or an interior mirror. The required mirrors should be secure and in good condition.

☐ 7. Check that the hand brake operates effectively without coming to the end of its working travel. The lever and its mechanism must be complete, securely mounted, unobstructed in its travel and in a sufficiently good condition to remain firmly in the "On" position even when knocked from side to side. The 30 cm rule on bodywork corrosion applies in the vicinity of the hand brake lever mounting.

☐ 8. The foot brake pedal assembly should be complete, unobstructed, and in a good working condition, including the pedal rubber (which should not have been worn smooth). There should be no excessive movement of the pedal at right angles to its normal direction. When fully depressed, the pedal should not be at the end of its travel. The pedal should not feel spongy (indicating air in the hydraulic system), nor should it tend to creep downwards while held under pressure (which indicates an internal hydraulic leak).

☐ 9. Seats must be secure on their mountings and seat backs must be capable of being locked in the upright position.

☐ 10. The law requires all models to be fitted with seatbelts for the driver and front passenger. These have to be three-point lap and diagonal belts. Rear seat belts are a requirement for vehicles first used after 31 March 1987 with three anchorage points for the 'outer' passengers, and at least a lap belt only for the centre passenger position. Examine seat belt webbing and fittings to make sure that all are in good condition and that anchorages are firmly attached to the vehicle's structure. Locking mechanisms should be capable of remaining locked, and of being released if required, when under load. Flexible buckle stalks (if fitted) should be free of corrosion, broken cable strands or other weaknesses. Note that any belts fitted which are not part of a legal requirements may be examined by the tester but will not form part of the official test.

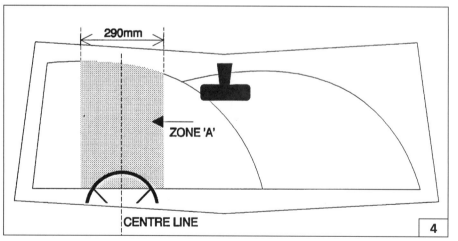

damage. Specialist windscreen companies can often repair a cracked screen for a lot less than the cost of replacement. Moreover, the cost of repair is often covered by comprehensive insurance policies. DIY repair kits are also available.

☐ 5. The horn control should be present, secure and readily accessible to the driver, and the horn should be loud enough to be heard by other road users. Gongs, bells and sirens are not permitted (except as part of an anti-theft device) and

☐ 11. On inertia reel belts, check that on retracting the belts, the webbing winds into the retracting unit automatically, albeit with some manual assistance to start with.

☐ 12. Note the point raised earlier regarding corrosion around seat belt anchorage points. The MoT tester will not carry out any dismantling here, but he will examine floor mounted anchorage points from underneath the vehicle if that is possible.

☐ 13. Before getting out of the vehicle, make sure that both doors can be opened from the inside.

Outside The Vehicle

☐ 14. Before closing the driver's door, check the condition of the inner sill. Usually the MoT tester will do this by applying finger or thumb pressure to various parts of the panel while the floor covering remains in place. For your own peace of mind, look beneath the sill covering, taking great care not to tear any covering. Then close the driver's door and make sure that it latches securely and repeat these checks on the nearside inner sill and door.

Now check all of the lights, front and rear, (and the number plate lights) while your assistant operates the light switches.

☐ 15. As we said earlier, you can carry out a rough and ready check on headlight alignment for yourself, although it will certainly not be as accurate as having it done for you at the MoT testing station. Drive your vehicle near to a wall, as shown. Check that your tyres are correctly inflated and the vehicle is on level ground.

Draw on the wall, with chalk:
• a horizontal line about 2 metres long, and at same height as centre of headlight lenses.
• two vertical lines about 1 metre long, each forming a cross with the horizontal line and the same distance apart as the headlight centres.
• another vertical line to form a cross on the horizontal line, midway between the others.

Now position your vehicle so that:
• it faces the wall squarely, and its centre line is in line with centre line marked on the wall.
• the steering is straight.
• headlight lenses are 5.0 metres (16 ft.) from the wall.

Switch on the headlights' 'main' and 'dipped' beams in turn and measure their centre points. You will be able to judge any major discrepancies in intensity and aim prior to having the beams properly set by a garage with beam measuring equipment.

Headlights should be complete, clean, securely mounted, in good working order and not adversely affected by the operation of another lamp, and these basic requirements affect all the lights listed below. Headlights must dip as a pair from a single switch. Their aim must be correctly adjusted and they should not be affected (even to the extent of flickering) when lightly tapped by hand. Each headlight should match its partner in terms of size, colour and intensity of light, and can be white or yellow.

☐ 16. Side lights should show white light to the front and red light to the rear. Lenses should not be broken, cracked or incomplete. Stop lights must be red, of course.

☐ 17. Check your indicators, doing what the MoT tester will do: turn on side lights and apply the brake lights while ensuring that the indicators still work properly, and that none of the lights interfere with each other, causing dimness or intermittent failure. Check side repeater lights, too.

☐ 18. Vehicles first used before 1 April 1986 do not have to have a hazard warning device, but if one is fitted, it must be tested, and it must operate with the ignition switch either on or off. The lights should flash 60-120 times per minute, and indicators must operate independently of any other lights.

☐ 19. There must be two red rear reflectors - always fitted by the manufacturers, of course! - which are clean and are securely and symmetrically fitted to the vehicle.

☐ 20. Your vehicle must have at least one rear fog light fitted to the centre or offside of the vehicle. If there are two, they must be spaced an equal distance from the centre. It must comply with the basic requirements (listed under headlights) and emit a steady red light. Its tell-tale light, inside the vehicle, must work to inform the driver that it is switched on.

☐ 21. There must be registration number plates at the front and rear of the vehicle and both must be clean, secure, complete and unobscured. Letters and figures must be correctly formed and correctly spaced and not likely to be misread due to an uncovered securing bolt or whatever. The year letter counts as a figure. The space between letters and figures must be at least twice that between adjacent letters or figures.

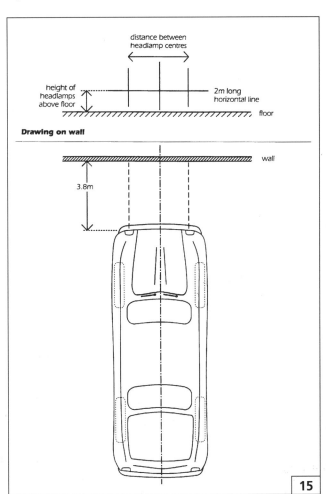

☐ 22. Number plate lights must be present, working, and must not flicker when tapped by hand, just as for other lights. Where more than one light or bulb was fitted as original equipment, all must be working.

Wheels And Tyres

The MoT tester will examine tyres and wheels while walking around the vehicle and again when he is underneath it.

☐ 23. Front tyres should match each other and rear tyres should match each other, both sets matching in terms of size, aspect ratio and type of structure. For example, you must never fit tyres of different sizes or types, such as cross-ply or radial, on the same 'axle' - both front wheels counting as 'on the same axle' in this context. If cross-ply or bias belted tyres are fitted to the rear of the car, you must not fit radial-ply tyres to the front. If cross-ply tyres are fitted to the rear, bias belted tyres should not be fitted to the front. (We recommend that you do not mix tyre types anywhere on the car.)

☐ 24. Failure of the test can be caused by a cut, lump, tear or bulge in a tyre, exposed ply or cord, a badly seated tyre, a re-cut tyre, a tyre fouling part of the vehicle, or a seriously damaged or misaligned valve stem which could cause sudden deflation of the tyre. To pass the test, the grooves of the tread pattern must be at least 1.6 mm deep throughout a continuous band comprising the central three-quarters of the breadth of tread, and round the entire outer circumference of the tyre.

We are grateful to Dunlop/SP Tyres for the photographs and information in this section.

☐ 24A. Modern tyres have tread wear indicators built into the tread groves (usually about eight of them spread equidistantly around the circumference). These appear as continuous bars running across the tread when the original pattern depth has worn down to 1.6 mm. There will be a distinct reduction in wet grip well before the tread wear indicators start to show, and you should replace tyres before they get to this stage, even though this is the legal minimum in the UK.

☐ 24B. Lumps and bulges in the tyre wall usually arise from accidental damage or even because of faults in the tyre construction. You should run your hand all the way around the side wall of the tyre, with the vehicle either jacked off the ground, or moving the vehicle half a wheels revolution, so that you can check the part of the tyre that was previously resting on the ground. Since you can't easily check the insides of the tyres in day-to-day use, it is even more important that you spend time carefully checking the inside of each tyre - the MoT tester will certainly do so! Tyres with bulges in them must be scrapped and replaced with new, since they can fail suddenly, causing your vehicle to lose control.

24B

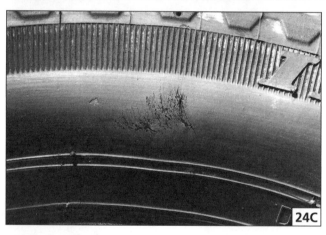

24C

☐ 24C. Abrasion of the tyre side wall can take place either in conjunction with bulging, or by itself, and this invariably results from an impact, such as the tyre striking the edge of a kerb or a pothole in the road. Once again, the tyre may be at imminent risk of failure and you should take advice from a tyre specialist on whether the abrasion is just superficial, or whether the tyre will need replacement.

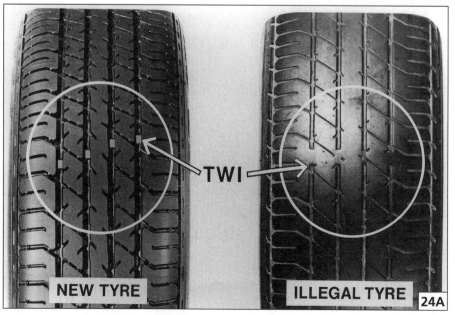

TWI

NEW TYRE

ILLEGAL TYRE

24A

☐ 24D. All tyres will suffer progressively from cracking, albeit in most cases superficially, due to the effects of sunlight. If old age has caused the tyres on your vehicle to degrade to this extent, replace them.

24D

☐ 24E. If the outer edges of the tread are worn noticeably more than the centre, the tyres have been run under inflated which not only ruins tyres, but causes worse fuel consumption, dangerous handling and is, of course, illegal.

Over-inflation causes the centre part of the tyre to wear more quickly than the outer edges. This is also illegal but in addition, it causes the steering and grip to suffer and the tyre becomes more susceptible to concussion damage.

24E

24F

☐ 24F. Incorrect wheel alignment causes one side of the tyre to wear more severely than the other. If your vehicle should hit a kerb or large pothole, it is worthwhile having the wheel alignment checked by a tyre specialist since this costs considerably less than new front tyres!

☐ 25. Road wheels must be secure and must not be badly damaged, distorted or cracked, or have badly distorted bead rims (perhaps due to "kerbing"), or loose or missing wheel nuts, studs or bolts.

☐ 26. Check the bodywork for any sharp edges or projections, caused by corrosion or damage, which could prove dangerous to other road users, including pedestrians.

☐ 27. Check that the fuel cap fastens securely and that its sealing washer is neither torn nor deteriorated, or its mounting flange damaged sufficiently to allow fuel to escape (for example, while the vehicle is cornering).

Under The Bonnet

☐ 28. The vehicle should have a Vehicle Identification Number fitted to the bodywork. This can be on a plate secured to the vehicle or, etched or stamped on the bodywork. See *Chapter 2, Buying Guide* for more information.

☐ 29. Check the steering rack or box for security by asking your assistant to turn the steering wheel from side to side (with the road wheels on the ground) while you watch what happens under the bonnet. Then, check for free play in the steering assembly as a whole. This is done by turning the steering wheel from side to side as far as possible without moving the road wheels - and measuring how far the steering wheel can be moved in this way. More than 75 mm (approx. 3 in.) of free play, on a steering box system, or 13 mm (approx. 0.5 in.), on a steering rack, at the perimeter of the steering wheel, due to wear in the steering components, is sufficient grounds for a test failure. Note that the free play is based on a steering wheel diameter of 380 mm (approx 15 in) and will be less for smaller steering wheels - which all of them virtually are! Also check for the presence and security of retaining and locking devices in the steering column assembly.

☐ 30. While peering under the bonnet, check that hydraulic master cylinders and reservoirs are securely mounted and not severely corroded or otherwise damaged. Ensure that the caps are present, that fluid levels are satisfactory and that there are no fluid leaks.

☐ 31. Also check that the brake servo is securely mounted and not damaged or corroded to an extent that would impair its operation. Vacuum pipes should be sound, that is, free from kinks, splits and excessive chafing and not collapsed internally.

☐ 32. Still under the bonnet have a thorough search for evidence of excessive corrosion, severe distortion or fracture in any load bearing panelling within 30 cm (12 in.) of important mounting points such as the master cylinder/servo mounting, front suspension mountings etc.

Under The Vehicle - Front End

☐ **33. SAFETY FIRST! On some occasions there is no alternative but for your assistant to sit in the vehicle whilst you go beneath. Therefore: 1) Place ramps as well as axle stands beneath the vehicle's structure so that it cannot fall. 2) Don't allow your assistant to move vigorously or get in or out of the vehicle while you are beneath it. If either of these are problematical, DON'T CARRY OUT CHECK 34 - leave it to your garage.**

☐ 34. Have an assistant turn the steering wheel from side to side while you watch for movement in the steering mechanism. Make sure that the rack or box mountings are secure, that the ball joints show no signs of wear and that the ball joint dust covers are in sound condition. Ensure that all split pins, locking nuts and so on are in place and correctly fastened, throughout the steering and suspension systems.

☐ 35. With each wheel raised in turn, spin the wheel listening for roughness in the bearings. There must be none.

☐ 36. Under the vehicle, check the condition of the front springs. Wearing goggles, use a stuff brush to clean off the mud and other debris so that you don't miss a hidden 'crack'. Make sure that all suspension mountings are sound.

☐ 37. Inspect the front shock absorbers. Their upper shrouds (outer casing) tend to rust. Any sign of leaks will cause failure of the test - look for weeping hydraulic fluid just below the lower edge of the upper shroud. Take a firm grip on the upper and lower shroud in turn with both hands and try to twist the damper to check for deterioration in the top and bottom mounting bushes.

☐ 38. With all four wheels on the ground, push down firmly a couple of times on each front wing of the vehicle, then let go at the bottom of the stroke. The vehicle should return to approximately its original level within two or three strokes. Continuing oscillations will earn your vehicle a 'failure' ticket for worn front shockers!

Under The Vehicle - Rear Suspension

☐ 39. Check the operation of the rear shock absorbers in the same way as the front (Check 38).

☐ 40. Check the rear wheel bearings as described in check 35.

☐ 41. Check the condition of the rear springs and suspension components as described in check 36.

☐ 42. Check the condition of the rear shock absorbers as described in check 37.

Braking System

☐ 43. The MoT brake test is carried out on a special 'rolling road' set-up, which measures the efficiency in terms of percentage. For the foot brake, the examiner is looking for 50 per cent; the hand brake must measure 25 per cent. Frankly, without a rolling road of your own, there is little that you can do to verify whether or not your vehicle will come up to the required figures. What you can do, though, is carry out an entire check of the brake system, which will also cover all other aspects the examiner will be checking, and be as sure as you can that the system is working efficiently.

IMPORTANT! See *Chapter 3, Servicing Your Car* for important information, including *SAFETY FIRST!* information before working on your vehicle's brakes.

☐ 44. The MoT examiner will not dismantle any part of the system, but you can do so. So, take off each front wheel in turn, and examine as follows:

Disc Brakes

Check the front brake discs themselves, looking for excessive grooving or crazing, the calliper pistons/dust seals (looking for signs of fluid leakage and deterioration of the seals), and the brake pads - ideally, replace them if less than approximately 3mm (1/8th in.) friction material remains on each pad - but check the recommendations in *Chapter 3*.

Drum Brakes

Remove each brake drum and check the condition of the linings (renew if worn down to anywhere near the rivet heads), the brake drum (watch for cracking, ovality and serious scoring, etc.) and the wheel cylinders. Check the cylinder's dust covers to see if they contain brake fluid. If so, or if it is obvious that the cylinder(s) have been leaking, replace them or - ONLY if the cylinder bore is in perfect condition - fit a new seal kit.

☐ 45. Ensure that the drum brake adjusters (where fitted) are free to rotate (i.e. not seized!). If they are stuck fast, apply a little penetrating oil (but if possible, only from behind the backplate; if you have to work inside the brake drum, take great care to avoid the risk of getting oil on the brake shoes), and gently work the adjuster backwards and forwards with a brake adjuster spanner. Eventually the adjusters should free and a little brake grease can be applied to the threads to keep them in this condition. Now rotate the adjuster until the brake shoes contact the drum (preventing the road wheel from turning), then reverse the adjustment just enough to allow the wheel to turn.

☐ 46. A similar procedure can be applied to the handbrake adjustment. Check that the handbrake applies the brakes fully, well before it reaches the end of its potential range of movement. Ensure that the handbrake lever remains locked in the 'on' position when fully applied, even if the lever is knocked sideways.

☐ 47. Closely check the state of ALL visible hydraulic pipework. If any section of the steel tubing shows signs of corrosion, replace it, for safety as well as to gain an MoT pass. Look too for leakage of fluid around pipe joints, and from the master cylinder. The fluid level in the master cylinder reservoir must also be at its correct level - if not, find out why and rectify the problem! At the front and rear of the vehicle, bend the flexible hydraulic pipes (by hand) near each end of each pipe, checking for signs of cracking. If any is evident, or if the pipes have been chafing on the tyres, wheels, steering or suspension components, replace them with new items, rerouting them to avoid future problems. Note also that where the manufacturers fitted a clip to secure a piece of pipe, then it must be present and the pipe must be secured by it.

☐ 48. Have an assistant press down hard on the brake pedal while you check all flexible pipes for bulges. As an additional check, firmly apply the foot brake and hold the pedal down for a few minutes. It should not slowly sink to the floor (if it does, you have a hydraulic system problem). Press and release the pedal a few times - it should not feel 'spongy' (due to the presence of air in the system). Now check the operation of the brake servo by starting the engine while the brake pedal is being held down. If all is well, as the vacuum servo starts to work, the pedal should move a short distance towards the floor. Check the condition of the servo unit and its hoses - all MUST be sound. If there is the risk of any problems with the braking system's hydraulics, have a qualified mechanic check it over before using the vehicle.

☐ 49. A test drive should reveal obvious faults (such as pulling to one side, due to a seized calliper piston, for example), but otherwise all will be revealed on the rollers at the MoT station...

Bodywork Structure

A structurally deficient vehicle is a dangerous vehicle, and rust can affect many important areas, including the sills, any 'outriggers' and the floorpan. Examine these areas carefully.

☐ 50. Essentially, fractures, cracks or serious corrosion in any load bearing panel or member (to the extent that the affected sections are weakened) need to be dealt with. In addition, failure will result from any deficiencies in the structural metalwork within 30 cm (12 in.) of the seat belt mountings, and also the steering and suspension component attachment points. Repairs made to any structural areas must be carried out by 'continuous' seam welding, and the repair should restore the affected section to at least its original strength.

☐ 51. The MoT examiner will be looking for metal which gives way under squeezing pressure between finger and thumb, and will use his wicked little 'Corrosion Assessment Tool' (i.e. a plastic-headed tool known as the 'toffee hammer'!), which in theory at least should be used for detecting rust by lightly tapping the surface. If scraping the surface of the metal shows weakness beneath, the vehicle will fail.

☐ 52. Note that the security of doors and other openings must also be assessed, including the hinges, locks and catches. Corrosion damage or other weakness in the vicinity of these

items can mean failure. All doors must latch securely. It must be possible to open both front doors from inside and outside the vehicle and rear doors from the outside only.

Exterior Bodywork

☐ 53. Look out for surface rust, or accident damage, on the exterior bodywork, which leaves sharp/jagged edges and which may be liable to cause injury. Ideally, repairs should be carried out by welding in new metal, but for non-structural areas, riveting a plate over a hole, bridging the gap with glass fibre/body filler or even taping over the gap can be legally acceptable, at least as far as the MoT test is concerned.

Fuel System

☐ 54. Another recent extension of the regulations brings the whole of the fuel system under scrutiny, from the tank to the engine. The system should be examined with and without the engine running, and there must be no leaks from any of the components. The tank must be securely mounted, and the filler cap must fit properly - 'temporary' caps are not permitted.

Emissions

☐ 55. In almost every case, a proper 'engine tune' will help to ensure that your vehicle is running at optimum efficiency, and there should be no difficulty in passing the test, unless your engine or its ancillaries are well worn.

All petrol engines are subject to the 'visual smoke emission' test. The engine must be fully warmed up, allowed to idle, then revved slightly. If smoke emitted is regarded by the examiner as being 'excessive', the vehicle will fail. Often smoke emitted during this test is as a result of worn valve stem seals, allowing oil into the combustion chambers during tickover, to be blown out of the exhaust as 'blue smoke' when the engine is revved. In practice, attitudes vary widely between MoT stations on this aspect of the test.

☐ 56. For diesel-engined vehicles a 'smoke' test also applies. Again, the engine must be fully warmed up, and allowed to idle, before being revved to around 2,500 rpm for 20 seconds (to 'purge' the system). If dense blue or black smoke is emitted for more than five seconds, the vehicle will fail. In addition, the exhaust smoke is tested. Problems will require **SPECIALIST SERVICE.**

GETTING THROUGH THE MOT

FACT FILE: VEHICLE EMISSIONS

PETROL ENGINED VEHICLES WITHOUT CATALYSER

Vehicles first used before 1 August 1973
- visual smoke check only.

Vehicles first used between 1 August 1973 and 31 July 1986
- 4.5% carbon monoxide and 1,200 parts per million, unburned hydrocarbons.

Vehicles first used between 1 August 1986 and 31 July 1992
- 3.5% carbon monoxide and 1,200 parts per million, unburned hydrocarbons.

PETROL ENGINED VEHICLES FITTED WITH CATALYTIC CONVERTERS

Vehicles first used from 1 August 1992
(K-registration on).

All have to be tested at an MoT Testing Station specially equipped to handle cars fitted with catalytic converters whether or not the vehicle is fitted with a 'cat'. If the test, or the garage's data, shows that the vehicle was not fitted with a 'cat' by the manufacturer, the owner is permitted to take the vehicle to a Testing Station not equipped for catalysed cars, if he/she prefers to do so (up to 1998-only). Required maxima are - 3.5% carbon monoxide and 1,200 parts per million, unburned hydrocarbons. The simple emissions test (as above) will be supplemented by a further check to make sure that the catalyst is maintained in good and efficient working order.

The tester also has to check that the engine oil is up to a specified temperature before carrying out the test. (This is because 'carbs' don't work properly at lower temperatures - ensure *your* engine is fully warm!)

DIESEL ENGINES' EMISSIONS STANDARDS

The Tester will have to rev your engine hard, several times. If it is not in good condition, he is entitled to refuse to test it. This is the full range of tests, even though all may not apply to your car.

Vehicles first used before 1 August, 1979

Engine run at normal running temperature; engine speed taken to around 2500 rpm (or half governed max. speed, if lower) and held for 20 seconds. FAILURE, if engine emits dense blue or black smoke for next 5 seconds, at tick-over. (NOTE: Testers are allowed to be more lenient with pre-1960 vehicles.)

Vehicles first used on or after 1 August, 1979

After checking engine condition, and with the engine at normal running temperature, the engine will be run up to full revs between three and six times to see whether your engine passes the prescribed smoke density test. (For what it's worth - 2.5k for non-turbo cars; 3.0k for turbo diesels. An opacity meter probe will be placed in your car's exhaust pipe and this is not something you can replicate at home.) Irrespective of the meter readings, the car will fail if smoke or vapour obscures the view of other road users.

IMPORTANT NOTE: The diesel engine test puts a lot of stress on the engine. It is IMPERATIVE that your car's engine is properly serviced, and the cam belt changed on schedule, before you take it in for the MoT test. The tester is entitled to refuse to test the car if he feels that the engine is not in serviceable condition and there are a number of pre-Test checks he may carry out.

CHAPTER 8 - FACTS & FIGURES

This Chapter serves two main purposes. In *Part I,* we aim to provide you with a guide to all the major production changes that have taken place, and second, we supply the 'Facts & Figures' you will need when servicing your car. In fact, *Part II* of this chapter, *Capacities and Settings,* will make essential reading when you come to carrying out servicing, since you will then need to know things like the correct spark plug gap, torque settings and a whole host of other adjustments and measurements.

PART I - MAJOR MILESTONES

As with virtually all Fords, the numbers of detail changes, special editions and minor modifications are staggering! Only the main ones are shown here.

Oct. 1982 - Sierra introduced as five-door Hatchback and Estate with 1.3, 1.6, and 2.0 litre OHC 4-cyl. engines, 2.3 litre V6 engine and a 2.3 litre diesel. Four-speed gearboxes fitted except on 2.3 diesel and 2.8 injection which have five-speed. (3-speed auto. option on 1.6 and up.) Dual-circuit brakes with front discs and rear drums; the 2.0 litre and larger engined cars have ventilated discs. Power steering available on diesel. Auto.transmission available on some models.

May 1983 - XR4i available with 2.8 litre V6 fuel-injected engine and five-speed close-ratio gearbox. Five-speed gearbox option on most 1.6 litre versions.

Oct. 1984 - New front-end styling, similar to Ghia/XR4i and all Hatchbacks have redesigned rear pillars. 1.6 models fitted with 1.6E-Max (economy) units as standard. New 4-speed auto.transmission replaces 3-speed unit with no auto. option on 1.3/1.6. New 1.8 litre engine introduced.

Mar. 1985 - XR 4x4i five-door with permanent 4WD (and optional ABS brakes from Oct.) replaces the three-door XR4i.

Mar. 1986 - 1.6, 1.8 and 2.0 LX introduced with uprated suspension and other extras. 2.8i Ghia 4x4 Estate introduced.

July 1986 - RS Cosworth with 2-litre turbo engine introduced.

Mar. 1987 - New front styling-bonnet dropping to bumber level, new indicators and deflectors on tailgate. Sierra Sapphire 4-door saloon range introduced, virtually identical to hatchback models.

Jan. 1988 - Sierra P100 Pick-up (replacing Cortina-based version) imported with 1 tonne payload.

Mar. 1988 - RS Cosworth now more powerful and available as Sapphire models. Hatch version discontinued. 1.8 litre CVH engine appears (June).

May 1989 - P100 now available with Turbo Diesel.

June 1989 - New 2-litre DOHC engine introduced in place of SOHC units.

Feb. 1990 - New radiator grilles on most models, with white front indicator lenses, smoked rears. 2-litre XR4x4 and Ghia Hatch and Saloon and 2-litre DOHC (non-turbo) XR4i Hatch introduced - but discontinued Aug. '91. (XR4x4i and GLS 4x4 with 2.9 engines continue.) New 1.8 turbo diesel replaces 2.3.

Aug. 1991 - Most models with body coloured bumpers and other detail changes inside and out. Catalyst option (unleaded) introduced progressively.

Apr. 1993 - All cars discontinued.

June 1994 - P100 Pick-up discontinued.

FACTS & FIGURES

PART II - CAPACITIES AND SETTINGS

Sierra 1.3 - 1982 to 1986:
Cubic capacity - 1294 cc OHC
Compression ratio - 9.0 : 1
Compression pressure - 11 to 13 bar (160 to 189 lbf/in^2)
Idle speed - 750 to 850 rpm
CO percentage - 1.0 to 2.0
Spark plug type - Motorcraft BF22X
Spark plug gap - 0.024 in. (0.6 mm)
Ignition timing - 12 degrees BTDC
Valve clearances: inlet - 0.008 in. (0.2 mm)
                                   exhaust - 0.010 in. (0.25 mm)

Sierra 1.6 - 1982 to 1986:
Cubic capacity - 1593 cc OHC
Compression ratio - 9.2 : 1
Compression pressure - 11 to 13 bar (160 to 189 lbf/in^2)
Idle speed - 750 to 850 rpm
CO percentage - 1.0 to 2.0
Spark plug type - Motorcraft BF22X
Spark plug gap - 0.024 in. (0.6 mm)
Ignition timing - 12 degrees BTDC
Valve clearances: inlet - 0.008 in. (0.2 mm)
                                   exhaust - 0.010 in. (0.25 mm)

Sierra and Sapphire 1.6i CAT - 1990 to 1993:
Cubic capacity - 1596 cc CVH
Compression ratio - 9.0 : 1
Compression pressure - 12 to 14 bar (174 to 203 lbf/in^2)
Idle speed - 850 to 950 rpm
CO percentage - Less than 0.5
Spark plug type - Motorcraft AGPR32CD1
Spark plug gap - 0.040 in. (1.0 mm)
Ignition timing - 8 to 12 degrees BTDC

Sierra 1.6 E-max - 1984 to 1987:6
Cubic capacity - 1597 cc OHC
Compression ratio - 9.5 : 1
Compression pressure - 11 to 13 bar (160 to 189 lbf/in^2)
Idle speed - 750 to 850 rpm
CO percentage - 0.75 to 1.75
Spark plug type - Motorcraft BRF22X
Spark plug gap - 0.024 in. (0.6 mm)
Ignition timing - 10 degrees BTDC
Valve clearances: inlet - 0.008 in. (0.2 mm)
                                   exhaust - 0.010 in. (0.25 mm)

Sierra and Sapphire 1.6 - 1987 to 1991:
Cubic capacity - 1597 cc OHC
Compression ratio - 9.5 : 1
Compression pressure - 11 to 13 bar (160 to 189 lbf/in^2)
Idle speed - 750 to 850 rpm
CO percentage - 1.0 to 2.0
Spark plug type - Motorcraft BRF32C
Spark plug gap - 0.030 in. (0.75 mm)
Ignition timing - 10 degrees BTDC
Valve clearances: inlet - 0.008 in. (0.2 mm)
                                   exhaust - 0.010 in. (0.25 mm)

Sierra and Sapphire 1.8 - 1988 to 1992:
Cubic capacity - 1769 cc CVH
Compression ratio - 9.3 : 1
Compression pressure - 11 to 13 bar (160 to 189 lbf/in^2)
Idle speed - 800 to 900 rpm manual
775 to 825 rpm automatic
CO percentage - 0.75 to 1.25
Spark plug type - Motorcraft AGPR32C1
Spark plug gap - 0.040 in. (1.00 mm)
Ignition timing - 20 degrees BTDC

Sierra and Sapphire 1.8 CAT - 1991 to 1992:
Cubic capacity - 1769 cc CVH
Compression ratio - 9.3 : 1
Compression pressure - 11 to 13 bar (160 to 189 lbf/in^2)
Idle speed - 800 to 900 rpm manual
775 to 825 rpm automatic
CO percentage - 0.75 to 1.25
Spark plug type - Motorcraft AGPR32C1
Spark plug gap - 0.040 in. (1.00 mm)
Ignition timing - 20 degrees BTDC

Sierra and Sapphire 1.8i CAT - 1992 to 1993:
Cubic capacity - 1769 cc CVH
Compression ratio - 9.3 : 1
Compression pressure - 11 to 13 bar (160 to 189 lbf/in^2)
Idle speed - 800 to 900 rpm
CO percentage - Less than 0.5
Spark plug type - Motorcraft AGPR32CD1
Spark plug gap - 0.040 in. (1.00 mm)
Ignition timing - Computer controlled

Sierra 1.8 - 1984 to 1987:
Cubic capacity - 1796 cc OHC
Compression ratio - 9.5 : 1
Compression pressure - 11 to 13 bar (160 to 189 lbf/in^2)
Idle speed - 825 to 925 rpm manual
750 to 850 rpm automatic
CO percentage - 0.75 to 1.75
Spark plug type - Motorcraft BRF22X
Spark plug gap - 0.024 in. (0.6 mm)
Ignition timing - 10 degrees BTDC
Valve clearances: inlet - 0.008 in. (0.2 mm)
                                   exhaust - 0.010 in. (0.25 mm)

Sierra and Sapphire 1.8 - 1987 to 1988:
Cubic capacity - 1796 cc OHC
Compression ratio - 9.5 : 1
Compression pressure - 11 to 13 bar (160 to 189 lbf/in^2)
Idle speed - 850 to 900 rpm
CO percentage - 0.75 to 1.75
Spark plug type - Motorcraft BRF22C
Spark plug gap - 0.030 in. (0.75 mm)
Ignition timing - 10 degrees BTDC
Valve clearances: inlet - 0.008 in. (0.2 mm)
                                   exhaust - 0.010 in. (0.25 mm)

FACTS & FIGURES

Sierra 2.0 - 1982 to 1987:
Cubic capacity - 1993 cc OHC
Compression ratio - 9.2 : 1
Compression pressure - 11 to 13 bar (160 to 189 lbf/in^2)
Idle speed - 750 to 850 rpm
825 to 925 rpm 1985 on
CO percentage - 0.75 to 1.75
Spark plug type - Motorcraft BRF32X
Spark plug gap - 0.024 in. (0.6 mm)
Ignition timing - 8 degrees BTDC
10 degrees BTDC 1985 on
Valve clearances: inlet - 0.008 in. (0.2 mm)
                                   exhaust - 0.010 in. (0.25 mm)

Sierra and Sapphire 2.0 - 1987 to 1989:
Cubic capacity - 1993 cc OHC
Compression ratio - 9.2 : 1
Compression pressure - 11 to 13 bar (160 to 189 lbf/in^2)
Idle speed - 825 to 875 rpm
CO percentage - 0.75 to 1.75
Spark plug type - Motorcraft BRF32C
Spark plug gap - 0.030 in. (0.75 mm)
Ignition timing - 10 degrees BTDC
Valve clearances: inlet - 0.008 in. (0.2 mm)
                                   exhaust - 0.010 in. (0.25 mm)

Sierra 2.0i - 1985 to 1987:
Cubic capacity - 1993 cc OHC
Compression ratio - 9.2 : 1
Compression pressure - 11 to 13 bar (160 to 189 lbf/in^2)
Idle speed - 825 to 925 rpm
CO percentage - 0.6 to 1.0
Spark plug type - Motorcraft BRF32X
Spark plug gap - 0.024 in. (0.6 mm)
Ignition timing - 12 degrees BTDC
Valve clearances: inlet - 0.008 in. (0.2 mm)
                                   exhaust - 0.010 in. (0.25 mm)

Sierra and Sapphire 2.0i - 1987 to 1989:
Cubic capacity - 1993 cc OHC
Compression ratio - 9.2 : 1
Compression pressure - 11 to 13 bar (160 to 189 lbf/in^2)
Idle speed - 825 to 925 rpm manual
750 to 850 rpm automatic
CO percentage - 0.6 to 1.0
Spark plug type - Motorcraft BRF22C
Spark plug gap - 0.03 in. (0.75 mm)
Ignition timing - 12 degrees BTDC
Valve clearances: inlet - 0.008 in. (0.2 mm)
                                   exhaust - 0.010 in. (0.25 mm)

Sierra and Sapphire 2.0 - 1989 to 1991:
Cubic capacity - 1998 cc DOHC
Compression ratio - 10.3 : 1
Compression pressure - 11 to 13 bar (160 to 189 lbf/in^2)
Idle speed - 825 to 875 rpm
CO percentage - 0.75 to 1.25
Spark plug type - Motorcraft AGPR32CD
Spark plug gap - 0.030 in. (0.75 mm)
Ignition timing - 12 degrees BTDC

Sierra and Sapphire 2.0i and 4x4 - 1989 to 1992:
Cubic capacity - 1998cc DOHC
Compression ratio - 10.3 : 1
Compression pressure - 11 to 13 bar (160 to 189 lbf/in^2)
Idle speed - 850 to 900 rpm
CO percentage - 1.0 to 1.5
Spark plug type - Motorcraft AGPR22CD
Spark plug gap - 0.030 in. (0.75 mm)
Ignition timing - 15 degrees BTDC

Sierra and Sapphire 2.0i CAT - 1989 to 1993:
Cubic capacity - 1998 cc DOHC
Compression ratio - 10.3 : 1
Compression pressure - 11 to 13 bar (160 to 189 lbf/in^2)
Idle speed - 850 to 900 rpm
CO percentage - Less that 0.5
Spark plug type - Motorcraft AGPR22CD
Spark plug gap - 0.030 in. (0.75 mm)
Ignition timing - N/A

Sierra 2.8i and 4x4 - 1983 to 1987:
Cubic capacity - 2792 cc V6
Compression ratio - 9.2 : 1
Compression pressure - Equal to, or greater than 11.5 bar (167 lbf/in^2)
Idle speed - 850 to 950 rpm
CO percentage - 1.0 to 1.5
Spark plug type - Motorcraft AGR22C
Spark plug gap - 0.025 in. (0.6 mm)
Ignition timing - 12 degrees BTDC
Valve clearances: inlet - 0.014 in. (0.35 mm)
                                   exhaust - 0.016 in. (0.4 mm)

Sierra 2.8i 4x4 1987 to 1989:
Cubic capacity - 2792 cc V6
Compression ratio - 9.2 : 1
Compression pressure - Equal to, or greater than 11.5 bar (167 lbf/in^2)
Idle speed - 850 to 950 rpm
CO percentage - 1.0 to 1.5
Spark plug type - Motorcraft AGR22C
Spark plug gap - 0.030 in. (0.75 mm)
Ignition timing - 12 degrees BTDC
Valve clearances: inlet - 0.014 in. (0.35 mm)
                                   exhaust - 0.016 in. (0.4 mm)

Sierra 2.9i 4x4 - 1989 to 1991:
Cubic capacity - 2933 cc OHV V6
Compression ratio - 9.5 : 1
Compression pressure - Equal to, or greater than 11.5 bar (167 lbf/in^2)
Idle speed - 850 to 950 rpm
CO percentage - 0.5 to 1.0
Spark plug type - Motorcraft AGPR32C
Spark plug gap - 0.030 in. (0.75 mm)
Ignition timing - 112 degrees BTDC
Valve clearances: inlet - 0.014 in. (0.35 mm)
                                   exhaust - 0.016 in. (0.4 mm)

Sierra 2.9i 4x4 CAT - 1990 to 1993:
Cubic capacity - 2933 cc OHV V6
Compression ratio - 9.0 : 1
Compression pressure - 11.5 to 12.5 bar (167 to 181 lbf/in^2)

Idle speed - 850 to 950 rpm
CO percentage - Less than 0.5
Spark plug type - Motorcraft AGRF42C1
Spark plug gap - 0.039 in. (1.0 mm)
Ignition timing - 15 degrees BTDC

DIESEL ENGINES

1.8 litre diesel:
Cubic capacity - 1753 cc
Compression ratio - 21.5 : 1
Compression pressure - 28 to 34 bar
Glow plugs - Champion CH147
Idle speed - 800 to 900 rpm

2.3 litre diesel:
Cubic capacity - 2304 cc
Compression ratio - 22.2 : 1
Compression pressure - 20 to 25 bar (290 to 360 lbf/in^2)
Glow plugs - Champion CH68
Idle speed - 875 to 900 rpm

CAPACITIES

Engine oil inc. filter:		Litres	Pints
Sierra 1.3	1982-86	3.75	6.6
Sierra & Sapphire 1.6	1982-91		
Sierra & Sapphire 1.8	1984-88		
Sierra & Sapphire 2.0	1982-89		
Sierra & Sapphire 1.6 CAT	1990-93	3.5	6.2
Sierra & Sapphire 1.8	1988-92	4.0	7.0
Sierra & Sapphire 1.8 CAT	1991-93		
Sierra & Sapph. 2.0/CAT & 4x4	1989-91	4.5	7.8
Sierra 2.8 & 2.9 4x4	1983-89	4.7	8.2

GEARBOX CAPACITIES

Ford do not generally issue capacity figures for their gearboxes since gearbox oil change is not part of their service schedule. Sierras and Sapphires have been fitted with a number of different gearbox types, each with a different capacity, some as low as 1 litre, others with up to 1.9 litres. The recommended quantity can best be established by filling up to the correct level as described in *Chapter 3*. However, you will need to obtain enough oil to do the job (whereas Ford dealerships have it 'on draft'). Bearing in mind that you can always use any left-overs for topping up later, we recommend that you start off with:

Manual gearboxes:		Litres	Pints
All models		2.0	3.5

Automatic gearbox - refill:		Litres	Pints
Sierra 1.6	1982-87	7.0	12.0
Sierra 2.0	1982-87		

Sierra & Sapphire 1.8 & 2.0 (inc. CAT & 4x4, all models)	1988-93	9.0	15.0

PETROL ENGINES

Cooling system:		Litres	Pints
ALL MODELS:			
Sierra & Sapph., All Models		8.0	14.1
EXCEPT:			
Sierra & Sapphire 1.6i CAT	1990-93	9.5	16.7
Sierra 2.8 & 2.9 4x4	1983-87	8.5	15.0
Sierra & Sapph. 2.0 CAT & 4X4	1989-93	7.3	12.8
Sierra & Sapphire 1.8	1988-93	8.7	15.3

Fuel tank:

All models - 60 litres (13.2 Gallons)

DIESEL ENGINES

1.8 litre	Litres	Pints
Engine oil with filter	4.5	7.9
Cooling system	9.5	16.7
Transmission oil	1.5	2.6

2.3 litre	Litres	Pints
Engine oil with filter	5.6	9.9
Cooling system	9.5	16.7
Transmission oil	1.9	3.3

Firing Order
All 4-cylinder engines   1 - 3 - 4 - 2
All 6-cylinder engines   1 - 4 - 2 - 5 - 3 - 6

Common torque wrench settings
Wheel nuts   74 lb.ft. (100 Nm)
Spark plugs   15 to 20 lb.ft. (20 to 28 Nm)
Sump plug   20 to 24 lb.ft. (28 to 35 Nm)

Tyre pressures:
There is an enormous number of different tyre sizes, specifications and pressures that are applicable to the Sierra range. We recommend, therefore, that you first consult you Ford Operator's Handbook. If you are in doubt about the correct tyre pressures to use, consult your local tyre specialist.

CHAPTER 9 - TOOLS & EQUIPMENT

Although good tools are not cheap, if you reckon their cost against what you would otherwise spend on professional servicing and repairs, your arithmetic should show you that it doesn't take long to recoup your outlay - and then to start showing a profit!

In fact, there is no need to spend a fortune all at once - most owners who do their own servicing acquire their implements over a long period of time. However, there are some items you simply cannot do without in order to properly carry out the work necessary to keep your car on the road. Therefore, in the following lists, we have concentrated on those items which are likely to be valuable aids to maintaining your car in a good state of tune, and to keep it running sweetly and safely and in addition we have featured some of the tools that are 'nice-to-have' rather than 'must have' because as your tool chest grows, there are some tools that help to make servicing just that bit easier and more thorough to carry out.

Two vital points - firstly always buy the best quality tools you can afford. 'Cheap and cheerful' items may look similar to more expensive implements, but

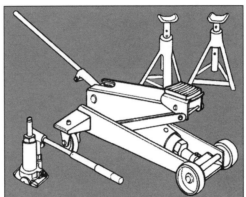

experience shows that they often fail when the going gets tough, and some can even be dangerous. With proper care, good quality tools will last a lifetime, and can be regarded as an investment. The extra outlay is well worth it, in the long run.

Over the years, there have been various nut/bolt/spanner designations. For many years British cars standardised on 'AF', a designation referring to the measurement 'across the flats' of the hexagon nut or bolt head, while the 'foreigners' were 'Metric'. While there are still many 'AF' cars around, all modern cars are 'Metric' of course, apart from American cars. (For the record, 'metric' sizes are also measured across their flats!). Be sure you know which designation applies to your car before you start buying. Your local motor accessory store should be able to advise, or you could all your local main dealer to make sure, if necessary.

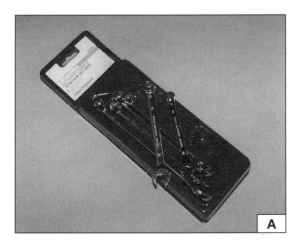

SPANNERS:

A. The two common types of spanner are the ring and the open-ended. The ring spanner grips practically all round the bolt, and is preferable where the bolt is really tight, for an open-ended spanner, merely straddling two flats of the bolt, could slip. On the other hand, the open-end is often quicker and easier to use - so this set of 'Combination' spanners, a ring at one end, open-ended the other, is a nice compromise!

All the tools featured here are available from your local High Street auto-accessory store or Super Store. Any special tools needed for your car are referred to in Chapter 3.

TOOLS & EQUIPMENT

B. While the 'flatness' of the combination spanners (or of a conventional open-ended spanner) is often useful, there are occasions when only the offset, or 'swan neck' of the conventional ring spanner will do the job - like when having to operate over the top of one bolt in order to undo another.

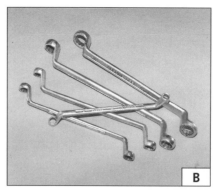

Unlike the combination spanners, the conventional ring and open-ended spanners will have a different size at each end.

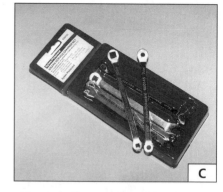

Usually, the AF sizes will rise in sixteenths of an inch, and the metrics by one millimetre - the following sizes will probably cover most of your needs:
AF - 3/8 x 7/16, 1/2 x 9/16, 5/8 x 11/16, 13/16 x 7/8
Metric - 10 x 11, 12 x 13, 14 x 15, 16 x 17

C. The sturdy specialist brake spanner used, for brake adjusters or bleed nipples, is undeniably a wise buy, as mentioned in the brake servicing text. You might not need the set as shown here, but you can choose individual sizes to suit your car, such as 1/4 in. square x 11/32 in. square or 1/4 in. hexagonal x 5/16 in. AF, or perhaps 8 x 10mm hexagonal - there are others.

D. A basic socket set should figure highly on your shopping list, for it will cover your basic spanner sizes and can often solve difficult access or extra-leverage problems. This one is a fairly sophisticated set, and includes a number of useful extras, such as spark plug spanners and Allen key and screwdriver bits. Don't buy more than you need, however, and don't be tempted by cheap, nasty - and often dangerous - market stall socket sets.

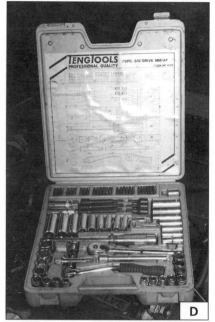

E. A torque wrench was also once a luxury, but nowadays it's practically essential, with specific torque settings quoted for many of the nuts and bolts used in modern car engineering. The example shown will cater for most applications, including adjustable wheel-bearing hub nuts, but even the next size up (30-150 lb/ft) in the DIY range will still fall short of the 200-odd lb/ft specified for some hub nuts!

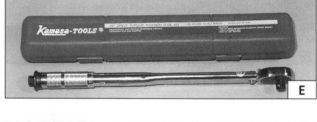

F. If you still need a plug spanner, and particularly if your engine features deep-set spark plugs, this Sykes-Pickavant 'extra long plug wrench', combining both 10mm and 14mm sizes, could be a boon. Some plugs are set deeper than the average length of a socket-set spark plug spanner, and if the socket set's extension bar is prone to leaving the spanner socket stuck on the plug, then you could have a problem ...

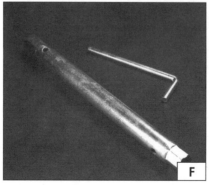

SCREWDRIVERS:

G. You will need a selection of screwdrivers, both flat-bladed and cross-headed, long ones, short ones, slim ones, fat ones ...

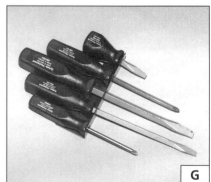

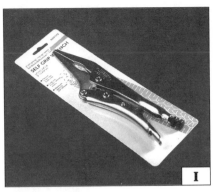

PLIERS:

H. Ordinary combination (or 'engineers') pliers are needed for general work, while a long-nosed pair are handy where access is tight. Their cutting edges are useful for stripping cable insulation, or for snipping wire or trimming split-pin lengths, but you might prefer a pair of specialist side-cutter pliers for such work.

I. Jolly useful as an extra pair of hands, or for gripping such as a rusty nut or bolt really tightly, is a self-grip wrench. This is a long-nose example, but there are also ordinary straight-jaw and round jaw versions.

SUNDRIES:

J. You'll need hammers, including the useful 1lb ball-pein type, plus a hefty copper hammer and maybe a soft (plastic-headed) hammer, too.

K. The wire brush should have brass bristles and as well as an ordinary set of feeler gauges, an 'ignition set' covers most plug and points gap sizes, and includes a points file and a spark plug gap setting tool.

L. You may need a grease gun (although virtually no modern cars have grease points) but you *will* want an oil can, and an oil funnel, and a container of sufficient capacity into which the engine oil can be drained.

M. You may also need a drain plug 'key' suitable for your car unless all the drain plugs are 'bolt'-type hexagons.

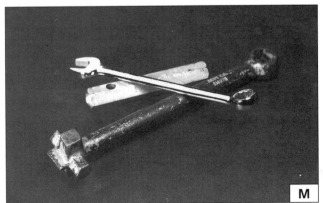

N. Well worthwhile, since some oil filters can be cussedly tight, is some sort of oil filter wrench - this chain-type is a nice example. In extreme cases, even these wrenches can fail to get a grip, in which case, drive an old screwdriver right through the filter and twist it loose.

O. A separate set of hand-held Allen keys is a good idea (they come in metric or Imperial sizes), and an adjustable spanner and a 'Junior' hacksaw will have their uses.

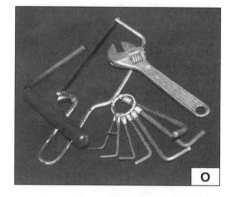

P. For your weekly maintenance checks, you'll need a tyre pressure gauge, tyre tread depth gauge and a footpump - which might, like the example here, have an integral pressure gauge. And whether you're wheel-changing at home or roadside, you will welcome the extremely useful Sykes-Pickavant 'Wheelmaster' wrench, which can be extended to give enough leverage to shift those wheel nuts or bolts that the average car-kit wheelbrace wouldn't even look at - see the wheel-change routine at the start of Chapter 3. Remember to carry the extendable wrench with you in the car!

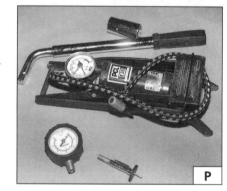

LIFTING:

Q. While the jack supplied with the car *might* be OK for emergency wheel-changes, you would soon tire of trying to use it for servicing operations. Here, you need a good trolley jack, and one of the latest on the market is this 2-ton lifting capacity 'Lift and Lock' example which, as its name suggests, has a built-in fail-safe locking device in the event of hydraulic failure.

R. No matter what sort of jack you use, it is ESSENTIAL that you should not venture beneath a car supported on a jack alone. Having raised it, you need to support it safely and securely. What you need now is definitely NOT house bricks (or any other such potentially dangerous items!) but rather axle stands or wheel-ramps. Adjustable-height stands are essential and both axle stands and ramps should be produced by a 'name' manufacturer, for safety's sake. If you don't need the wheels off, it can be argued that the ramps offer better stability - though you'll benefit from some assistance when it comes to driving upon them. See the start of *Chapter 3*.

TUNING AIDS:

S. As we have said earlier in this chapter and within the servicing sections, the tuning aids that are now available to the DIY market have become practically invaluable 'musts' for the dedicated home mechanic. Any of the Gunson's collection shown here would soon prove their worth. Top of the tree, of course, is their 'Gastester Professional' - don't let its designation suggest that it's not for DIY use, for although it's expensive a group of friends sharing its cost would find their outlay well worth the benefits offered by the unit's Exhaust Gas 'CO' functions, plus its Voltage, Dwell and RPM modes. If it's pure 'multi-meter' you're after, then their 'Digimeter 320' is a tidy little hand-held unit, with clear digital read-outs for such as Volts (DC and household AC) and Amps, Ohms, rpm, and Dwell (degrees and per cent), and its sophistication extends to Frequency, Period and Pulsewidth testing (handy for fuel injection systems), as well as Diode, Resistance and Continuity testing. Also by Gunson's is the powerful 'Timestrobe' xenon timing light, the now not so new, but still novel 'Colortune' and (not shown) the 'Carbalancer'. The latter two devices are virtually invaluable when it comes to carburettor tuning.

APPENDIX 1
RECOMMENDED CASTROL LUBRICANTS

ENGINE OIL

PETROL ENGINES

Engine (all models except Cosworth)

1982 to 1986:
Castrol GTX (15W/50): A 'superior' multi-grade engine oil that is certainly suitable for newer vehicles requiring an SAE 15W/50 or 20W/50 viscosity oil, but which is particularly appropriate for older technology engines and high-mileage vehicles, where working clearances might be higher than average.

1987-on:
Castrol GTX2 (15W/40): Suits newer vehicles, including turbo-charged, where this viscosity is recommended.

Castrol GTX3 Lightec (10W/40): Specially formulated for multi-valve, high-technology engines, including turbos, where a light viscosity oil has been recommended.

DIESEL ENGINES

All models:
Castrol GTD (15W/40): Specially formulated for the particular demands of all diesel engines, including turbo-charged.

GEARBOX OIL

MANUAL TRANSMISSION

All models
Castrol Syntrax Universal, except:

1989 to 1993 2.0i DOHC and 4x4
Castrol FMT

AUTOMATIC TRANSMISSION

Castrol Dexron R III

POWER STEERING
Castrol TQ Dexron R III

BRAKE FLUID
Castrol Super Disc

BRAKE MECHANISM
Areas of metal-to-metal contact

Proprietary brand of high melting point brake grease such as Castrol PH Grease - not conventional high point melting grease.

CV JOINTS
Castrol Moly Grease

FRONT AND REAR DIFFERENTIALS
Castrol Syntrax Universal

WHEEL BEARINGS
Castrol LM Grease

LOCKS AND HINGES
Castrol Everyman

ELECTRICAL CONNECTIONS
Castrol DWF

NUT AND BOLT RELEASE
Castrol Easing oil

COOLING SYSTEM
Castrol Antifreeze and Summer Coolant

CASTROL ANTIFREEZE: Recommended for use in petrol or diesel engine cooling systems, with aluminium or cast engines. Its formulation of mono ethylene glycol and corrosion inhibitors makes it suitable for all-year-round use, and because it contains no phosphate it is reckoned that the problems of deposits in some modern uprated engines are eliminated. A 33 per cent concentration will protect down to minus 17 degrees C.

APPENDIX 2
SPECIALISTS & SUPPLIERS
FEATURED IN THIS BOOK

All of the products and specialists listed below have contributed in various ways to this book. All of the consumer products used are available through regular high street outlets or by mail order from specialist suppliers.

Castrol (UK) Ltd., Burmah House, Pipers Way, Swindon, Wiltshire, SN3 1RE. Tel: 01793 452222
Contact Castrol's Consumer Technical Department Help Line on the above number for advice on lubrication recommendations.

Dinol (GB) Ltd., Dinol House, 98 Ock Street, Abingdon, Oxford, OX14 5DH. Tel: 01235 530677
Suppliers of Dinitrol rust proofing fluids, and are equipped to carry out rustproofing on vehicles.

Douglas Seaton Ltd., West Hendford, Yeovil, Somerset, BA22 2AG.
Tel: 01935 27421

Ford Motor Co. Ltd., Eagle Way, Warley, Brentwood, Essex, CM13 3BW. Tel: 01277 253000
See your local main dealer in Yellow Pages for Ford parts.

Gunson Ltd., Coppen Road, Dagenham, Essex, RM8 1NU. Tel: 0181 984 8855
Electrical and electronic engine tuning equipment.

HPI Autodata, HP Information plc, Dolphin House, P O Box 61, New Street, Salisbury, Wiltshire, SP1 2TB. Tel: 01722 422422
Before buying any used car, check it out with HPI Autodata.

Kamasa Tools, Saxon Industries, Lower Everland Road, Hungerford, Berkshire, RG17 0DX. Tel: 01488 684545
Wide range of hand and power tools, some of which were used in this book.

Moff Motors Ltd., Castle Cary, Somerset, BA7 7PF. Tel: 01963 350310

NGK Spark Plugs (UK) Ltd., 7-8-9 Garrick Industrial Centre, Hendon, London, NW9 6AQ. Tel: 0181 202 2151
Top quality spark plugs.

SP Tyres UK Ltd., Fort Dunlop, Birmingham, B24 9QT. Tel: 0121 384 4444
Manufacturers of Dunlop tyres.

Sykes-Pickavant Group plc, Kilnhouse Lane, Lytham St Annes, Lancs, FY8 3DU. Tel: 01253 721291
Wide range of hand tools and specialist equipment, some of which were used in this book.

Waste Oil Disposal
There are 1,300 listed waste oil disposal sites in the UK alone. PLEASE don't foul the environment by tipping waste oil into the drains or the ground. Find your nearest oil disposal point by running the National Rivers Authority on FREEPHONE 0800 663366.

APPENDIX 3
SERVICE HISTORY

This Chapter helps you keep track of all the servicing carried out on your vehicle and can even save you money! A vehicle with a Service History is always worth more than one without, and you can make full use of this section, even if you have a garage or mechanic carry out the work for you. It enables you to specify the jobs you want to have carried out to your vehicle and, of course, it enables you to keep that all-important Service History. And even if your vehicle doesn't have a 'history' going back to when it was new, keeping this Chapter complete will add to your vehicle's value when you come to sell it. Mind you, it obviously won't be enough to just to tick the boxes: keep all your receipts when you buy oil, filters and other consumables or parts. That way, you'll also be able to return any faulty parts if needs be.

Buying Parts

Before carrying out a service on your car, you will need to purchase the right parts. Please refer to **Chapter 2, Buying Guide** for information on how to buy the right parts at the right prices and for information on how to find your car's 'identity numbers'; information that you will need in order to buy the right parts, first time!

Month, whichever comes first, is repeated at each one of the following Service Intervals. The same applies to the **6,000 Miles or Six Months** interval: much of it is repeated at **12,000 Miles or Twelve Months.** Every time a Job or set of Jobs is 'repeated' from an earlier Interval, we show it in a tinted area on the page. You can then see more clearly which jobs are unique to the level of Service Interval that you are on.

The Job Lists

Wherever possible, the Jobs listed in this section have been placed in a logical order or placed into groups that will help you make progress on the car. We have tried to save you too much in the way of unnecessary movement by grouping jobs around areas of the car. Therefore, at each Service Interval, you will see the work grouped into Jobs that need carrying out in The Engine Bay, Around The Car or Under The Car.

You'll also see space at each Service Interval for you to write down the date, price and seller's name every time you buy consumables or accessories. And once again, do remember to keep your receipts! There's also space for you to date and sign the Service Record or for a garage's stamp to be applied.

As you move through the Service Intervals, you will notice that the work carried out at say, **1,500 Miles or Every**

You will also find that all the major Intervals, right up to the 'longest', contain Jobs that are unique to that Service Interval. That's why we have continued this Service History right up to the **36,000 Miles or every Three Years** interval. So now, you will be able to service your car and keep a full record of the work, in the knowledge that your car has been looked after as well as anyone could wish for!

Important Note!

The Service Jobs listed here are intended as a check list and a means of keeping a record of your vehicle's service history, **not** as a set of instructions for working on your car. It is most important that you refer to **Chapter 3, Servicing Your Car** for full details of how to carry out each Job listed here and for essential SAFETY information and, see also, **Chapter 1, Safety First!**.

EVERY 500 MILES, WEEKLY OR BEFORE A LONG JOURNEY

This list is shown, complete, only once. It would have been a bit much to have provided the list 52 times over for use once a week throughout the year! Each job is, however, included with every longer Service list from 3,000 miles/Three Months-on so that each of the 'weekly' Jobs is carried out as part of every service.

Every 500 Miles - The Engine Bay

☐ Job 1. Engine oil level.

☐ Job 2. Check coolant level.

☐ Job 3. Check brake fluid level.

☐ Job 4. Check battery electrolyte.

☐ Job 5. Check screenwash level.

Every 500 Miles - Around the Car

☐ Job 6. Check tyre pressures.

☐ Job 7. Check headlights, sidelights and front indicators.

☐ Job 8. Rear lights and indicator bulbs.

☐ Job 9. Interior light bulbs.

☐ Job 10. Number plate light bulbs.

☐ Job 11. Side repeater bulbs.

☐ Job 12. Check horns.

☐ Job 13. Check windscreen wipers.

☐ Job 14. Windscreen washers.

EVERY 1,500 MILES - OR EVERY MONTH, WHICHEVER COMES FIRST

These Jobs are similar to the 500 Mile Jobs but don't need carrying out quite so regularly. Once again, these Jobs are not shown with a separate listing for each 1,500 miles/1 Month interval but they are included as part of every 3,000 miles/Three Months Service list and for every longer Service interval.

Every 1,500 Miles - Around the Car

☐ Job 15. Check tyres.

☐ Job 16. Check spare tyre.

☐ Job 17. Wash bodywork.

☐ Job 18. Touch-up paintwork.

☐ Job 19. Radio aerial.

☐ Job 20. Valet interior.

☐ Job 21. Improve visibility.

Every 1,500 miles - Under the Car

☐ Job 22. Clean mud traps.

EVERY 3,000 MILES - OR THREE MOHTHS, WHICHEVER COMES FIRST

All the Service Jobs in the tinted area have been carried forward from earlier service intervals and are to be repeated at this service.

Every 3,000 miles - The Engine Bay

First carry out all Jobs listed under earlier Service intervals as applicable.

☐ Job 1. Engine oil level.

☐ Job 2. Check coolant level.

☐ Job 3. Check brake fluid level.

☐ Job 4. Check battery electrolyte.

☐ Job 5. Check screenwash level.

☐ Job 23. Generator drive belt.

☐ Job 24. Check brake/fuel lines.

☐ Job 25. **DIESEL ENGINES ONLY** Drain fuel filter.

Every 3,000 miles - Around The Car

First carry out all Jobs listed under earlier Service intervals as applicable.

☐ Job 6. Check tyre pressures.

☐ Job 7. Check headlights, sidelights and front indicators.

☐ Job 8. Rear lights and indicator bulbs.

☐ Job 9. Interior light bulbs.

☐ Job 10. Number plate light bulbs.

☐ Job 11. Side repeater bulbs.

☐ Job 12. Check horns.

☐ Job 13. Check windscreen wipers.

☐ Job 14. Windscreen washers.

☐ Job 15. Check tyres.

☐ Job 16. Check spare tyre.

☐ Job 17. Wash bodywork.

☐ Job 18. Touch-up paintwork.

Job 19. Radio aerial.

Job 20. Valet interior.

Job 21. Improve visibility.

Job 26. Check tightness of wheel nuts.

Job 27. Check brake/fuel lines.

Job 28. Check handbrake adjustment.

Job 29. Check door/tailgate seals.

Job 30. Check windscreen.

Job 31. Rear view mirrors.

Every 3,000 miles - Under the Car

First carry out all Jobs listed under earlier Service intervals as applicable.

Job 22. Clean mud traps.

Job 32. Check exhaust system for leaks/damage.

Job 33. Check exhaust system mountings.

Job 34. Check steering rack gaiters.

Job 35. **4X4 MODELS ONLY** Check drive shaft gaiters.

Job 36. Check steering joints.

Job 37. Check suspension ball joints.

Job 38. **P100 PICK-UP ONLY** Check rear springs.

Job 39. Check underside for leaks.

Every 3,000 miles - Road Test

Job 40. Clean controls/check instruments.

Job 41. Check brakes and steering.

Job 42. Check throttle pedal operation.

Date serviced:...

Carried out by:...
Garage Stamp or signature:

Parts/Accessories purchased (date, parts, source) ....

....

....

....

....

EVERY 6,000 MILES - OR EVERY SIX MONTHS, WHICHEVER COMES FIRST

All the Service Jobs in the tinted area have been carried forward from earlier service intervals and are to be repeated at this service.

Every 6,000 miles - The Engine Bay

First carry out all Jobs listed under earlier Service intervals as applicable.

Job 2. Check coolant level.

Job 3. Check brake fluid level.

Job 4. Check battery electrolyte.

Job 5. Check screenwash level.

Job 23. Generator drive belt.

Job 24. Check brake/fuel lines.

Job 25. **DIESEL ENGINES ONLY** Drain fuel filter.

Job 43. Change engine oil.

Job 44. Change engine oil filter.

Job 45. Check/adjust spark plugs.

Job 46. Check ignition timing.

Job 47. Lubricate throttle controls.

Job 48. Check coolant radiator matrix.

Job 49. Check engine coolant.

Job 50. Check water pump for leaks.

Job 51. **MANUAL TRANSMISSION ONLY** Check manual gearbox oil.

Job 52. **AUTOMATIC TRANSMISSION ONLY** Automatic transmission fluid.

Job 53. Check rear axle oil level.

Job 54. Check power steering fluid level (if fitted).

Job 55. Check valve clearances.

Job 56. Check steering column coupling.

Job 57. Check fuel injection pipes and sensor wires.

Job 58. Check exhaust emission.

Job 59. Adjust idle speed and mixture setting.

Job 60. Replace fuel filter.

Job 61. Check ignition components.

Every 6,000 miles - Around the Car

First carry out all Jobs listed under earlier Service intervals as applicable.

- [ ] Job 6. Check tyre pressures.
- [ ] Job 7. Check headlights, sidelights and front indicators.
- [ ] Job 8. Rear lights and indicator bulbs.
- [ ] Job 9. Interior light bulbs.
- [ ] Job 10. Number plate light bulbs.
- [ ] Job 11. Side repeater bulbs.
- [ ] Job 12. Check horns.
- [ ] Job 13. Check windscreen wipers.
- [ ] Job 14. Windscreen washers.
- [ ] Job 15. Check tyres.
- [ ] Job 16. Check spare tyre.
- [ ] Job 17. Wash bodywork.
- [ ] Job 18. Touch-up paintwork.
- [ ] Job 19. Radio aerial.
- [ ] Job 20. Valet interior.
- [ ] Job 21. Improve visibility.
- [ ] Job 26. Check tightness of wheel nuts.
- [ ] Job 27. Check brake/fuel lines.
- [ ] Job 28. Check handbrake adjustment.
- [ ] Job 29. Check door/tailgate seals.
- [ ] Job 30. Check windscreen.
- [ ] Job 31. Rear view mirrors.

Every 6,000 miles - Under the Car

- [ ] Job 22. Clean mud traps.
- [ ] Job 32. Check exhaust system for leaks/damage.
- [ ] Job 33. Check exhaust system mountings.
- [ ] Job 34. Check steering rack gaiters.
- [ ] Job 35. **4X4 MODELS ONLY** Check drive shaft gaiters.
- [ ] Job 36. Check steering joints.
- [ ] Job 37. Check suspension ball joints.
- [ ] Job 38. **P100 PICK-UP ONLY** Check rear springs.
- [ ] Job 39. Check underside for leaks.

Every 6,000 miles - Road Test

- [ ] Job 40. Clean controls/check instruments.
- [ ] Job 41. Check brakes and steering.
- [ ] Job 42. Check throttle pedal operation.

EVERY 9,000 MILES - OR EVERY NINE MONTHS, WHICHEVER COMES FIRST

All the Jobs at this Service Interval have been carried forward from earlier Service Intervals and are to be repeated at this service.

Every 9,000 miles - The Engine Bay

- [ ] Job 1. Engine oil level.
- [ ] Job 2. Check coolant level.
- [ ] Job 3. Check brake fluid level.
- [ ] Job 4. Check battery electrolyte.
- [ ] Job 5. Check screenwash level.
- [ ] Job 23. Generator drive belt.
- [ ] Job 24. Check brake/fuel lines.
- [ ] Job 25. **DIESEL ENGINES ONLY** Drain fuel filter.

- [ ] Job 62. Check seat belts.
- [ ] Job 63. Lubricate locks and hinges.
- [ ] Job 64. Lubricate bonnet release mechanism.
- [ ] Job 65. Check seats.
- [ ] Job 66. Test shock absorbers.
- [ ] Job 67. Check/replace front disc brake pads.
- [ ] Job 68. Check/replace rear disc pads.
- [ ] Job 69. Check/adjust/renew rear drum brakes.
- [ ] Job 70. Check brake proportioning valve.

Date serviced:...

Carried out by: ....
Garage Stamp or signature:

Parts/Accessories purchased (date, parts, source) ....

....

....

....

....

Every 9,000 miles - Around The Car

First carry out all Jobs listed under earlier Service intervals as applicable.

- [ ] Job 6. Check tyre pressures.
- [ ] Job 7. Check headlights, sidelights and front indicators.
- [ ] Job 8. Rear lights and indicator bulbs.
- [ ] Job 9. Interior light bulbs.
- [ ] Job 10. Number plate light bulbs.
- [ ] Job 11. Side repeater bulbs.
- [ ] Job 12. Check horns.
- [ ] Job 13. Check windscreen wipers.
- [ ] Job 14. Windscreen washers.
- [ ] Job 15. Check tyres.
- [ ] Job 16. Check spare tyre.
- [ ] Job 17. Wash bodywork.
- [ ] Job 18. Touch-up paintwork.
- [ ] Job 19. Radio aerial.
- [ ] Job 20. Valet interior.
- [ ] Job 21. Improve visibility.
- [ ] Job 26. Check tightness of wheel nuts.
- [ ] Job 27. Check brake/fuel lines.
- [ ] Job 28. Check handbrake adjustment.
- [ ] Job 29. Check door/tailgate seals.
- [ ] Job 30. Check windscreen.
- [ ] Job 31. Rear view mirrors.

Every 9,000 miles - Under the Car

- [ ] Job 22. Clean mud traps.
- [ ] Job 32. Check exhaust system for leaks/damage.
- [ ] Job 33. Check exhaust system mountings.
- [ ] Job 34. Check steering rack gaiters.
- [ ] Job 35. 4X4 MODELS ONLYS ONLY Check drive shaft gaiters.
- [ ] Job 36. Check steering joints.
- [ ] Job 37. Check suspension ball joints.
- [ ] Job 38. P100 PICK-UP ONLY Check rear springs.
- [ ] Job 39. Check underside for leaks.

Every 9,000 miles - Road Test

- [ ] Job 40. Clean controls/check instruments.
- [ ] Job 41. Check brakes and steering.
- [ ] Job 42. Check throttle pedal operation.

Date serviced:...

Carried out by:..
Garage Stamp or signature:

Parts/Accessories purchased (date, parts, source) ....
....
....
....
....

EVERY 12,000 MILES - OR EVERY TWELVE MONTHS, WHICHEVER COMES FIRST

All the Service Jobs in the tinted area have been carried forward from earlier service intervals and are to be repeated at this service.

Every 12,000 miles - The Engine Bay

First carry out all Jobs listed under earlier Service intervals as applicable.

- [ ] Job 1. Engine oil level.
- [ ] Job 2. Check coolant level.
- [ ] Job 3. Check brake fluid level.
- [ ] Job 4. Check battery electrolyte.
- [ ] Job 5. Check screenwash level.
- [ ] Job 23. Generator drive belt.
- [ ] Job 24. Check brake/fuel lines.
- [ ] Job 25. DIESEL ENGINES ONLY Drain fuel filter.
- [ ] Job 43. Change engine oil.
- [ ] Job 44. Change engine oil filter.
- [ ] Job 45. Check/adjust spark plugs.
- [ ] Job 46. Check ignition timing.
- [ ] Job 47. Lubricate throttle controls.
- [ ] Job 48. Check coolant radiator matrix.
- [ ] Job 49. Check engine coolant.
- [ ] Job 50. Check water pump for leaks.
- [ ] Job 51. MANUAL TRANSMISSION ONLY Check manual gearbox oil.
- [ ] Job 52. AUTOMATIC TRANSMISSION ONLY Automatic transmission fluid.
- [ ] Job 53. Check rear axle oil level.
- [ ] Job 54. Check power steering fluid level (if fitted).
- [ ] Job 55. Check valve clearances.
- [ ] Job 56. Check steering column coupling.
- [ ] Job 57. Check fuel injection pipes and sensor wires.
- [ ] Job 58. Check exhaust emission.
- [ ] Job 59. Adjust idle speed and mixture setting.
- [ ] Job 61. Check ignition components.

☐ Job 71. Check camshaft timing belt and condition.

☐ Job 72. **SIERRAS FROM 1992 ONLY** Emission control equipment.

☐ Job 73. **CARBURETTOR MODELS ONLY** Renew air filter element.

☐ Job 74. **FUEL INJECTION MODELS ONLY** Renew air filter element.

☐ Job 75. **DIESEL ENGINES ONLY** Renew air filter element.

☐ Job 76. Check/renew fuel filter.

☐ Job 77. Check coolant hoses.

☐ Job 78. Check power steering and hoses.

☐ Job 79. Check air conditioning operation (if fitted).

☐ Job 80. Battery terminals.

☐ Job 81. **DIESEL ENGINES ONLY** Check clean glow plugs.

☐ Job 82. Check visible electrical wiring for security.

Every 12,000 miles - Around the Car

First carry out all Jobs listed under earlier Service intervals as applicable.

☐ Job 6. Check tyre pressures.

☐ Job 7. Check headlights, sidelights and front indicators.

☐ Job 8. Rear lights and indicator bulbs.

☐ Job 9. Interior light bulbs.

☐ Job 10. Number plate light bulbs.

☐ Job 11. Side repeater bulbs.

☐ Job 12. Check horns.

☐ Job 14. Windscreen washers.

☐ Job 15. Check tyres.

☐ Job 16. Check spare tyre.

☐ Job 17. Wash bodywork.

☐ Job 18. Touch-up paintwork.

☐ Job 19. Radio aerial.

☐ Job 20. Valet interior.

☐ Job 21. Improve visibility.

☐ Job 26. Check tightness of wheel nuts.

☐ Job 27. Check brake/fuel lines.

☐ Job 28. Check handbrake adjustment.

☐ Job 29. Check door/tailgate seals.

☐ Job 30. Check windscreen.

☐ Job 31. Rear view mirrors.

☐ Job 62. Check seat belts.

☐ Job 63. Lubricate locks and hinges.

☐ Job 64. Lubricate bonnet release mechanism.

☐ Job 65. Check seats.

☐ Job 66. Test shock absorbers.

☐ Job 67. Check/replace front disc brake pads.

☐ Job 68. Check/replace rear disc pads.

☐ Job 69. Check/adjust/renew rear drum brakes.

☐ Job 70. Check brake proportioning valve.

☐ Job 83. Toolkit and jack.

☐ Job 84. Check wheel bearings.

☐ Job 85. Check headlamp alignment.

☐ Job 86. Check/replace wiper blades.

☐ Job 87. Check steering and suspension.

☐ Job 88. Replace alarm remote batteries.

Every 12,000 miles - Under the Car

First carry out all Jobs listed under earlier Service intervals as applicable.

☐ Job 22. Clean mud traps.

☐ Job 32. Check exhaust system for leaks/damage.

☐ Job 33. Check exhaust system mountings.

☐ Job 34. Check steering rack gaiters.

☐ Job 35. **4X4 MODELS ONLY** Check drive shaft gaiters.

☐ Job 36. Check steering joints.

☐ Job 37. Check suspension ball joints.

☐ Job 38. **P100 PICK-UP ONLY** Check rear springs.

☐ Job 39. Check underside for leaks.

☐ Job 89. Inspect underside and clear drain holes.

☐ Job 90. Check prop shaft U.J.s and driveshafts.

Every 12,000 miles - Road Test

☐ Job 40. Clean controls/check instruments.

☐ Job 41. Check brakes and steering.

☐ Job 42. Check throttle pedal operation.

Date serviced:..

Carried out by: ....

Garage Stamp or signature:

Parts/Accessories purchased (date, parts, source) ....

....

....

....

....

EVERY 15,000 MILES - OR EVERY FIFTEEN MONTHS, WHICHEVER COMES FIRST

All the Jobs at this Service Interval have been carried forward from earlier Service Intervals and are to be repeated at this service.

Every 15,000 miles - The Engine Bay

- [ ] Job 1. Engine oil level.
- [ ] Job 2. Check coolant level.
- [ ] Job 3. Check brake fluid level.
- [ ] Job 4. Check battery electrolyte.
- [ ] Job 5. Check screenwash level.
- [ ] Job 23. Generator drive belt.
- [ ] Job 24. Check brake/fuel lines.
- [ ] Job 25. **DIESEL ENGINES ONLY** Drain fuel filter.

Every 15,000 miles - Around The Car

First carry out all Jobs listed under earlier Service intervals as applicable.

- [ ] Job 6. Check tyre pressures.
- [ ] Job 7. Check headlights, sidelights and front indicators.
- [ ] Job 8. Rear lights and indicator bulbs.
- [ ] Job 9. Interior light bulbs.
- [ ] Job 10. Number plate light bulbs.
- [ ] Job 11. Side repeater bulbs.
- [ ] Job 12. Check horns.
- [ ] Job 13. Check windscreen wipers.
- [ ] Job 14. Windscreen washers.
- [ ] Job 15. Check tyres.
- [ ] Job 16. Check spare tyre.
- [ ] Job 17. Wash bodywork.
- [ ] Job 18. Touch-up paintwork.
- [ ] Job 19. Radio aerial.
- [ ] Job 20. Valet interior.
- [ ] Job 21. Improve visibility.
- [ ] Job 26. Check tightness of wheel nuts.
- [ ] Job 27. Check brake/fuel lines.
- [ ] Job 28. Check handbrake adjustment.
- [ ] Job 29. Check door/tailgate seals.
- [ ] Job 30. Check windscreen.
- [ ] Job 31. Rear view mirrors.

Every 15,000 miles - Under the Car

- [ ] Job 22. Clean mud traps.
- [ ] Job 32. Check exhaust system for leaks/damage.
- [ ] Job 33. Check exhaust system mountings.
- [ ] Job 34. Check steering rack gaiters.
- [ ] Job 35. **4X4 MODELS ONLY** Check drive shaft gaiters.
- [ ] Job 36. Check steering joints.
- [ ] Job 37. Check suspension ball joints.
- [ ] Job 38. **P100 PICK-UP ONLY** Check rear springs.
- [ ] Job 39. Check underside for leaks.

Every 15,000 miles - Road Test

- [ ] Job 40. Clean controls/check instruments.
- [ ] Job 41. Check brakes and steering.
- [ ] Job 42. Check throttle pedal operation.

Date serviced:..

Carried out by:..
Garage Stamp or signature:

Parts/Accessories purchased (date, parts, source) ....

....

....

....

....

SERVICE HISTORY

EVERY 18,000 MILES - OR EVERY EIGHTEEN MONTHS, WHICHEVER COMES FIRST

All the Jobs at this Service Interval have been carried forward from earlier Service Intervals and are to be repeated at this service.

Every 18,000 miles - The Engine Bay

- [ ] Job 2. Check coolant level.
- [ ] Job 3. Check brake fluid level.
- [ ] Job 4. Check battery electrolyte.
- [ ] Job 5. Check screenwash level.
- [ ] Job 23. Generator drive belt.
- [ ] Job 24. Check brake/fuel lines.
- [ ] Job 25. **DIESEL ENGINES ONLY** Drain fuel filter.
- [ ] Job 43. Change engine oil.
- [ ] Job 44. Change engine oil filter.
- [ ] Job 45. Check/adjust spark plugs.
- [ ] Job 46. Check ignition timing.
- [ ] Job 47. Lubricate throttle controls.
- [ ] Job 48. Check coolant radiator matrix.
- [ ] Job 49. Check engine coolant.
- [ ] Job 50. Check water pump for leaks.
- [ ] Job 51. **MANUAL TRANSMISSION ONLY** Check manual gearbox oil.
- [ ] Job 52. **AUTOMATIC TRANSMISSION ONLY** Automatic transmission fluid.
- [ ] Job 53. Check rear axle oil level.
- [ ] Job 54. Check power steering fluid level (if fitted).
- [ ] Job 55. Check valve clearances.
- [ ] Job 56. Check steering column coupling.
- [ ] Job 57. Check fuel injection pipes and sensor wires.
- [ ] Job 58. Check exhaust emission.
- [ ] Job 59. Adjust idle speed and mixture setting.
- [ ] Job 60. Replace fuel filter.
- [ ] Job 61. Check ignition components.

Every 18,000 miles - Around the Car

First carry out all Jobs listed under earlier Service intervals as applicable.

- [ ] Job 6. Check tyre pressures.
- [ ] Job 7. Check headlights, sidelights and front indicators.
- [ ] Job 8. Rear lights and indicator bulbs.
- [ ] Job 9. Interior light bulbs.
- [ ] Job 10. Number plate light bulbs.
- [ ] Job 11. Side repeater bulbs.
- [ ] Job 12. Check horns.
- [ ] Job 14. Windscreen washers.
- [ ] Job 15. Check tyres.
- [ ] Job 16. Check spare tyre.
- [ ] Job 17. Wash bodywork.
- [ ] Job 18. Touch-up paintwork.
- [ ] Job 19. Radio aerial.
- [ ] Job 20. Valet interior.
- [ ] Job 21. Improve visibility.
- [ ] Job 26. Check tightness of wheel nuts.
- [ ] Job 27. Check brake/fuel lines.
- [ ] Job 28. Check handbrake adjustment.
- [ ] Job 29. Check door/tailgate seals.
- [ ] Job 30. Check windscreen.
- [ ] Job 31. Rear view mirrors
- [ ] Job 62. Check seat belts.
- [ ] Job 63. Lubricate locks and hinges.
- [ ] Job 64. Lubricate bonnet release mechanism.
- [ ] Job 65. Check seats.
- [ ] Job 66. Test shock absorbers.
- [ ] Job 67. Check/replace front disc brake pads.
- [ ] Job 68. Check/replace rear disc pads.
- [ ] Job 69. Check/adjust/renew rear drum brakes.
- [ ] Job 70. Check brake proportioning valve.

Every 18,000 miles - Under the Car

First carry out all Jobs listed under earlier Service intervals as applicable.

- [ ] Job 22. Clean mud traps.
- [ ] Job 32. Check exhaust system for leaks/damage.
- [ ] Job 33. Check exhaust system mountings.
- [ ] Job 34. Check steering rack gaiters.
- [ ] Job 35. **4X4 MODELS ONLY** Check drive shaft gaiters.
- [ ] Job 36. Check steering joints.
- [ ] Job 37. Check suspension ball joints.
- [ ] Job 38. **P100 PICK-UP ONLY** Check rear springs.
- [ ] Job 39. Check underside for leaks.

Every 18,000 miles - Road Test

- [ ] Job 40. Clean controls/check instruments.
- [ ] Job 41. Check brakes and steering.
- [ ] Job 42. Check throttle pedal operation.

Date serviced: ....

Carried out by: ....
Garage Stamp or signature:

Parts/Accessories purchased (date, parts, source) ....
....
....
....
....

EVERY 21,000 MILES - OR EVERY TWENTY ONE MONTHS, WHICHEVER COMES FIRST

All the Jobs at this Service Interval have been carried forward from earlier Service Intervals and are to be repeated at this service.

Every 21,000 miles - The Engine Bay

- [ ] Job 1. Engine oil level.
- [ ] Job 2. Check coolant level.
- [ ] Job 3. Check brake fluid level.
- [ ] Job 4. Check battery electrolyte.
- [ ] Job 5. Check screenwash level.
- [ ] Job 23. Generator drive belt.
- [ ] Job 24. Check brake/fuel lines.
- [ ] Job 25. **DIESEL ENGINES ONLY** Drain fuel filter.

Every 21,000 miles - Around the Car

First carry out all Jobs listed under earlier Service intervals as applicable.

- [ ] Job 6. Check tyre pressures.
- [ ] Job 7. Check headlights, sidelights and front indicators.
- [ ] Job 8. Rear lights and indicator bulbs.
- [ ] Job 9. Interior light bulbs.
- [ ] Job 10. Number plate light bulbs.
- [ ] Job 11. Side repeater bulbs.
- [ ] Job 12. Check horns.
- [ ] Job 13. Check windscreen wipers.
- [ ] Job 14. Windscreen washers.
- [ ] Job 15. Check tyres.
- [ ] Job 16. Check spare tyre.
- [ ] Job 17. Wash bodywork.
- [ ] Job 18. Touch-up paintwork.
- [ ] Job 19. Radio aerial.
- [ ] Job 20. Valet interior.
- [ ] Job 21. Improve visibility.
- [ ] Job 26. Check tightness of wheel nuts.
- [ ] Job 27. Check brake/fuel lines.
- [ ] Job 28. Check handbrake adjustment.
- [ ] Job 29. Check door/tailgate seals.
- [ ] Job 30. Check windscreen.
- [ ] Job 31. Rear view mirrors.

Every 21,000 miles - Under the Car

- [ ] Job 22. Clean mud traps.
- [ ] Job 32. Check exhaust system for leaks/damage.
- [ ] Job 33. Check exhaust system mountings.
- [ ] Job 34. Check steering rack gaiters.
- [ ] Job 35. **4X4 MODELS ONLY** Check drive shaft gaiters.
- [ ] Job 36. Check steering joints.
- [ ] Job 37. Check suspension ball joints.
- [ ] Job 38. **P100 PICK-UP ONLY** Check rear springs.
- [ ] Job 39. Check underside for leaks.

Every 21,000 miles - Road Test

- [ ] Job 40. Clean controls/check instruments.
- [ ] Job 41. Check brakes and steering.
- [ ] Job 42. Check throttle pedal operation.

Date serviced:..

Carried out by:...
Garage Stamp or signature:

Parts/Accessories purchased (date, parts, source) ....
....
....
....
....

EVERY 24,000 MILES - OR EVERY TWO YEARS, WHICHEVER COMES FIRST

All the Service Jobs in the tinted area have been carried forward from earlier service intervals and are to be repeated at this service.

Every 24,000 miles - The Engine Bay

First carry out all Jobs listed under earlier Service intervals as applicable.

☐ Job 1. Engine oil level.

☐ Job 2. Check coolant level.

☐ Job 4. Check battery electrolyte.

☐ Job 5. Check screenwash level.

☐ Job 23. Generator drive belt.

☐ Job 24. Check brake/fuel lines.

☐ Job 25. **DIESEL ENGINES ONLY** Drain fuel filter.

☐ Job 43. Change engine oil.

☐ Job 44. Change engine oil filter.

☐ Job 45. Check/adjust spark plugs.

☐ Job 46. Check ignition timing.

☐ Job 47. Lubricate throttle controls.

☐ Job 48. Check coolant radiator matrix.

☐ Job 50. Check water pump for leaks.

☐ Job 51. **MANUAL TRANSMISSION ONLY** Check manual gearbox oil.

☐ Job 52. **AUTOMATIC TRANSMISSION ONLY** Automatic transmission fluid.

☐ Job 53. Check rear axle oil level.

☐ Job 54. Check power steering fluid level (if fitted).

☐ Job 55. Check valve clearances.

☐ Job 56. Check steering column coupling.

☐ Job 57. Check fuel injection pipes and sensor wires.

☐ Job 58. Check exhaust emission.

☐ Job 59. Adjust idle speed and mixture setting.

☐ Job 60. Replace fuel filter.

☐ Job 61. Check ignition components.

☐ Job 71. Check camshaft timing belt and condition.

☐ Job 72. **SIERRAS FROM 1992 ONLY** Emission control equipment.

☐ Job 73. **CARBURETTOR MODELS ONLY** Renew air filter element.

☐ Job 74. **FUEL INJECTION MODELS ONLY** Renew air filter element.

☐ Job 75. **DIESEL ENGINES ONLY** Renew air filter element.

☐ Job 76. Check/renew fuel filter.

☐ Job 77. Check coolant hoses.

☐ Job 78. Check power steering and hoses.

☐ Job 79. Check air conditioning operation (if fitted).

☐ Job 80. Battery terminals.

☐ Job 81. **DIESEL ENGINES ONLY** Check clean glow plugs.

☐ Job 82. Check visible electrical wiring for security.

☐ Job 93. **V6 ENGINE ONLY** Replace crankcase emission valve.

☐ Job 94. **DIESEL ENGINES ONLY** Clean/replace engine oil filler cap.

☐ Job 96. Change engine coolant.

Every 24,000 miles - Around the Car

First carry out all Jobs listed under earlier Service intervals as applicable.

☐ Job 6. Check tyre pressures.

☐ Job 7. Check headlights, sidelights and front indicators.

☐ Job 8. Rear lights and indicator bulbs.

☐ Job 9. Interior light bulbs.

☐ Job 10. Number plate light bulbs.

☐ Job 11. Side repeater bulbs.

☐ Job 12. Check horns.

☐ Job 13. Check windscreen wipers.

☐ Job 14. Windscreen washers.

☐ Job 15. Check tyres.

☐ Job 16. Check spare tyre.

☐ Job 17. Wash bodywork.

☐ Job 18. Touch-up paintwork.

☐ Job 19. Radio aerial.

☐ Job 20. Valet interior.

☐ Job 21. Improve visibility.

☐ Job 26. Check tightness of wheel nuts.

☐ Job 27. Check brake/fuel lines.

☐ Job 28. Check handbrake adjustment.

☐ Job 29. Check door/tailgate seals.

☐ Job 30. Check windscreen.

☐ Job 31. Rear view mirrors.

☐ Job 62. Check seat belts.

☐ Job 63. Lubricate locks and hinges.

☐ Job 64. Lubricate bonnet release mechanism.

☐ Job 65. Check seats.

☐ Job 66. Test shock absorbers.

☐ Job 67. Check/replace front disc brake pads.

☐ Job 68. Check/replace rear disc pads.

☐ Job 69. Check/adjust/renew rear drum brakes.

☐ Job 70. Check brake proportioning valve.

☐ Job 83. Toolkit and jack.

☐ Job 84. Check wheel bearings.

☐ Job 85. Check headlamp alignment.

☐ Job 86. Check/replace wiper blades.

☐ Job 87. Check steering and suspension.

☐ Job 88. Replace alarm remote batteries.

☐ Job 92. Check brake discs/drums and calipers.

☐ Job 95. Adjust brake bands

Every 24,000 miles - Under the Car

First carry out all Jobs listed under earlier Service intervals as applicable.

☐ Job 22. Clean mud traps.

☐ Job 32. Check exhaust system for leaks/damage.

☐ Job 33. Check exhaust system mountings.

☐ Job 34. Check steering rack gaiters.

☐ Job 35. **4X4 MODELS ONLY** Check drive shaft gaiters.

☐ Job 36. Check steering joints.

☐ Job 37. Check suspension ball joints.

☐ Job 38. **P100 PICK-UP ONLY** Check rear springs.

☐ Job 39. Check underside for leaks.

☐ Job 89. Inspect underside and clear drain holes.

☐ Job 90. Check prop shaft U.J.s and driveshafts.

☐ Job 91. Replace brake fluid.

Every 24,000 miles - Road Test

☐ Job 40. Clean controls/check instruments.

☐ Job 41. Check brakes and steering.

☐ Job 42. Check throttle pedal operation.

EVERY 27,000 MILES - OR EVERY TWENTY SEVEN MONTHS, WHICHEVER COMES FIRST

All the Jobs at this Service Interval have been carried forward from earlier Service Intervals and are to be repeated at this service.

Every 27,000 miles - The Engine Bay

☐ Job 1. Engine oil level.

☐ Job 2. Check coolant level.

☐ Job 3. Check brake fluid level.

☐ Job 4. Check battery electrolyte.

☐ Job 5. Check screenwash level.

☐ Job 23. Generator drive belt.

☐ Job 24. Check brake/fuel lines.

☐ Job 25. **DIESEL ENGINES ONLY** Drain fuel filter.

Date serviced:...

Carried out by: ....
Garage Stamp or signature:

Parts/Accessories purchased (date, parts, source) ....

Every 27,000 miles - Around the Car

First carry out all Jobs listed under earlier Service intervals as applicable.

- [ ] Job 6. Check tyre pressures.
- [ ] Job 7. Check headlights, sidelights and front indicators.
- [ ] Job 8. Rear lights and indicator bulbs.
- [ ] Job 9. Interior light bulbs.
- [ ] Job 10. Number plate light bulbs.
- [ ] Job 11. Side repeater bulbs.
- [ ] Job 12. Check horns.
- [ ] Job 13. Check windscreen wipers.
- [ ] Job 14. Windscreen washers.
- [ ] Job 15. Check tyres.
- [ ] Job 16. Check spare tyre.
- [ ] Job 17. Wash bodywork.
- [ ] Job 18. Touch-up paintwork.
- [ ] Job 19. Radio aerial.
- [ ] Job 20. Valet interior.
- [ ] Job 21. Improve visibility.
- [ ] Job 26. Check tightness of wheel nuts.
- [ ] Job 27. Check brake/fuel lines.
- [ ] Job 28. Check handbrake adjustment.
- [ ] Job 29. Check door/tailgate seals.
- [ ] Job 30. Check windscreen.
- [ ] Job 31. Rear view mirrors.

Every 27,000 miles - Under the Car

- [ ] Job 22. Clean mud traps.
- [ ] Job 32. Check exhaust system for leaks/damage.
- [ ] Job 33. Check exhaust system mountings.
- [ ] Job 34. Check steering rack gaiters.
- [ ] Job 35. **4X4 MODELS ONLY** Check drive shaft gaiters.
- [ ] Job 36. Check steering joints.
- [ ] Job 37. Check suspension ball joints.
- [ ] Job 38. **P100 PICK-UP ONLY** Check rear springs.
- [ ] Job 39. Check underside for leaks.

Every 27,000 miles - Road Test

- [ ] Job 40. Clean controls/check instruments.
- [ ] Job 41. Check brakes and steering.
- [ ] Job 42. Check throttle pedal operation.

Date serviced:...

Carried out by:...
Garage Stamp or signature:

Parts/Accessories purchased (date, parts, source) ....

....

....

....

....

EVERY 30,000 MILES - OR EVERY THIRTY MONTHS, WHICHEVER COMES FIRST

All the Jobs at this Service Interval have been carried forward from earlier Service Intervals and are to be repeated at this service.

Every 30,000 miles - The Engine Bay

- [ ] Job 2. Check coolant level.
- [ ] Job 3. Check brake fluid level.
- [ ] Job 4. Check battery electrolyte.
- [ ] Job 5. Check screenwash level.
- [ ] Job 23. Generator drive belt.
- [ ] Job 24. Check brake/fuel lines.
- [ ] Job 25. **DIESEL ENGINES ONLY** Drain fuel filter.
- [ ] Job 43. Change engine oil.
- [ ] Job 44. Change engine oil filter.
- [ ] Job 45. Check/adjust spark plugs.
- [ ] Job 46. Check ignition timing.
- [ ] Job 47. Lubricate throttle controls.
- [ ] Job 48. Check coolant radiator matrix.
- [ ] Job 49. Check engine coolant.
- [ ] Job 50. Check water pump for leaks.
- [ ] Job 51. **MANUAL TRANSMISSION ONLY** Check manual gearbox oil.
- [ ] Job 52. **AUTOMATIC TRANSMISSION ONLY** Automatic transmission fluid.
- [ ] Job 53. Check rear axle oil level.
- [ ] Job 54. Check power steering fluid level (if fitted).
- [ ] Job 55. Check valve clearances.
- [ ] Job 56. Check steering column coupling.
- [ ] Job 57. Check fuel injection pipes and sensor wires.
- [ ] Job 58. Check exhaust emission.
- [ ] Job 59. Adjust idle speed and mixture setting.
- [ ] Job 60. Replace fuel filter.
- [ ] Job 61. Check ignition components.

Every 30,000 miles - Around the Car

First carry out all Jobs listed under earlier Service intervals as applicable.

- [ ] Job 6. Check tyre pressures.
- [ ] Job 7. Check headlights, sidelights and front indicators.
- [ ] Job 8. Rear lights and indicator bulbs.
- [ ] Job 9. Interior light bulbs.
- [ ] Job 10. Number plate light bulbs.
- [ ] Job 11. Side repeater bulbs.
- [ ] Job 12. Check horns.
- [ ] Job 14. Windscreen washers.
- [ ] Job 15. Check tyres.
- [ ] Job 16. Check spare tyre.
- [ ] Job 17. Wash bodywork.
- [ ] Job 18. Touch-up paintwork.
- [ ] Job 19. Radio aerial.
- [ ] Job 20. Valet interior.
- [ ] Job 21. Improve visibility.
- [ ] Job 26. Check tightness of wheel nuts.
- [ ] Job 27. Check brake/fuel lines.
- [ ] Job 28. Check handbrake adjustment.
- [ ] Job 29. Check door/tailgate seals.
- [ ] Job 30. Check windscreen.
- [ ] Job 31. Rear view mirrors.
- [ ] Job 62. Check seat belts.
- [ ] Job 63. Lubricate locks and hinges.
- [ ] Job 64. Lubricate bonnet release mechanism.
- [ ] Job 65. Check seats.
- [ ] Job 66. Test shock absorbers.
- [ ] Job 67. Check/replace front disc brake pads.
- [ ] Job 68. Check/replace rear disc pads.
- [ ] Job 69. Check/adjust/renew rear drum brakes.
- [ ] Job 70. Check brake proportioning valve.

Every 30,000 miles - Under the Car

First carry out all Jobs listed under earlier Service intervals as applicable.

- [ ] Job 22. Clean mud traps.
- [ ] Job 32. Check exhaust system for leaks/damage.
- [ ] Job 33. Check exhaust system mountings.
- [ ] Job 34. Check steering rack gaiters.
- [ ] Job 35. **4X4 MODELS ONLY** Check drive shaft gaiters.
- [ ] Job 36. Check steering joints.
- [ ] Job 37. Check suspension ball joints.
- [ ] Job 38. **P100 PICK-UP ONLY** Check rear springs.
- [ ] Job 39. Check underside for leaks.

Every 30,000 miles - Road Test

- [ ] Job 40. Clean controls/check instruments.
- [ ] Job 41. Check brakes and steering.
- [ ] Job 42. Check throttle pedal operation.

EVERY 33,000 MILES - OR EVERY THIRTY THREE MONTHS, WHICHEVER COMES FIRST

All the Jobs at this Service Interval have been carried forward from earlier Service Intervals and are to be repeated at this service.

Every 33,000 miles - The Engine Bay

- [ ] Job 1. Engine oil level.
- [ ] Job 2. Check coolant level.
- [ ] Job 3. Check brake fluid level.
- [ ] Job 4. Check battery electrolyte.
- [ ] Job 5. Check screenwash level.
- [ ] Job 23. Generator drive belt.
- [ ] Job 24. Check brake/fuel lines.
- [ ] Job 25. **DIESEL ENGINES ONLY** Drain fuel filter.

Date serviced:..

Carried out by: ....
Garage Stamp or signature:

Parts/Accessories purchased (date, parts, source) ....

Every 33,000 miles - Around The Car

First carry out all Jobs listed under earlier Service intervals as applicable.

- [ ] Job 6. Check tyre pressures.
- [ ] Job 7. Check headlights, sidelights and front indicators.
- [ ] Job 8. Rear lights and indicator bulbs.
- [ ] Job 9. Interior light bulbs.
- [ ] Job 10. Number plate light bulbs.
- [ ] Job 11. Side repeater bulbs.
- [ ] Job 12. Check horns.
- [ ] Job 13. Check windscreen wipers.
- [ ] Job 14. Windscreen washers.
- [ ] Job 15. Check tyres.
- [ ] Job 16. Check spare tyre.
- [ ] Job 17. Wash bodywork.
- [ ] Job 18. Touch-up paintwork.
- [ ] Job 19. Radio aerial.
- [ ] Job 20. Valet interior.
- [ ] Job 21. Improve visibility.
- [ ] Job 26. Check tightness of wheel nuts.
- [ ] Job 27. Check brake/fuel lines.
- [ ] Job 28. Check handbrake adjustment.
- [ ] Job 29. Check door/tailgate seals.
- [ ] Job 30. Check windscreen.
- [ ] Job 31. Rear view mirrors.

Every 33,000 miles - Under the Car

- [ ] Job 22. Clean mud traps.
- [ ] Job 32. Check exhaust system for leaks/damage.
- [ ] Job 33. Check exhaust system mountings.
- [ ] Job 34. Check steering rack gaiters.
- [ ] Job 35. **4X4 MODELS ONLY** Check drive shaft gaiters.
- [ ] Job 36. Check steering joints.
- [ ] Job 37. Check suspension ball joints.
- [ ] Job 38. **P100 PICK-UP ONLY** Check rear springs.
- [ ] Job 39. Check underside for leaks.

Every 33,000 miles - Road Test

- [ ] Job 40. Clean controls/check instruments.
- [ ] Job 41. Check brakes and steering.
- [ ] Job 42. Check throttle pedal operation.

Date serviced:..

Carried out by:..
Garage Stamp or signature:

Parts/Accessories purchased (date, parts,

source) ....

....

....

....

EVERY 36,000 MILES - OR EVERY THREE YEARS, WHICHEVER COMES FIRST

All the Service Jobs in the tinted area have been carried forward from earlier service intervals and are to be repeated at this service.

Every 36,000 miles - The Engine Bay

First carry out all Jobs listed under earlier Service intervals as applicable.

- [ ] Job 1. Engine oil level.
- [ ] Job 2. Check coolant level.
- [ ] Job 3. Check brake fluid level.
- [ ] Job 4. Check battery electrolyte.
- [ ] Job 5. Check screenwash level.
- [ ] Job 23. Generator drive belt.
- [ ] Job 24. Check brake/fuel lines.
- [ ] Job 25. **DIESEL ENGINES ONLY** Drain fuel filter.
- [ ] Job 43. Change engine oil.
- [ ] Job 44. Change engine oil filter.
- [ ] Job 45. Check/adjust spark plugs.
- [ ] Job 46. Check ignition timing.
- [ ] Job 47. Lubricate throttle controls.
- [ ] Job 48. Check coolant radiator matrix.
- [ ] Job 49. Check engine coolant.
- [ ] Job 50. Check water pump for leaks.
- [ ] Job 51. **MANUAL TRANSMISSION ONLY** Check manual gearbox oil.
- [ ] Job 52. **AUTOMATIC TRANSMISSION ONLY** Automatic transmission fluid.
- [ ] Job 53. Check rear axle oil level.
- [ ] Job 54. Check power steering fluid level (if fitted).
- [ ] Job 55. Check valve clearances.
- [ ] Job 56. Check steering column coupling.
- [ ] Job 57. Check fuel injection pipes and sensor wires.
- [ ] Job 58. Check exhaust emission.
- [ ] Job 59. Adjust idle speed and mixture setting.
- [ ] Job 60. Replace fuel filter.
- [ ] Job 61. Check ignition components.
- [ ] Job 71. Check camshaft timing belt and condition.

☐ Job 72. **SIERRAS FROM 1992 ONLY** Emission control equipment.

☐ Job 73. **CARBURETTOR MODELS ONLY** Renew air filter element.

☐ Job 74. **FUEL INJECTION MODELS ONLY** Renew air filter element.

☐ Job 75. **DIESEL ENGINES ONLY** Renew air filter element.

☐ Job 76. Check/renew fuel filter.

☐ Job 77. Check coolant hoses.

☐ Job 78. Check power steering and hoses.

☐ Job 79. Check air conditioning operation (if fitted).

☐ Job 80. Battery terminals.

☐ Job 81. **DIESEL ENGINES ONLY** Check clean glow plugs.

☐ Job 82. Check visible electrical wiring for security.

☐ Job 97. Replace camshaft drive belt.

☐ Job 98. Renew HT leads.

Every 36,000 miles - Around the Car

☐ Job 6. Check tyre pressures.

☐ Job 7. Check headlights, sidelights and front indicators.

☐ Job 8. Rear lights and indicator bulbs.

☐ Job 9. Interior light bulbs.

☐ Job 10. Number plate light bulbs.

☐ Job 11. Side repeater bulbs.

☐ Job 12. Check horns.

☐ Job 13. Check windscreen wipers.

☐ Job 14. Windscreen washers.

☐ Job 15. Check tyres.

☐ Job 16. Check spare tyre.

☐ Job 17. Wash bodywork.

☐ Job 18. Touch-up paintwork.

☐ Job 19. Radio aerial.

☐ Job 20. Valet interior.

☐ Job 21. Improve visibility.

☐ Job 26. Check tightness of wheel nuts.

☐ Job 27. Check brake/fuel lines.

☐ Job 28. Check handbrake adjustment.

☐ Job 29. Check door/tailgate seals.

☐ Job 30. Check windscreen.

☐ Job 31. Rear view mirrors.

☐ Job 62. Check seat belts.

☐ Job 63. Lubricate locks and hinges.

☐ Job 64. Lubricate bonnet release mechanism.

☐ Job 65. Check seats.

☐ Job 66. Test shock absorbers.

☐ Job 67. Check/replace front disc brake pads.

☐ Job 68. Check/replace rear disc pads.

☐ Job 69. Check/adjust/renew rear drum brakes.

☐ Job 70. Check brake proportioning valve.

☐ Job 83. Toolkit and jack.

☐ Job 84. Check wheel bearings.

☐ Job 85. Check headlamp alignment.

☐ Job 86. Check/replace wiper blades.

☐ Job 87. Check steering and suspension.

☐ Job 88. Replace alarm remote batteries.

Every 36,000 miles - Under the Car

First carry out all Jobs listed under earlier Service intervals as applicable.

☐ Job 22. Clean mud traps.

☐ Job 32. Check exhaust system for leaks/damage.

☐ Job 33. Check exhaust system mountings.

☐ Job 34. Check steering rack gaiters.

☐ Job 35. **4X4 MODELS ONLY** Check drive shaft gaiters.

☐ Job 36. Check steering joints.

☐ Job 37. Check suspension ball joints.

☐ Job 38. **P100 PICK-UP ONLY** Check rear springs.

☐ Job 39. Check underside for leaks.

☐ Job 89. Inspect underside and clear drain holes.

☐ Job 90. Check prop shaft U.J.s and driveshafts.

☐ Job 99. Rustproofing.

Every 36,000 miles - Road Test

☐ Job 40. Clean controls/check instruments.

☐ Job 41. Check brakes and steering.

☐ Job 42. Check throttle pedal operation.

Date serviced:..

Carried out by: ....
Garage Stamp or signature:

Parts/Accessories purchased (date, parts, source) ....
....
....
....
....